THE COMMON TRADITION

OF THE

SYNOPTIC GOSPELS.

THE COMMON TRADITION

OF THE

SYNOPTIC GOSPELS

IN THE TEXT OF THE REVISED VERSION

BY

EDWIN A. ABBOTT, D.D.,

FORMERLY FELLOW OF ST. JOHN'S COLLEGE, CAMBRIDGE,

AND

W. G. RUSHBROOKE, M.L.,

FORMERLY FELLOW OF ST. JOHN'S COLLEGE, CAMBRIDGE.

Wipf & Stock
PUBLISHERS
Eugene, Oregon

Wipf and Stock Publishers
199 W 8th Ave, Suite 3
Eugene, OR 97401

The Common Tradition of the Synoptic Gospels in the Text of the Revised Version
By Abbott, Edwin A. and Rushbrooke, W. G.
ISBN: 1-59752-460-3
Publication date 2/10/2006
Previously published by Macmillan and Co., 1884

INTRODUCTION.

I.—TO THE GENERAL READER.

1.—THE OBJECT OF THIS BOOK.

TURNING over the pages of this Harmony of the Synoptic Gospels the reader will at once notice a number of words in **black type**. On examination, he will find that the same, or nearly the same black type recurs in each of the three columns representing Mark, Matthew, and Luke; or, in other words, that this black type exhibits the matter common to the first three Evangelists. If he will then take the trouble to run his eye over the black type, taken by itself, he will perceive that these words, though extracted out of narratives, constitute a kind of narrative by themselves, a Tradition of the words and deeds of Christ. Since this Tradition is common to the first three Gospels, it may, for convenience, be called the Common or Triple Tradition.

The object of this book is to place before English readers this Common Tradition, as being a tradition *earlier than any of our existing Gospels*, and consequently exhibiting the closest approximation we possess to some parts of the original narrative from which our Gospels are derived.[1]

Of course the importance of this Tradition depends upon the fact that the three Evangelists borrowed independently from it. When any judge, or jury, is engaged in weighing evidence, special importance will naturally be attached to all such statements as are made not by one witness, but by several, *provided they have had no communication with one another*. A fact stated by one witness

---

[1] It is intended, in due course, to publish a separate volume containing the "Double Tradition," that is to say, the portions of the Synoptic narrative common to Mark and Matthew, Mark and Luke, Matthew and Luke; and also the passages peculiar to each of the three Synoptists.

alone may be accepted if the witness himself is generally credible: but obviously all such once-supported evidence stands on an entirely different footing from evidence twice or thrice independently supported. Admitting the honesty of the witness, we may doubt his exactness of statement, his acuteness of observation, his power of distinguishing facts from inferences. These, and other causes combine to make us assent to the maxim of the Levitical Law, "In the mouth of two or three witnesses shall every word be established." And as regards statements of supreme importance, we may accept the dictum of Philo—which has also been adopted by the author of the Epistles of St. John (1 John v. 8, 9)—that: "A sacred matter is tested by three witnesses." For these reasons the Tradition common to our three earliest Gospels assumes a very high importance, on the hypothesis that the three Evangelists bear independent testimony to its pre-existence and authority.

Closely though the Synoptists in some passages agree, yet the independence of their testimony requires in these days no proof. Few reasonable sceptics now assert, as early Christian Fathers once did, that "Mark abbreviated Matthew and Luke," or that any one of the three first Evangelists had before him the work of either of the other two. Proof, if proof were needed, might easily be derived from a perusal of the pages of the following Harmony, which would shew a number of divergences, half-agreements, incomplete statements, omissions, incompatible, as a whole, with the hypothesis of borrowing. And, therefore, the unlearned reader may rest assured that at least no suspicion of collusion or dependence between the three earliest writers of the life of Christ need impair his acceptance of the Triple or Common Tradition.

But the independence of the three witnesses does not prevent one of the three from being earlier than the other two, and from approximating more closely than the rest to the Original Tradition from which all three are descended. On this point there has been difference of opinion: but the general consent of competent critics has, of late years, pointed toward Mark as the earliest of the three Evangelists. Or rather, to speak more accurately, it is believed that the Gospel of St. Mark *contains* a closer approximation to the Original Tradition, than is *contained* in the other Synoptists. Parts of St. Mark's Gospel are so full and ample on small and special points, as to suggest that the writer sometimes added a good deal from his own knowledge to the Tradition which he had before him; but for the most part it will be found that Mark contains very little which is not found either in Matthew or in Luke.

It is possible to demonstrate that, at all events in some passages, Mark *contains the whole of a Tradition from which Matthew and Luke borrowed parts;* but the proof, though not complicated, requires a little more reflection than is usually given to statements made in a mere introduction of this kind. However, the reader will have little difficulty in appreciating it, if he will give a moment's consideration to the following proposition :—

In the case of three narratives A, B, and C (e.g. Mark, Matthew, and Luke), *if A contains much that is common to A and B alone, and much that is common to A and C alone, and* all that is common to B and C, *it follows generally that A contains the whole of some narrative from which B and C have borrowed parts.*

The important clause in this proposition is that " A contains all that is common to B and C," in other words, that Mark contains (as happens in some passages) *all that is common to Matthew and Luke.* For how could this happen (to the extent to which it occasionally happens, not amounting to a word or phrase or two, but to a considerable part of the whole) on the supposition that Mark borrowed from Matthew and Luke? Mark could only have achieved such a result *by carefully underlining all the words common to Matthew's and Luke's narratives*, and by then writing a narrative of his own, which should *include all these words* and yet preserve the natural style of an original composition. "The difficulty of doing this is enormous, and will be patent to any one who will try to perform a similar literary feat himself. To embody *the whole* of even one document in a narrative of one's own without copying it *verbatim*, and to do this in a free and natural manner, requires no little care; but to take two documents, to put them side by side and analyse their common matter, and then to write a narrative, graphic, abrupt, and in all respects the opposite of artificial, which shall contain every word that is common to both—this would be a *tour de force* even for a skilful literary forger of these days, and may be dismissed as an impossibility for the writer of the Second Gospel." [1]

But if Mark did not combine Matthew and Luke, it follows that (since the resemblance is far too close to be accounted for as accidental) Matthew and Luke must have borrowed from Mark, or —if that hypothesis be dismissed, as it must be—from some common tradition which is embodied in Mark. This will explain all the phenomena of the Triple Tradition. The two later writers, *borrowing independently from the Original Tradition (which is contained in Mark)* would agree with one another *only so far as they borrowed*, or in other words *would contain nothing in common which was not also in Mark.* For the rest, Matthew would borrow this, and Luke that; so that when all that had been borrowed from Mark,[2] was deducted from Mark, very little would be left that

---

[1] *Encyclopædia Britannica*, vol. x. p. 791, article "Gospels."
[2] When we speak of "borrowing from Mark," we mean "borrowing from the Original Tradition contained in Mark:" and this expression will be occasionally used for brevity.

Where Matthew and Luke agree in slight deviations from Mark, they probably used some "similar edition" of the Original Tradition, from which there had

could be set down as peculiar to Mark. Hence (in the following Harmony), when the reader looks down the left-hand column which represents the "portions peculiar to Mark," he need not be surprised at sometimes finding little but a group of words such as "and," "straightway," "that," and the other mannerisms of the Evangelist. This paucity of "peculiar matter" is a tribute to the faithfulness with which Mark followed, without enlarging, the Original Tradition.

From the superiority of Mark's Gospel, in respect of date, it must not be inferred that his narrative, wherever it covers the same ground, enables us to dispense with those of Matthew and Luke. On the contrary, it is sometimes extremely abrupt and obscure, and apparently has been so confused as to require illustration by means of the other two Synoptists. Take for example the following passage:—

MARK XIV. 65.	MATTHEW XXVI. 67, 68.	LUKE XXII 63, 64
And some began to spit on him, and to cover his face, and to buffet him, and to say unto him, Prophesy: and the officers received him with blows.	Then did they spit in his face and buffet him, but others smote him, saying, (68) Prophesy to us, thou Christ, who is it that smote thee?	And the men that held him, mocked him; (64) and covering his eyes (Gr. him) they asked him saying, Prophesy, Who is it that smote thee?

Here the meaning of the mocking command to "prophesy" is not clear in Mark's narrative. It suggests the question "Prophesy? About what?" And we are also left to ask, "What was the object of 'covering his face'?"

Still more obscure is Matthew. For here we find Jesus requested by the soldiers to "prophesy" who smote him; yet, so far as Matthew's narrative goes, we cannot in the least understand how there could be any difficulty in telling, without any recourse to "prophesy," who it was that smote Jesus, since the smiters (so far as Matthew informs us) were visible. It is reserved for Luke, the latest of the three Synoptists, to make all clear by combining the *two* traditions, 1st, the *blindfolding;* 2nd, the command to prophesy *who it was that smote him*, when blindfolded.

Yet the very obscurity and abruptness of Mark's Gospel are indications of the early date at which it was committed to writing; for what is obscure and abrupt in an early tradition may naturally be corrected by later editors into what is clear and smooth; but no one would be tempted to substitute abrupt obscurity for original clearness and smoothness.

been removed some of the abruptnesses perceptible in Mark's form of the Tradition.

Where Matthew and Luke agree, and Mark is altogether wanting, they borrowed from some document or tradition, containing the parables and longer discourses of Christ.

A comparison of the Gospel of Luke, in the original, with that of St. Mark would place beyond doubt the conclusion that the educated physician who composed the third of our Synoptic Gospels, altered many words and expressions in the Earlier Tradition, in conformity with a more exact and polite usage: but in most instances a knowledge of Greek is required to appreciate such a demonstration. One or two examples, however, may be made intelligible to the English reader. In the Stilling of the Tempest (see pp. 32–35) Matthew and Mark speak of Jesus, on the lake of Gennesaret, "rebuking the *sea*" (Mark iv. 39, Matthew viii. 26) and describe how "even the wind and the *sea*" obey Jesus. In both cases Luke uses "water" or "waters." This might be thought an accident, but it is not. For in the Exorcism of the Gadarene (pp. 36, 37), whereas Mark and Matthew use the word "sea" (Mark v. 13, Matthew viii. 32), Luke uses "lake;" and this makes clear the motive of his correction. He objects to the application of the word "sea," where "lake" is more appropriate. Again in Mark ii. 4–9, 11, 12 we find four times repeated a word "bed," concerning which it is said by the grammarian Phrynichus that "only the *canaille* use this word;" consequently Matthew (ix. 2) and Luke (v. 18) substitute for it (pp. 10–13) the word "couch;"[1] and when Luke finds himself compelled to repeat the word, he resorts to the word "little couch" (Luke v. 19, 24) rather than employ a word condemned by polite usage

But these trifling, though frequent, peculiarities of grammatical expression are insignificant, as compared with the differences of *thought*, which may be noted in the following pages, distinguishing the earlier from the later Evangelists. It is a cogent proof of the early date of Mark that this Gospel contains many expressions, which, although no doubt historically accurate, would be likely to be stumbling-blocks in the way of weak believers; so that they are omitted in the later Gospels, and would not have been tolerated except in a Tradition of extreme antiquity. For example, after Mark has described, in language closely resembling that of Matthew, the return of Jesus to his home at Nazareth, the two Evangelists conclude thus (see pp. 40, 41):—

MARK VI. 5.	MATTHEW XIII. 58.
And **he could there do no mighty work,** save that he laid his hands upon a few sick folk and healed them. And he marvelled because of their unbelief.	And **he did not many mighty works there** because of their unbelief.

---

[1] This is one of the few cases in which the Revisers (very justifiably avoiding the charge of pedantry) have not attempted to represent in English the differences of the Greek words. It will be noted that in pp. 10, 11, although the word "bed" is used by all three Synoptists, it is not printed in black type. This indicates that, though the English is the same in all three, the Greek is not the same.

A somewhat similar divergence is found (pp. 8, 9) in a passage common to the three Evangelists, immediately following the account of the healing of Peter's wife's mother:—

MARK I. 32-34	MATTHEW VIII 16.	LUKE IV. 40, 41.
And at even, when the sun did set, **they brought unto him all that were sick**, and them that were possessed with devils...(41) And he healed **many** that were sick with divers diseases...	And when even was come, **they brought unto him many possessed with devils**; and he cast out the spirits with a word, and healed **all** that were sick.	And when the sun was setting, **all they that had any sick with divers diseases brought them unto him**; and he laid his hands on **every one** of them and healed them

No one can fail to see a kind of climax here, ascending from the earlier to the later Evangelists. In Mark's narrative "*all* that were sick" are brought to Jesus; but *not* "all," only "many," are healed. But, in Matthew, "many" are brought, and "the spirits" are cast out, and "*all* that were sick" are healed; and similarly in Luke "*all* they that had *any* sick" bring them and Jesus lays his hands on "*every one* of them and heals them." Obviously it is far more likely that the more restricted statement was the earliest of the three, and was amplified (in accordance with a very natural tendency, to prevent the supposition that the acts of healing performed by Jesus were sometimes of a tentative or partial nature) than that the fuller statements of Matthew and Luke were curtailed in the earlier days of the Church by an increasing exactness of criticism. Many other instances might be mentioned of "stumbling-blocks" existing in the early version of St. Mark, and removed in later Gospels; but it must suffice to refer to one only, the attempt made by the friends of Jesus to lay hands on him "for they said, He is beside himself" (Mark iii. 21, see p. 20).

The reader will now understand why, in this Harmony, a departure has been made from the usual order of the Gospels, and the narrative of Mark is printed first. The reason is, that Mark's Gospel, being the earliest, is advantageously studied first, in a comparison of the three Synoptists.

If we possessed the Original Gospel from which our existing Gospels are derived, we should probably be able to understand in what way many of the discrepancies between our Evangelists arose from a difference of *interpretation*. In the last section of this Introduction (see p. xxvi.) the writer proposes to give a few, out of a very large number, of interesting variations, tending to support this explanation of many of the synoptic divergences; namely, that (in many parts) the three narratives were derived from one common tradition; that this tradition was probably Greek; and that, in any case, this tradition was variously *interpreted*, by difference of punctuation, transposition, or other slight changes, so as to give rise to three more or less divergent narratives. Meanwhile, one word on the *à priori* probability of the hypothesis.

INTRODUCTION.

It is possible that for some time the Evangelistic records were handed down not in writing, but by means of oral tradition, like the Mishna of the Jews; which is said to have been editorially arranged about the end of the second century, but not committed to writing till afterwards. A tradition intended to be handed down orally might naturally aim at brevity; and the following extract from a condensed and interesting essay on the Mishna will shew that, at all events in Jewish tradition, brevity was occasionally accompanied by its proverbial danger, obscurity. "Dr. Schiller Szinnessy says: 'The language of the Mishna, although pure, and indeed purer than the language of several books of the Bible, was so concise and terse that it could not be understood without a commentary.' This elliptical style may perhaps be compared to that of *a telegram, which has to be expanded before it can be understood*. For instance, in the following quotation the words in brackets are part of the expansion and have no counterpart in the Hebrew:—

"[*Damages awarded to her in compensation for*] insult or injury belong to her, Rabbi Judah ben Bethera saith: [*if the injury inflicted on her is*] hidden, two-thirds [*of the damages recovered*] belong to her and one-third to him [*the husband*]."[1]

Without the words in brackets this passage would read thus: "Insult or injury belong to her. Rabbi Judah ben Bethera saith hidden two-thirds belong to her, and one third to him." No doubt the context would to some extent elucidate the meaning of such a passage; but still, remembering that the Gospels and the Mishna sprang from the same national source, we may not unprofitably ask ourselves, as we cast our eyes along the black type of the Common Tradition in the following pages, "Is it not possible that the condensed narrative which we can pick out of the three Synoptic records represents the 'elliptical style' of the earliest Gospel notes or Memoirs, which needed to be 'expanded' before they could be used for the purposes of teaching, and which might naturally be expanded with various and sometimes divergent amplifications?" We shall recur to this hypothesis later on (see p. xxvi.); but the fuller discussion of it almost necessitates some reference to the Greek text, and for the present it must suffice to say that there are good reasons for supposing that the brevity and obscurity of several portions of the Original Memoirs, and especially of those portions which contain dialogue, may account for many of the existing differences in the Synoptic Gospels.

[1] *The Mishna as Illustrating the Gospels*, by W. H. Bennett, B.A. (M.A. London), Fry Hebrew Scholar of St. John's College, Cambridge, and Tyrwhitt University Scholar. (Cambridge: Deighton, Bell, and Co. London: George Bell and Sons, 1884.)

2.—ON THE REVISED TEXT OF THE NEW TESTAMENT.

By the kind permission of the Oxford and Cambridge Delegates of the respective University Presses, we have been allowed to use the Revised Text in the following pages; to the very great advantage of those readers who seek to approach as closely as possible to the exact meaning of the words of Christ.

In an Introduction addressed to "the general reader," it would be out of place to enter into detail concerning the faithfulness of the Revised Version to the Greek Gospels: but one or two popular objections may be briefly discussed.

It is alleged that the New Version is less rhythmical than the old, and that it has introduced a number of needless changes which jar upon the ear and throw over the general style an air of pedantry. For example in Matthew v. 26, "Thou shalt by no means come out thence, till thou have paid the last farthing," certainly sounds unrhythmical as compared with the Old Version "till thou have paid the uttermost farthing."

Both in this and other passages it is probable that the Revisers would have done more wisely to insert in the margin, and not in the text, changes introduced not for necessity, but for consistency, *i.e.* for the purpose of always rendering the same Greek word by the same English word. The popular instinct—which, in respect of English, is a much more faithful guide than the taste of those who have given much time to Greek and Latin composition and very little to the serious study of their own language—readily detects any combination of ancient and modern phraseology, and rejects the mixture as unpleasing. "The last farthing" suggests to us, at present, the modern phrase, "one's last shilling," and, in its ancient and venerable context, raises a feeling of incongruity.

But time will help to dissipate this objection. The modern and vernacular expressions of to-day become recognized in the second generation, respectable in the third, and venerable in the fourth or fifth. It cannot be too often repeated that the same charge of want of rhythm, which is now brought against the Version of the nineteenth century, was also brought two centuries and a half ago, against that Authorized Version which all English-speaking peoples now agree in regarding as one of the purest fountains of their language. The Revised Version of the New Testament was not made simply or mainly for the present, but also for future ages, and it may be not unreasonably hoped that the twentieth century will not have passed away without covering multitudes of what we must needs now think defects under those pleasing associations which we are in the habit of calling the "veil of antiquity." And some little sacrifice of the mere pleasure of the ear may fairly be

INTRODUCTION. xiii

demanded from the general reader of the Bible if thereby the Book is made, for all time, a more faithful interpreter of the Divine Word.

But a second and far more serious charge has been brought against the Revisers, that they have erroneously altered the text of the Greek Testament in conformity with certain Manuscripts, ancient indeed but not so ancient as some of the Fathers on whose evidence they have set comparatively little store; and, more particularly, that they have been led by this erroneous system to omit passages of Scripture, and even to throw doubt on no less than twelve consecutive verses which have hitherto formed the conclusion of St. Mark's Gospel, Mark xvi. 9–20. These verses are not, it is true, cancelled by the Revisers, nor are they even relegated to the margin; but an interval is left between them and the eighth verse of the sixteenth chapter, as if to say that they are of the nature of an Appendix; and the opinion of the Revisers is indicated by a marginal note stating that "the two oldest Greek manuscripts, and some other authorities, omit from verse 8 to the end. Some other authorities have a different ending to the Gospel."

The controversy on these verses is of such deep interest—both because of the importance of the particular passage itself, and because the discussion illustrates the general principles upon which the Revisers have proceeded—that we shall make no apology for giving a summary of the argument and the evidence on both sides. But some preliminary considerations claim our attention.

First, it must be remembered that the tendency in the earliest periods of the Church was decidedly in favour of amplifying rather than curtailing the Gospels. The most common way of doing this was to supplement one Gospel by another. To take the first instance that comes to hand. In the description of Jesus walking on the sea, in Mark vi. 47, we read merely that "the ship was in the midst of the sea;" but Matthew (xiv. 24) tells us that "the ship was many furlongs distant from the land, *being tossed* by the waves." Hence a MS. adds *in Mark also* the words "being tossed." "The number of such instances in the older MSS. is legion," says Professor Sanday,[1] and therefore we need not mention another of this kind.

But there was another method of supplementing the Gospels, not so easily detected, namely, by additions derivable from oral tradition, or from the suggestions of scribes. Sometimes these amplifications were on a small scale and consist of little more than the reduplication of various readings. For example, in Mark vi. 33, after the words "ran there together on foot from all the cities," there appears to have been a variation in the text :—

---

[1] *Gospel of the Second Century*, p. 68. The best and amplest instances of this kind of corruption will be found in the marginal notes of the Revisers on Luke xi. 2-4, the passage containing the Lord's prayer.

(1) One very early text, represented by our two most ancient MSS. reads "and they outwent them."

(2) Another very early text, mostly current in the West, and therefore called for convenience the Western text, reads "and they came together there."

(3) A third text, represented by a great number of MSS. of respectable antiquity, *combines the two readings*, with slight modification, thus: "and they outwent them and came together to him."

It is easy to see how this amplification and "mixing of texts" might occur. A various reading might be placed at first in the margin of a MS.; then it might be transferred to the text, perhaps written between the lines; finally it might be inserted in the text itself. The same anxiety which makes us reluctant now to give up a word *that may possibly be a part* of the sacred narrative would be present in the minds of most readers and scribes from the earliest times, urging them to give each interpolation "the benefit of the doubt." And thus in all but a few of the best MSS., copied from the best originals by the most faithful and intelligent scribes, the process of amplification would go on. Hence it follows that, in order to determine the true reading in any case, the *character* as well as the *number*, of the ancient MSS must be considered; and a very few MSS., of *good character*, will outweigh a large number of those MSS., even though ancient, which habitually "mix readings."

But we have not yet dealt with interpolations, properly so called, that is to say, insertions of new matter. Of these there are not many, or at least not many that can now be detected: but what there are, appear to be of very early date, probably inserted in times when the first three Gospels, not yet being recognized as supremely authoritative or "Canonical," were treated by the scribes with a freedom not tolerated in later times. "By the end of the second century," says Dr. Sanday, "the Gospels exhibit a text which bears the marks of frequent transcription and advanced corruption."[1] And he quotes Dr. Scrivener as saying that "It is no less true to fact than paradoxical in sound, that the worst corruptions to which the New Testament has ever been subjected originated within a hundred years after it was composed; that Irenæus, and the African Fathers, and the whole Western (with a portion of the Syrian) Church, used far inferior manuscripts to those employed by Stunica, or Erasmus, or Stephens, thirteen centuries later, when moulding the *Textus Receptus*." Irenæus himself directly attests the diver-

---

[1] *Gospel of the Second Century*, p. 328.

sity of the copies of the New Testament in his day; for in speaking of the book of the Apocalypse (which he declares, and probably with truth, to have been written in the days of Domitian, "almost in our time")[1] he tells us that the number of the Beast (Rev. viii. 18) is variously given in different MSS., and he distinguishes some as "good and ancient." So rapidly did one generation of MSS. succeed another; and so speedily did the sacred autographs pass into utter oblivion.

An ancient text therefore, is, in itself, no security for an uninterpolated text. As individual MSS. depend for their weight, not upon their mere antiquity, but upon their *character;* so it must be with groups of MSS. representing the early texts used in different Churches; and it becomes necessary to ask, Which text is most given to interpolations?

All agree that this fault is most frequently to be found in the Western text, that is to say the text used by Irenæus, the African Fathers and the whole Western Church. "The chief and most constant characteristic of the Western readings is a love of paraphrase. Words, clauses, and even whole sentences were changed, omitted, and inserted with astonishing freedom. . . . . . Another equally important characteristic is a disposition *to enrich the text at the cost of its purity, by alterations or additions taken from traditional and perhaps from apocryphal* or other *non-biblical* sources.'[2] To the same effect speaks Dr. Scrivener in describing the ancient MS. called Codex Bezæ (presented by Beza to the University of Cambridge) which best represents the Western text: "The most striking feature of Codex D" (a brief method of denoting the Codex Bezæ) "is *its habitual tendency to interpolation.*" At the same time he maintains that these interpolations were very early, and that "the Text of the Codex Bezæ as it stands at present, is, in the main, identical with one that was current both in the East and West as early as the second century of our era. It may very well have been brought into Gaul by Irenæus and his Asiatic contemporaries about A.D. 170."[3]

Of the numerous interpolations of the Codex Bezæ two must suffice. After Matthew xx. 28, it inserts the following passage:—

"But seek ye to become great from being little; and, from being greater, to become less. And when ye enter in and are invited to sup, sit ye not down in the prominent places, lest at some time a more illustrious than thou come in, and the host (*lit.* the supper-inviter) say to thee, Go yet lower. But if thou take thy seat in the inferior place, and there come in one inferior to thee, the host will say to thee, Go yet higher; and this shall be expedient for thee."

---

[1] This is disputed by many, but (I believe) on insufficient grounds.
[2] Westcott and Hort, *New Testament*, vol. ii. p. 122, from which work most of this section is borrowed.
[3] *Bezae Codex Cantabrigiensis,* Ed. Scrivener, p. xlix.

INTRODUCTION.

Again, in the place of Luke vi. 5, which he transposes to a place between vi. 10 and vi. 11, the scribe of Codex D, sets down the following story :—

"On the same day, seeing a certain man working on the sabbath, he said unto him, Man, if thou knowest what thou doest, blessed art thou ; but if thou knowest not, cursed art thou and a transgressor of the law."

As to that portion of the Acts of the Apostles which is preserved in the Codex Bezæ Dr. Scrivener says, "While the general course of the history and the spirit of the work remain the same as in our commonly received text, we perpetually encounter long passages in Codex Bezæ which resemble that text only as a loose and explanatory paraphrase recalls the original from which it sprang."

The reader will require no further quotations, and no argument at all, to convince him that the evidence of the Western Text, as represented by the Codex Bezæ, is almost worthless in support of any passage omitted by the two or three ancient MSS. representing the early non-Western text. Here, as before, not the *number* of MSS. but their *character*, will determine the question ; and, even though an interpolation may have spread from the Western text into later texts, and may have been so generally adopted, as to find its way into a multitude of those respectable but not first-rate MSS. which are convicted of the practice of "mixing readings," the concurrent testimony of this mass of witnesses will not avail against that of a comparatively small body of witnesses of superior character.

The testimony of the Fathers must evidently be judged in the same way. We must inquire not only into their date, but into their *character*, that is to say, into their practice of quoting from an accurate or from a corrupt text, and also into their opportunities for distinguishing between a corrupt and incorrupt text. Take for example Origen in the third century and Irenæus in the second. Both writers recognize the corrupt nature of the text of the New Testament in their days; but Origen was a learned and scholarly critic, working in Alexandria, a centre of literature and learning, with abundant means of comparing MSS. from all parts of the world ; Irenæus, on the other hand, spent the active part of his life at Lyons, and is not notable for scholarship or critical acumen ; he is besides known to have *used the Western text*.[1] Obviously

[1] The text used by Irenæus is not always easy to determine, as the Latin translator of his Greek works, who has alone preserved the greater part of his writings, may very often have rendered the Greek quotations from the New Testament by corresponding quotations from some old Latin version, current and known to the translator—just as, if we were translating into English a French book containing quotations from the Vulgate, we should render them into quotations from our English version. But Westcott and Hort, while fully recognizing this fact, agree in assigning to him a Western text : "Secure knowledge of the character of the text of the New Testament used by Irenæus himself,

INTRODUCTION. xvii

therefore the testimony of Origen will go for much, and that of Irenæus (early though he was) must go for very little, in determining any question of interpolation.

Nor can it be maintained that Irenæus, though he laboured under the disadvantage of employing for the most part a corrupt and interpolated text, was likely to be prevented by any inherent accuracy, and critical insight, from adopting any serious interpolation. Several remarkable faults in the single volume of his extant works attest his uncritical nature. For example, he quotes (iii. 20, 4) as from Isaiah, a passage which he elsewhere (v. 31, 1) attributes to Jeremiah, but which is really found in neither prophet;[1] and in the same chapter he quotes Habakkuk in conformity neither with the Hebrew nor the LXX.; Jeremiah also receives from him (v. 35, 1) credit for a long passage extracted from Baruch iv. 36. His remarks in the way of Hebrew criticism (ii. 35, 3) induce the commentator Massuet to write that "Some ignoramus appears here to have imposed upon our friend Irenæus, who was not very conversant with Hebrew." These mistakes are all from the Old Testament, with which we might suppose our author to be less familiar than with the New.[2] But even in referring to the Gospels he makes mistakes, and occasionally very strange ones. For example, in describing the raising up of the daughter of Jairus (ii. 24, 4), he says that Jesus suffered no one to go in, save Peter and James, and the father and mother of the maiden—omitting John. Again, after quoting Matthew xi. 27, "No man knoweth the Son but the Father, &c." (and similarly Luke x. 22), he continues, "Thus hath Matthew set it down, and Luke in like manner, *and Mark the very same*"—whereas Mark altogether omits this passage. He mentions Jesus as raising up "the deceased daughter of *the high-priest*," meaning, by "high-priest," Jairus, the ruler of the synagogue (v. 13, 1); and in describing the raising up of the young man, the son of a widow (Luke vii. 12), he writes as follows: "For [the Scripture] saith, 'The Lord took the hand of the dead man, and said to him, Young man, I say unto thee, Arise. And the dead man sat up; and he commanded that something should be given him to eat; and he delivered him to his mother.'" Now the words of Luke, who alone records this incident, are: "And he came nigh and touched the bier: and the bearers stood still. And he said, Young

---

can of course be obtained only from the Greek extracts, and from such readings, extant only in Latin, as are distinctly fixed by the context; and it is solely from these materials that we have described his text as definitely Western" (*New Testament*, vol. ii. p. 160).

[1] It was probably found in some interpolated version. Justin Martyr accuses the Jews of removing it from the Bible (Clarke's *Irenæus*, iii. 20, 5).

[2] The merely numerical error of "three spies" for "two" received by Rahab the harlot (iv. 20, 12) is of trifling importance as compared with the errors mentioned above.

b

man, I say unto thee, Arise. And he that was dead sat up and began to speak. And he gave him to his mother." We see, therefore, that Irenæus, while professing to quote, omits two incidents, viz. the touching of the bier, and the young man's beginning to speak, and inserts two, viz. the taking of the young man by the hand, and the precept to give him something to eat. There can be hardly a doubt that Irenæus is here influenced by that amalgamating tendency which we mentioned above as the source of constant interpolation, introducing into the miracle of Nain two of the incidents recorded in the raising of the daughter of Jairus. In any case these errors can by no possibility be attributed to the Latin translator. Irenæus himself must be held responsible for them; and his critical weight must be diminished accordingly.

After these preliminary considerations as to the method on which the Revisers have proceeded, the early occurrence of corruption in the text of the New Testament, the general tendency to amplify rather than to curtail, the necessity for weighing the character as well as the antiquity of MSS., and the special liability of the Western text (which was used by Irenæus) to ancient but arbitrary interpolation—we pass now to the discussion of the particular passage for the omission of which the Revisers have been censured. It may be called for convenience—

3.—THE APPENDIX TO ST. MARK'S GOSPEL.

This name has been given to verses 9–20 of the sixteenth chapter of St. Mark, beginning "Now when he was risen," and ending with the words "the signs that followed. Amen."

Of the internal evidence, derived from style, the reader now addressed is supposed incapable of judging; but it would be generally admitted by all competent and unbiased critics that Westcott and Hort rather understate than exaggerate the case when they pronounce their conclusion that the differences of style between the Appendix and the Gospel "produce an impression unfavourable to authorship," *i.e.* to the genuineness of the passage.

But concerning another kind of internal evidence the ordinary English reader is quite competent to judge, and that is the discontinuity between the Gospel and the Appendix. Mark xvi. 8 describes Mary Magdalene, another Mary and Salome, who had come to visit the sepulchre "very early on the first day of the week" (xvi. 2), as fleeing from the sepulchre in fear. What is needed is a continuation, such as we find in the parallel passage in Matthew xxviii. 9 : "And behold Jesus met them." But, instead of this, the very next verse introduces Mary *as though she had never been mentioned before;* repeats "the first day of the week," as though the date had not just been given; makes no mention of the manner in which her terror-stricken flight was arrested; and leaves us in complete ignorance of what happened to the other woman who accompanied Mary in her flight :—

"8. And they" (*i e.* Mary Magdalene and the rest) "went out and fled from the tomb; for trembling and astonishment had come upon them; and they said nothing to any one; for they were afraid.

9. *Now when he was risen early on the first day of the week, he appeared first to Mary Magdalene, from whom he had cast out seven devils.*"

The italicized words might stand suitably in a catalogue of the appearances of Jesus after the Resurrection (and in such an account there would be a fitness both in the use of the word "first," and in the insertion of the day on which the Resurrection took place), but they are wholly out of place here in a continuation of the narrative of the visit of Mary Magdalene and her companions to the sepulchre.

But it may be asked, If there is really this manifest discontinuity between the Gospel and the Appendix, and if the Appendix is an interpolation, how can we suppose that the interpolator could not have devised some more continuous interpolation? The reply is, that in all probability the Appendix was not written specially for this purpose, but was a fragment from some very ancient document or tradition, inserted here to fill a gap. We can hardly suppose that the Gospel of St. Mark was intended to end with the words in verse 8, "for they were afraid." Either the Gospel was left incomplete, or the earliest copy, or copies, of the Gospel must have been by some accident mutilated. In either case the temptation to supply the gap would be very great indeed; but a scribe might naturally feel reluctant to compose a conclusion of his own, and would prefer to insert a fragment from some ancient tradition, even though it did not exactly fit the place to be filled.

We have actual evidence that scribes in very early times *did attempt* to fill the gap at the end of St. Mark's Gospel by composing appendices of different kinds. A manuscript, generally called Codex L, which, although ascribed to the eighth century, is nevertheless believed by scholars to represent an extremely pure text, and was said by Griesbach to agree remarkably with the text used by the great scholar Origen, adds the following short Appendix after verse 8 :—

"The following passage also has a kind of currency (or is current in some places.)

"But all these things that had been commanded to them, they narrated briefly to the companions of Peter. And after these things, Jesus also himself, from the east even to the west, sent forth by their means the holy and incorruptible preaching of eternal salvation."[1]

---

[1] A similar Appendix is found in a Latin manuscript called the *Codex Taurinensis*, representing a version made in the fifth century.

The Manuscript then continues thus :—

"But there is also this passage current, after the (sentence), For they were afraid :—"

and it then proceeds to give the whole of the passage, Mark xvi. 9, which we have called above the Longer Appendix.

This testimony is extremely important, as shewing that the Manuscript that has handed down to us one of our purest texts, recognizes, first, the incompleteness of Mark's Gospel, and secondly, the existence of two unauthoritative supplements, giving the precedence to the shorter of the two, and placing it above the Longer Appendix, which in our Unrevised Version was printed as an integral part of St. Mark's Gospel.

How natural it would be to insert some Appendix, and how difficult to resist its spreading from one MS. to another, may be inferred from our own reluctance to suppose that a Gospel could be issued to the world incomplete and omitting (except so far as it is stated in the account of "a vision of angels" to women) the cardinal fact of all Gospels, the attestation of the resurrection of Christ. Irenæus expresses a prejudice almost universal among Christians when he writes that : "Since God hath made all things of an orderly and compact structure, it needs must have been that the form of the Gospel also should be well ordered and well harmonized" (iii. 11, 9); and such a prejudice is almost incompatible with the acceptance of St. Mark's Gospel in its incomplete shape. The same Father very frankly sets forth another criterion of truth, by no means uncommon even in these days, viz., that it is "necessary." He declares that if any one could oppose Luke on the ground that he was ignorant of the truth, such a one would be "convicted of casting aside the Gospel of which he claims to be a disciple." And why? "Because through Luke we have come to the knowledge of very many, and these the *more necessary* facts of the Gospel, such as the birth of John, the story of Zacharias, &c." (iii. 14, 3). Again Eusebius, who wrote as a professed critic in the fourth century, speaking of this very passage—which he himself rejects, as not being found "in the accurate copies"—nevertheless admits the existence of a large class of men who will not "dare to reject anything whatever that has *any kind of currency* in the Scriptures." The most striking instance of the tendency of "necessary," that is to say edifying, matter, to spread from one to a multitude of MSS., is afforded by the doxology of the Lord's Prayer. The words "for thine is the kingdom, the power and the glory for ever and ever. Amen," have no place in the Lord's Prayer as recorded either by Matthew or by Luke, and are excluded from our Revised Text. They are omitted by all Greek commentators on the Lord's Prayer (except Chrysostom and his followers), and by all Latin commentators; and one writer expressly defends them as being "the final ascription *added by the holy luminaries and masters of the Church:*" yet to this day they are regarded by millions of Christians as being the words of Christ, and they are found in all but four of the most ancient MSS.[1]

We need not therefore be surprised at finding that the Longer Appendix is contained in seven ancient MSS. of respectable antiquity and in a great multitude of others; and that Irenæus expressly quotes from it as a part of the Gospel of St. Mark. On the first point it is sufficient to say that these MSS. are not of that superior class which is free from interpolations and "mixed readings." On the second point we need merely repeat that the uncritical nature of Irenæus and the character of the Western text, which he employed, render his testimony almost worthless in favour of any passage supposed to be interpolated.

On the other side we have a mass of external evidence, positive and negative, which, having regard to the strong tendency in favour of the interpolation, we can hardly regard as other than irresistible. The passage is omitted by the two oldest and most trustworthy MSS.; and one of these, the Codex Vaticanus, leaving a blank space in a manner not usual in the conclusion of any other book in the Codex, indicates that the scribe was aware of the gap at the end of the Gospel, but did not know of any genuine matter wherewith to fill the gap. A third most excellent MS. (Codex L) has been shown to contain the Longer Appendix, as the inferior of two non-canonical interpolations.

The critic Eusebius, writing in the fourth century, declares that the passage is "not found in the accurate copies"; and the great commentator Jerome, although in his earlier writings he twice quotes it, yet twenty-four years afterwards adopts the view of Eusebius, and says that "almost all Greek copies omit this section."

The negative evidence is perhaps still more cogent. For the passage contains texts which, on such subjects as the appearances of Jesus after the Resurrection, the necessity of Baptism, the Ascension of Jesus, and the Sitting at the right hand of God, could hardly fail to be occasionally used, if not for illustration, at all events for controversy; yet neither Cyril of Jerusalem (A.D. 350) in his exhaustive quotations of passages concerning the Sitting at the right hand of God, nor Tertullian (A.D. 200) nor Cyprian (A.D. 250) in their controversies concerning the necessity of Baptism, make any reference to any passage in the Longer Appendix. Indeed, with the single exception of the untrustworthy testimony of Irenæus, not a single Latin or Greek writer can be shown to

---

[1] A form of the doxology is found even in the *Teaching of the Twelve Apostles*, composed during the second century.

INTRODUCTION.

have made any use of the Appendix before the Nicene Council in 325 A.D.[1]

The only argument of the slightest weight against the overwhelming mass of evidence internal and external, is that there are not only differences of style between the Appendix and the Gospel, but also one or two apparent or real discrepancies of fact, and that these discrepancies might have led scribes to omit the passage. But the answer to this argument is complete. The scribes of the MSS. of the New Testament resort occasionally to the omission of a phrase, or a sentence, in order to escape from a supposed discrepancy, but never to the wholesale cancelling of a large section of the text; nor could any, even the most audacious of cancellers, dream of "so violent a remedy as the excision of the last twelve verses of a Gospel, *leaving a sentence incomplete*. . . . . Remedial omissions on this scale, and having such results, are unknown."[2]

The Greek student will find all the evidence on both sides of the question, stated in much fuller detail, and carefully and dispassionately weighed, in the second volume of Westcott and Hort's edition of the New Testament, wherein they arrive at the conclusion that the passage is an interpolation (*Notes on Select Readings*, pp. 28—49); but we believe that the general reader, reviewing this popular summary of the controversy, and taking into consideration the general tendency to interpolate; the special temptation to complete an incomplete Gospel; the internal evidences of style and discontinuity; the uncritical character of the only early Father (Irenæus) who quotes this passage, and the corrupt nature of the text which he habitually employs; the inferior character of the MSS. which insert the passage as compared with the excellence of the MSS. which omit it; the direct condemnation pronounced by Eusebius and deliberately repeated by Jerome in his later years; and lastly, the fact that a passage so rich in controversial texts, is not used by a single early Father (except Irenæus) up to 325 A.D., will have no difficulty in

---

[1] It has been suggested that Justin Martyr may have used the Appendix, because he speaks of "that strong word which his Apostles preached everywhere, having gone forth from Jerusalem," which he may have borrowed from Mark xvi. 20, "But they, having gone forth from Jerusalem, preached everywhere." But the employment of words of such common occurrence (compare "teaching everywhere," Matt. xxi. 28; 1 Cor. iv. 17) can prove nothing.

And the North African bishop, Vincentius of Thibaris (256 A.D.), can be shown to be quoting, not Mark xvi. 18, but, in all probability, Matt. x. 6. See Westcott and Hort, as above.

[2] Westcott and Hort, ii. 49. As to the supposition that the passage may have been omitted because of some misinterpretation of the word "end" in the margin, used to denote the "end" of a church lesson, and misunderstood to mean the "end" of the Gospel—it will be found refuted by Westcott and Hort (ii. 49); and it would not have been mentioned in a popular summary like this, except as a specimen of the desperate shifts to which those must resort who could defend this indefensible interpolation.

understanding and appreciating the reasons which have forced the Revisers to print the passage as an Appendix, and not as a portion of the original Gospel of St. Mark.

4.—ON THE PART PLAYED BY CRITICISM IN THE DEVELOPMENT OF THE CHRISTIAN RELIGION.

Some of those who assent to the reasoning in the last section may regret that they are obliged to do so. "Would it not be better to have had no Gospel of St. Mark at all," they may be inclined to exclaim, "rather than that the Church should have used the Gospel as a complete work for more than a thousand years, and now at last find that it has been deceived?" And when it is pointed out to them that this is but one—though the most important—of hundreds of passages containing various readings, or interpolations, each of which indicates that some individual, or congregation, or group of congregations, was under some error less or greater; and that even in the Lord's Prayer the Church has been permitted to remain for many centuries at least so far in error as to attribute to our Lord, and to repeat as His, words which were innocently added by later scribes—some may be inclined to go still further in their despair, and to ask, "Would it not have been better to have had but one Gospel, not needing to be harmonized with two or three others; with no interpolations to be rejected, no various readings to be discussed, no difficulties to be solved? Is it right or reasonable that a religion of Love should be surrounded with intellectual difficulties, over and above the moral difficulty of conforming the emotions to its dictates?"

Certainly if the object of Providence had been to lay down a law, or even to place on record a number of deeds and words to be exactly imitated, in either case a single Gospel would seem to have been best. Or, if the Divine purpose had been that the Christian religion should remain one and the same for ever, in form as well as in spirit, uninfluenced by the growth of knowledge and scientific criticism—then also it would have been better that Constantine should have destroyed every Codex of the Gospels but one (even though that one were the interpolated Codex Bezæ), and that henceforth all faults and corruptions of scribes should have been made impossible by uniform supervision. And such, or somewhat such, has been the fate of the Koran. But not such has been the way of Providence in the diffusion of the Christian Gospels; and surely it behoves believers in Providence to ask whether, after all, the Koran has wholly gained, and the New Testament wholly lost, the one from its uniformity, the other from its manifold variations.

INTRODUCTION.

In the opinion of the writer (although the thought may seem to savour too much of the old Evangelical school) there has been a distinct gain for the Christian religion from the uncertainty and variations of the text of the Christian books. In almost all ages, certainly in the earliest, the divergence of manuscripts has furnished some protection against bondage to the letter; and still more valuable have been the variations in Christ's words, as recorded in the several Gospels. It has been a benefit to the Christian religion that it has developed with the Renaissance, and that it has been aided by the growth of literature and criticism to free itself from corruptions and superstitions. If on the one hand there has resulted, and is likely to result in a far greater degree hereafter, some uncertainty respecting the exact nature of minor details of the Gospel History, the consequent mental detachment from the mere letter of the New Testament may help to attach us more firmly to the Spirit of Him from whom the New Testament derives all its vitality. Our faith in Jesus of Nazareth as the eternal Son of God and Redeemer of the world is not, or ought not to be, based upon historical details which may be shaken to-morrow by the discovery of the book-case of a Christian of the second century in Pompeii, but upon the broad and incontestable evidence afforded by the character and teaching of Christ, and upon the marvellous triumphs over evil which we discern in experience and in history wherever His Spirit has been faithfully followed.

Nor ought any moderately thoughtful observer of the ways of Truth to be in the least distressed if, looking back upon the history of the Christian Church, he seems to see, in every manifestation of the truth, some admixture of falsehood and more of illusion; much din of controversy and hubbub of apologetics often drowning the still small voice of pure religion; the way towards the ideal by no means a straight road, but a narrow and winding path, leading to a number of Promised Lands, each of which in turn proves to be no real Promised Land at all, but only a minor eminence whence to discern the far-off highest height of all. As it was in Astronomy—perhaps the noblest of intellectual pursuits in the sphere of natural science—so may it well be in the search after religious truths. We are led to truth through illusion.

"All the works of Divine Providence in the world," says Francis Bacon, "are wrought by winding and roundabout ways—where one thing seems to be doing, and another is doing really—as in the selling of Joseph into Egypt and the like." So it has assuredly been in the history of the Christian Church. Who is the great witness to the resurrection of Jesus? Is it, as St. Peter puts it, one of the men "which have companied with us all the time that the Lord Jesus went in and went out among us"?—is it one of these that "must become a witness with us of His resurrection"? Not so. It is the thirteenth Apostle, the man who knew not Christ in the flesh, and could be no eye-witness to any of His deeds—who was selected by Providence to be the earliest and most weighty witness (so far as concerns the testimony of the authors of our sacred books) to the fundamental fact of Christianity. There is no more striking contrast between the attempted symmetry of human plans in councils and convocations, and the startling irregularity of Divine plans, than is to be found in the absolute obscurity which attends the history of the formally elected twelfth Apostle, and the world-renowned achievements of the informally summoned thirteenth!

We ought to take comfort from these considerations. God does not make—it is an Evil Being that makes—falsehood, error, and illusion; but God does make falsehood, error, and illusion, stepping-stones to a higher truth than could be attained without them. In the attainment of all blessings, we shall ever find that we do not reach our first-desired object in its entirety; but the portion that we actually attain is really better for us. And so it is in the search after religious truth. When we were children we could not stop short of desiring to believe that the whole of the letter of the Bible was absolutely true, but concerning the spirit of it we knew and cared little or nothing. Now we must be content to accept part of the letter of the Bible; but the result will be not loss but gain, if we penetrate all the more deeply to the spirit of the sacred Book.

II.—TO THE STUDENT OF THE GREEK TESTAMENT.

1.—THE OBJECT OF THE BOOK.

While exhibiting to the general reader the Common Tradition of the Synoptic Gospels, this Harmony is also intended to enable the student of the Greek Testament—provided that he has so much knowledge of the Greek language as may fairly be expected from a pupil in the Fifth and Sixth Forms of first-grade schools—to follow with exactness the agreements, divergencies, and peculiarities of the Synoptic Writers.

The work is a translation of the first part of Mr. Rushbrooke's *Synopticon*, which, by means of different colours and types, sets before the Greek student in a strikingly intelligible manner all the curious phenomena of the first three Gospels; but *Synopticon*, owing to the great expense of producing it, is necessarily a very costly work, far above the means of boys at school. And yet the study of any one Gospel must always be most incomplete and unsatisfactory, unless it is illustrated by such a comparison of the other two as the student is enabled to make by means of *Synopticon*. It has therefore seemed desirable to publish an English translation of that work so arranged as to enable any Greek student, with a little pains and attention, to make a Synopticon for himself in the following way :—

Take a pen with red ink, and, omitting the black type, underline, in columns 2 and 3, all the words common to Mark and Matthew;[1] then, with black ink, underline, in columns 2 and 4, all the words common to Mark and Luke; lastly, in columns 3 and 4, underline with pencil or blue ink all such words as are common to Matthew and Luke. It will of course follow that all words not underlined and not in black type in any column are peculiar to the Evangelist whose name stands at the head of that column; and thus the student will have before him :—

(1) Black type, the Common Tradition of the first three Gospels.

(2) Underlined with red, the additions common to Mark and Matthew.

(3) Underlined with black, the additions common to Mark and Luke.

(4) Underlined with blue, the additions common to Matthew and Luke.

(5) Ordinary type, in each Gospel, the additions peculiar to that Gospel.

The Revised Version presents much greater facilities than the unrevised for a work of this kind, because the general exactness and consistency of the translation enables the Greek student to reproduce the original from the English with much greater ease and certainty. The cases are few in which any inconsistency of the Revisers in rendering parallel passages might place some obstacle in the way of reproducing the original Greek; and wherever any difficulty of this kind has been observed, a note of it is made in the left-hand column.

One or two short statements may explain the principles upon which the Harmony is composed, and especially the arrangement of the black type :—

I. Similar English words are not printed black, *e.g.* "bed" (Mark i. 4; Matthew ix. 2; Luke v. 18) when they represent different words in the Greek (Mark, κράββατος ; Matthew and Luke, κλίνη).

These cases are of very rare occurrence.

---

[1] The black type is supposed to be omitted in the rest of the following directions, so that "all the words" means "all except those in black type."

INTRODUCTION. xxvii

II. Dissimilar English words are printed black when they represent Greek words similar in part or whole.

III. But where a Greek word, similar only in part, is represented by a *group* of English words, there a portion of the group is left in ordinary type, so as to indicate that the Greek original is not wholly similar.

IV. An asterisk calls attention to minute differences in the Greek, which are not exhibited in the English.

V. A note of interrogation signifies possibilities of different arrangement.

2.—THE CONFUSION OF THE COMMON TRADITION.

Nothing remains but to give one or two instances of the manner in which the book may be used for the elucidation of one Gospel by the others, and for the detachment of the mind from those parts of the Gospel narrative which must be regarded as less certain than the rest.

We have seen above (p. xi.) that in some cases the Mishna is obscure owing to its brevity; and some of its dicta have been compared to telegrams which require "expansion" in order to make them intelligible. Now let us suppose that the earliest records upon which the Gospels are based consisted of brief notes occasionally resembling the Mishna in respect of obscurity: on that supposition, where might we most reasonably expect, in the dialogues and doctrine of Christ, to find some difference of interpretation arising from the original brevity? Is it not in the assignment of different parts of the dialogue to different interlocutors, the words "he said" or "they say" being omitted in the original—much as, in modern novels, a dialogue is sometimes written down without the insertion of words defining the speaker in each case, because the context may be supposed to render such definition needless, and because paragraphs, inverted commas, and other punctuation (devices unknown to the earliest Greek MSS.) help to elucidate the meaning? We will now proceed to give one or two instances of confusion of this kind, arising from the variations in the assignment of dialogue.

Take for example the conclusion of the parable of the Lord of the Vineyard. Jesus puts a question, asking, "What will the Lord of the vineyard do to the wicked servants?" An answer is returned that "He will destroy them." But the Evangelists *differ*

xxviii INTRODUCTION.

as to who makes this answer, whether the Pharisees, or Jesus replying to himself:

MARK XII. 9, 10.	MATTHEW XXI 40–42	LUKE XX. 15–17.
What will the Lord of the vineyard do? He will come and destroy the husbandmen and give the vineyard to others. (10) Have ye not even read the Scripture, The stone, &c.	When therefore the Lord of the vineyard cometh, what will he do to those husbandmen? (41) **They say to him**, He will miserably destroy those miserable men, and will let out the vineyard to other husbandmen, who shall render him the fruits in their seasons. (42) **Jesus saith unto them**, Have ye not even ever read the Scripture, The stone, &c.	What then will the Lord of the vineyard do to them? He will come and destroy those husbandmen and give the vineyard to others And when they heard (this) they said, God forbid. (17) But he looked on them and said, What then is this that is written, The stone, &c.

Here probably Mark most faithfully represents the Original Memoirs, in which the dialogue was written down without any assignment of different parts to different speakers:

(1) "What will the Lord of the vineyard do?"

(2) "He will destroy those husbandmen."

(3) "Have ye not read the Scripture, &c.?"

But it is by no means improbable that Matthew may exhibit the most intelligent *interpretation* of these Memoirs in assigning the second speech to the Pharisees. And it is noteworthy that Luke, although he adopts Mark's assignment, nevertheless feels that the third speech follows so abruptly on the second that he introduces *some intervening remark on the part of the Pharisees*, "God forbid;" to which the third speech comes from Jesus as a retort.

Take another instance from the conclusion of the dialogue between Jesus and the Pharisees concerning divorce: and in this case reversing the process of the last paragraph, let us start from what we may suppose to have been the Original Memoirs, and work onward to the shape which it has assumed in our Gospels. The Greek student will not require to be reminded that there was neither punctuation nor distinction of capital letters in the writing of the first century; he will also be aware that the Greek for "what?" and "why?" is often the same ($\tau \iota$), and that the verb may stand either at the beginning, or at the end, or in any other part of the sentence. Suppose then that the Memoirs of the Apostles contained some note of this kind arranged in the short lines which are found in the earlier and Greek MSS:—

WHAT } DID MOSES COMMAND
WHY
TO GIVE A BILL OF DIVORCEMENT
AND TO PUT HER AWAY HE
SUFFERED FOR THE HARD-
NESS OF YOUR HEARTS

INTRODUCTION.   xxix

Obviously this may be interpreted in two ways :—

(1)
Jesus. What did Moses command?
Pharisees To give a bill of divorcement and to put her away he suffered.
Jesus For the hardness of your hearts (he suffered this).

(2)
Pharisees. Why then did Moses command to give a bill of divorcement and to put her away?
Jesus. He suffered (it) for the hardness of your hearts.

Now see these two different interpretations actually given by Mark and Matthew :—

MARK X. 3–5.
[*And he answered and said unto them,*] What did Moses command [*you? And they said, Moses*] suffered to write a bill of divorcement and to put her away. [*But Jesus said*] for the hardness of your heart [*he wrote you this commandment*].

MATTHEW X. 7–8.
[*They say unto him,*] Why then did Moses command to give a bill of divorcement and to put her away? [*He saith unto them, Moses*] for the hardness of your heart suffered [*you to put away your wives*].

In the following instance Matthew and Mark reverse their treatment of the Tradition ; and what Matthew expresses in a continuous speech, Mark breaks up into a rapid dialogue. It is contained in a passage in which Jesus makes mention of the feeding of the four thousand and of the five thousand (Mark viii. 17–21, Matthew xvi. 9–11), interesting and important because it describes one among several occasions (perhaps more numerous than are generally supposed) in which Jesus uses metaphorical language as to "leaven" and "bread," which was completely misunderstood by his disciples.

Following the same method as before, we may suppose the Original Tradition to have run thus :—

> DO YE NOT YET PERCEIVE
> NEITHER REMEMBER THE FIVE
> LOAVES FOR THE FIVE THOUSAND
> HOW MANY BASKETS FULL OF
> FRAGMENTS TOOK YE[1] UP THE
> SEVEN LOAVES FOR THE FOUR THOU-
> SAND HOW MANY BASKETS OF FRAG-
> MENTS TOOK YE UP[1] DO YE NOT
> YET PERCEIVE

This might be variously interpreted thus :—

(1)
Do ye not yet perceive neither remember? The five loaves for the five thousand? How many baskets took ye up?[1] The seven for the four thousand? How many baskets took ye up? Do ye not yet perceive?

(2)
Do ye not yet perceive neither remember the five loaves for the five thousand (and) how many baskets ye took up,[1] (neither) the seven loaves for the four thousand and how many baskets ye took up?[1] How is it ye do not perceive?

The former of these two interpretations naturally passes into another stage when the abrupt questions are amplified so as to be more in conformity with grammar, and when answers are inserted

---

[1] The Greek for the verb is the same, whether predicatively or interrogatively used.

in reply to the questions; and thus we have the actual versions of Mark and Matthew:—

MARK VIII. 17-21.	MATTHEW XVI. 9-11.
Do ye not yet perceive neither............remember? [*When I brake*] the five loaves for the five thousand, how many baskets full of fragments took ye up? [*They say to him, Twelve. When*[1]] the seven for the four thousand, how many baskets of fragments took ye up? [*They say to him, Seven. And he said to them,*] Do ye not yet understand?	Do ye not yet perceive neither remember the five loaves of the five thousand, and how many baskets ye took up, neither the seven loaves of the four thousand and how many baskets ye took up? How is it that ye do not understand [*that I spake not to you concerning bread?*]

Take now another instance in which there is no variation as to the speaker; but, by the interchange of a relative for an interrogative pronoun, and of a statement for a question, a complete change is made in the sense:—

MARK VI. 19.	LUKE IX. 9.
But Herod when he heard (thereof) said, John, whom I beheaded, he (it. this, $οὗτος$) is risen.	And Herod said, John I beheaded, but who is this?

If the reader will compare the context of these passages, he will find that, whereas both Matthew and Mark assign to Herod the statement that John had risen from the dead, Luke assigns it to "some"; so that the final words of Herod, while in Mark they represent a positive statement, in Luke represent nothing beyond the question of a bewildered man.

Again, in the same passage, compare the following statements:—

MARK VI. 19-21.	MATTHEW XIV. 5.	LUKE IX. 7.
(Herodias) desired to kill him (i.e. John): and she could not, (20) for Herod feared John, knowing that he was a righteous man, and a holy, and kept him safe. (21) And when he heard him, he was much perplexed, and he heard him gladly.	And when he (Herod) desired to kill him, he feared the multitude, because they counted him as a prophet.	Now Herod the tetrarch heard of all that was done, and he was much perplexed, because that it was said by some, &c.

Is it not obvious that some confusion has here arisen from diverse interpretations of the Original Memoirs? It would appear that they contained some brief notes to this effect:—

"desired to kill him . . . feared."

—perhaps supplemented by a further tradition as to "keeping" or "guarding" John, or "regarding" him as a prophet.

But while one Evangelist makes Herodias, another makes Herod, "desire to kill John;" and, in the one, Herodias is prevented by Herod, in the other it is Herod who is prevented by the multitude. Again, in Mark, Herod fears "John"; in Matthew he fears "the multitude."

Lastly, whereas Mark represents Herod as being "perplexed" by

---

[1] It is perhaps a mark of the abruptness of the Original Tradition that the words "I brake" are not repeated here.

the prophetic utterances of John, Luke represents him as being "perplexed" by the rumours of the multitude *about* John.

Few critics conversant with the Gospels would doubt that the close similarity between some parallel passages in them necessitates the hypothesis of a Greek, not an Aramaic, Original Tradition, at least so far as concerns these passages. But it may be of use to call the student's attention to a passage which appears especially well adapted to prove that hypothesis.

MARK XIV. 49.	MATTHEW XXVI. 55.	LUKE XXII. 53.
I was daily with you in the temple teaching.	I sat daily in the temple teaching.	When I was daily with you in the temple.

The Greek for "was" in Mark is here HMHN, a non-classical form not used elsewhere by this Evangelist. But this word, according as it is pronounced with a rough or smooth breathing, may mean "I was," or "I sat." Now the breathings are not inserted in the ancient MSS. so that the word is perfectly ambiguous; and indeed the two words have actually been confused in a play of Sophocles (*Trachiniæ*, 24; see *New Phrynichus*, p. 241). Hence, we need not be surprised that while Matthew renders the word "I sat" (ἐκαθεζόμην) Luke renders it "I was," but avoids the non-classical form by using the participle (ὄντος μου). This appears to indicate a confusion arising from a common use of an Original Greek Tradition, containing the word HMHN, retained by Mark, but altered by Matthew in the sense "I sat," and by Luke in the sense "I was."

One more instance may be given, of a nature more conjectural:

MARK II. 16.	MATTHEW IX. 11.	LUKE V. 30.
And the scribes of the Pharisees, when they saw that he ate with the publicans and sinners, said unto his disciples, Why (ὅτι) doth he eat and drink with the publicans and sinners?¹	And when the Pharisees saw it, they said unto his disciples, Why eateth your Master with the publicans and sinners?	But the Pharisees and their scribes began to murmur against his disciples, saying, Why do ye eat with the publicans and sinners?

Incidentally we may first note here that whereas Matthew records that "the Pharisees," and Mark that "the Scribes *of* the Pharisees" were the speakers, Luke combines both traditions by mentioning "the Pharisees and their Scribes."

But we note in the next place the variations, (1) Mark, "Why doth *he* eat?"; (2) Matthew, "Why eateth *your Master?*" (3) Luke, "Why do *ye* eat?"

It is possible that the Original Tradition was, "And the Scribes of the Pharisees said to the disciples, Why doth he eat (ἐσθίει) with the publicans and sinners?"

---

¹ Of course ὅτι ought not, in good Greek, to mean "why," but I cannot help believing that here, as well as in ix. 11 and ix. 28, Mark uses it so. The sense demands it, and in all three places the parallel passages in Matthew have "why" (τί, or διὰ τί).

This abrupt introduction of the reference to Jesus, as the mere implied subject of the verb, was removed or amended, in Mark, by inserting the introductory clause "when they saw that he ate, &c.," so as to prepare the way for the speech of the Pharisees; in Matthew, by the insertion of the subject "your Master," it being a frequent habit of Matthew to insert a subject where Mark omits one. But in the next place, the editor, or one of the editors, of the earliest Gospel (Mark's) inserted "drink," because, as a matter of fact, Jesus both ate and drank with sinners. Such an insertion as this is very common. Those who compare the Greek with the Hebrew Version of the Old Testament will find that many scribes are unwilling that any one should "eat" without "drinking" also; and accordingly (Robertson Smith, *Lectures on the Septuagint*, p. 90) sometimes a Hebrew scribe (1 Sam. i. 9), sometimes a Greek scribe (2 Sam. xii. 21) adds "drinking" to the textual "eating."

It is probable therefore that a new form of the Tradition would be, "Why doth he both eat and drink?" (ἐσθίει τε καὶ πίνει; comp. Luke xii. 45, ἐσθίειν τε καὶ πίνειν). Now it is easy to see, even in ordinary Greek characters, that εσθιειτε, "he both eateth," is easily confused with εσθιετε, "ye eat." Let us also remember that the diphthongs in the Hellenistic writing were often sadly confused; so that as a matter of fact, in this present passage, D reads εσθιεται και πινεται, and a corrector in C has εσθιετε και πινεται, meaning to represent the 2nd pers. pl.; and this constant practice with D and other ancient MSS. is also found in early inscriptions; and hence a confusion between εσθιειτε and one of the forms of the 2nd pers. pl. would be aided. When εσθιειτε had once been corrupted into εσθιετε, it would be necessary to alter πινει also into the 2nd pers. pl.; but, as the word και follows πινει in Luke's tradition, πινεικαι might easily be mistaken for πινεται, a form of πινετε; and hence we are led to the conclusion that, without any arbitrary alteration of the Tradition, Luke might have found the reading ἐσθίετε καὶ πίνετε, and might have preferred it, as avoiding the abruptness which characterizes the tradition retained by Mark.[1]

The next instance will contain less of the conjectural element, and will afford demonstrative evidence that Matthew has borrowed, not from Mark, but from some Common Tradition, probably Greek, from which Mark has also borrowed. It is taken from the Dis-

---

[1] This conjecture is inserted as being worthy of consideration; but it must not be forgotten that elsewhere Luke uses the second person where Matthew and Mark use the third.—See Mark ii. 19 and 24. In Isaiah ix. 2, "the people that sat in darkness *hath seen* a great light," the LXX. reads "see ye" (ἴδετε); and it would be interesting to enquire whether there are many other such instances in the LXX., and whether they can be explained by some error natural in translation.

course uttered by Jesus on the Mount of Olives, a short time before the Crucifixion, concerning the Last Days:

MARK XIII 9, 10.	MATTHEW XXIV. 9, 14.
...they shall deliver you up to councils...and before governors and kings shall ye stand for my sake **for a testimony unto them** εἰς μαρτύριον αὐτοῖς). (10) **And unto all the nations** ¹ (καὶ εἰς πάντα τὰ ἔθνη) must the Gospel be first preached.	Then shall they deliver you up... (14) And this Gospel of the kingdom shall be preached in the whole world **for a testimony to all the nations** (πᾶσιν τοῖς ἔθνεσιν).

So far, it would be a mere conjecture, though a probable conjecture, that the Original Tradition was:

> YE SHALL STAND FOR MY SAKE FOR
> A TESTIMONY UNTO THEM AND TO
> ALL THE NATIONS MUST THE GOSPEL
> BE PREACHED

—and that Matthew connected the words "for a testimony unto" with "nations," while Mark connected them with the word "them," and gave "nations" a different connection. But the parallel passage in Matthew, though it contains many similarities with that in Mark, does not follow Mark so closely as to make this conjecture by any means a certainty. Fortunately, however, we find another passage in Matthew x. 17-22, where *the whole of Mark's Discourse on the Mount of Olives is faithfully followed*, although, strange to say, it is assigned to *quite a different period in the life of Christ*, viz. *when He is for the first time sending out the Twelve Apostles;* the close agreement of the two passages may be easily seen:

MARK XIII. 9-11.	MATTHEW X. 17-19.
(*Discourse on the Mount of Olives*)	(*The Sending forth of the Twelve.*)
...they shall deliver you up to councils, and in synagogues shall ye be beaten, and before governors and kings shall ye stand for my sake **for a testimony unto them** .(10) **And unto all the nations** must the Gospel be first preached. (11) And when they lead you and deliver you up, &c.	...they will deliver you up to councils; and in their synagogues they will scourge you; (18) yea and before governors and kings shall ye be brought for my sake, **for a testimony to them and to the nations** (καὶ τοῖς ἔθνεσιν). (19) But when they deliver you up, &c.

Can any Greek scholar, or can even any ordinary English reader, after comparing these passages, retain a particle of doubt that the words italicised above—"for a testimony unto them and unto all the nations"—represent an Original Tradition, variously interpreted by Mark and Matthew?

Mark took the words "unto all the nations" with the following words, and interpreted the tradition thus: "Unto all the nations must the Gospel be first preached."

Matthew has *two versions* of the Original Tradition, which he assigns to different periods in the life of Christ.

¹ The order of the Revised Version has been altered so as to correspond with the order of the Greek.

The word "nations" (ἔθνη) is translated by the Revisers "nations," when preceded by "all the"; when it is preceded by "the," they render it "Gentiles."

c

xxxiv   INTRODUCTION.

In the earlier of these (x. 18) he connects the words "to the nations" with the foregoing words; and as the subsequent words of the Tradition, "the Gospel must first be preached," now lose their meaning, he omits them.

In his later version (xxiv. 14) he retains the omitted words "the Gospel shall be preached;" but he seems to have connected the words of the Tradition thus: "for a testimony to them and to the nations shall the gospel be preached." But, in his later context, the words "to them" make no sense; and it becomes necessary to modify the sentence thus, "the Gospel shall be preached to the nations for a testimony to them," or, more shortly, "the Gospel shall be preached for a testimony to the nations," which is the interpretation he actually adopts.

In the following passage there is probably an interesting confusion between πολύς, many, and πόλις, a city. It is in the parable of the talents or pounds:—

MATTHEW XXV. 21, 23.	LUKE XIX 17, 19.
His lord said unto him, Well done, good and faithful servant: thou hast been faithful over a few things, I will set thee **over many things**...thou hast been faithful over a few things, I will set thee **over many things**.	And he said unto him, Well done, thou good servant: because thou wast found faithful in a very few things, have thou authority **over ten cities**...Be thou also **over five cities**.

For "over" Matthew has ἐπί, but Luke ἐπάνω; but this peculiarity of Luke's style does not prevent us from recognizing that ἐπί was the original, just as ὑπό is the original in Mark iv. 21, "*under* the bed," Matthew v. 15, Luke xi. 33, "*under* the bushel," but is altered by Luke, in one of his two versions of the passage, into ὑποκάτω.

The Original Tradition was probably "over many things," ΕΠΙΠΟΛΛΩΝ; but, since Ι meant "ten," this might easily be confused with ΕΠΙΙΠΟΛΕΩΝ, "over ten cities." Again, ΕΠΙ was spelt in the earliest MSS. indifferently ΕΠΙ or ΕΠΕΙ [1]; and, since Ε meant "five," ΕΠΕΙΠΟΛΛΩΝ "over many things," might equally well be confused with ΕΠΙΕΠΟΛΕΩΝ, "over five cities."

It is possible that a somewhat similar confusion may explain the discrepancy between the following passages:—

MARK V. 20.	LUKE VIII. 39.
And he went his way and began to publish **in Decapolis** (ἐν τῇ Δεκαπόλει) how great things Jesus had done for him.	And he went his way publishing **throughout the whole city** (καθ' ὅλην τὴν πόλιν) how great things Jesus had done for him.

---

[1] An amusing instance of the variation in the spelling of ἐπί is to be found in the various interpretations of the first word of Irenæus' *Treatise against Heresies*. It was επι or επει: Epiphanius read επι and interpreted it "against"; the Latin translator read επει and interpreted it "since."

INTRODUCTION.

Now the word Decapolis means TEN CITY, and just as TEN CITY might be easily confused with THE CITY so might "Decapolis" be confused with "the city" in the following way. Deca-, meaning "ten," might be mistaken by an unlearned copyist for the numeral "ten," and might be denoted by the letter I : consequently ΕΝΤΗΔΕΚΑΠΟΛΕΙ would be written ΕΝΤΗΙΠΟΛΕΙ, which could be interpreted by an educated reader in no other way than as meaning ἐν τῇ πόλει, "in the city."[1]

In the narrative of the Transfiguration, Matthew attributes to St. Peter an egotistic utterance not found in Mark and Luke, and explicable from confusion :—

MARK IX. 5.	MATTHEW XVII. 4.	LUKE IX. 33.
And Peter answereth and said unto Jesus, Rabbi, it is good for us to be here, and **let us make** three tabernacles, one for thee, and one for Moses, and one for Elijah.	And Peter answered and said unto Jesus, Lord, it is good for us to be here : **If thou wilt, I will make here** three tabernacles, one for thee, and one for Moses, and one for Elijah	...Peter said unto Jesus, Master, it is good for us to be here, **and let us make** three tabernacles, one for thee, and one for Moses, and one for Elias.

The Original Tradition, preserved by Mark and Luke, was "let us make," ΠΟΙΗϹΩΜΕΝ ; but this was wrongly interpreted in the Tradition which finds expression in Matthew's Gospel, as if it were *in two words*, ΠΟΙΗϹΩ ΜΕΝ : then the word ΜΕΝ, appearing to make no sense, was changed into its correlative ΔΕ, and ΠΟΙΗϹΩ ΔΕ was easily changed (and the more easily because there is ΩΔΕ in the preceding line) into ΠΟΙΗϹΩΔΕ, *i.e.* "I will make here." The intolerable egotism of this reading—"*I will* make"—forced the Editor of this Gospel to insert at least the qualification "if thou wilt" ; and hence the present erroneous version of Matthew.

These specimens of certain or probable confusion of the Original Tradition shall be concluded by one of greater importance, which the writer can offer only as a conjecture, and must needs offer with the knowledge that many learned scholars have declared that the day of conjectures, unsupported by evidence of MSS., is now passed as regards the criticism of the New Testament. And so it probably is, as regards all the other books of the New Testament ; but the peculiar advantages afforded by three independent narratives derived from one Common Tradition have been as yet so little utilized that this dictum does not hold good concerning the Synoptic Gospels, or rather concerning the Original Tradition from which the Synoptic Gospels have jointly borrowed.

The passage in question is taken from Luke's account of the Mission of the Seventy (x. 4, 5) :—"Carry no purse, no wallet, no

---

[1] Even if the confusion did not arise in this way, it seems probable that there is a confusion of some kind, and that πόλις was separated from δέκα by some corruption that points to a Greek Original.

shoes, and salute no man by the way" (μὴ βαστάζετέ βαλλάντιον μὴ πήραν, μὴ ὑποδήματα, καὶ μηδένα κατὰ τὴν ὁδὸν ἀσπάσησθε).

Now in the first place we note that Luke's account of the Mission of the Seventy contains *many sayings which Matthew sets down under the Mission of the Twelve.* For example Luke inserts (x. 2) "The harvest truly is plenteous &c." (Matthew ix. 37, 38); Luke inserts (x. 3) "Behold I send you forth as sheep, &c." (Matthew x. 16); Luke inserts (x. 5, 6) the precept to pronounce a blessing on a house, if there be in it any "son of peace," or, as Matthew expresses it, "any one worthy," (Matthew, x. 11, 12, 13); Luke inserts (x. 9, 11) the precept to proclaim "The kingdom of God is at hand" (Matthew x. 7); Luke inserts (x. 12), "I say unto you that it shall be more tolerable for Sodom, &c." (Matthew x. 15). Indeed, comparing Matthew x. 9—15 with Luke ix. 3—5 (both of which passages describe the Mission of the Twelve), we may almost say that *whatever Luke has omitted from Matthew's tradition, under the heading of the Mission of the Twelve, he has inserted under the heading of the Mission of the Seventy.*[1] But there is one important exception: Matthew's account of the Mission of the Twelve contains a precept to "salute" a house on entering it; Luke, in his Mission of the Twelve, omits it, and yet does not insert it (not at least in the same words) in our present version of the Mission of the Seventy.

One more point of importance needs to be noted before we proceed to our conjecture. As to the precept of Jesus to the Apostles to take nothing with them on their journey, there seems to have been some difference of interpretation in the times of our Evangelists—some having made an exception in favour of "a staff," as Mark does; others, as Luke, making no exception; others, as Matthew, endeavouring to dissipate the difficulty by substituting, for the word "take," another word "procure," as if the precept did not forbid taking with one what one had, but only forbade *procuring anything expressly for the journey:*

MARK VI. 8	MATTHEW X. 9, 10.	LUKE IX. 3.
...that they should **take** (αἴρωσιν) **nothing for their journey,** save a staff only; no bread, no wallet, no money (Gr. brass) in their purse.	**Get** you (κτήσησθε) no gold, nor silver, nor brass for your purses (ζώνας), no wallet **for your journey,** &c.	**Take** (αἴρετε) nothing **for your journey,** neither staff, nor wallet, nor bread, nor money (Gr. silver).

It will be observed, however, that, in spite of other differences, the Synoptists all agree in connecting the precept of the Lord as to the wallet, &c. *with the words "for the journey"* (Matthew and Mark, εἰς ὁδόν: Luke, εἰς τὴν ὁδόν).

---

[1] Luke omits in ix. 3 the mention of "gold" and "brass" for the "purses," and he does not *in the same words* supply the omission in x. 4, but he does so *virtually*, by adding "Carry not *purse.*"

INTRODUCTION.

We now return to the passage under discussion (Luke x. 4, 5), which we will arrange in the order of the Greek; we will also substitute the word "journey" for "way," so as to be uniform with the translation in the last paragraph; and we will place immediately after it the words that follow :—

> CARRY NO PURSE NO WALLET
> NO SHOES AND NO ONE ON THE
> JOURNEY SALUTE BUT INTO WHAT-
> SOEVER HOUSE YE ENTER. . . . .

As to the "purse," we can now perhaps explain Luke's insertion of it, for we find that Matthew, x. 9, makes mention of "purses" although the Greek word is different; and we have seen that, *whatever Luke in the Mission of the Twelve omits from Matthew's Tradition, he inserts in the Mission of the Seventy.* But where, in Luke's Mission of the Seventy can we find Matthew's precept to "salute" the house? And where, in Luke's Mission of the Seventy can we find the precept to "take nothing" connected with the words "for" or "on" the "journey"? Since he thinks it necessary to repeat, in the Mission of the Seventy, the instructions about the "wallet" and "sandals" given to the Twelve, it seems strange that he should omit the qualifying words "for the journey"!

Even the English reader will probably perceive that if, in the second line, "no one" could be changed into "nothing," (in other words, if MHΔENA could be changed into MHΔEN) and if "but" could be transposed (which in Greek involves the transposition of a single letter Δ) all would become clear, and we should have—

> CARRY NO PURSE NO WALLET
> NO SHOES AND NOTHING ON
> THE JOURNEY BUT SALUTE
> WHATSOEVER HOUSE YE
> ENTER INTO. . . . .

Undoubtedly there is some little roughness in this reading; the word "and," before "nothing," is unnecessary and weak; and we should naturally expect rather "carry no purse, no wallet, no shoes—nothing on the journey;" also ἀσπάσησθε would have to be altered to ἀσπάσασθε; and the order of words, ἀσπάσασθε δ' εἰς ἥν ἂν εἰσέλθητε οἰκίαν,—though partly justified by Luke xxiv. 1, φέρουσαι ἃ ἡτοίμασαν ἀρώματα, and John vi. 14, ἰδόντες ὃ ἐποίησε σημεῖον,—is not so usual, or so smooth, as that in Luke's text, which is also found in Luke x. 8 and 10. But the reader must carefully observe that we are not attempting to *emend Luke*, but to *restore the text of some Tradition from which Luke undoubtedly borrowed, and which is identical with many parts of Matthew*; and it is quite possible to demonstrate, by comparison with Matthew, that this Tradition has been corrupted *in some way, and at some time,* without being able to show the precise time or way in which the corruption took place, whether orally or through documents; and whether it was erroneously interpreted by Luke, or by preceding editors, or by Luke in conjunction with others. In the course of such a transmission many misunderstandings and alterations might easily occur, and especially if there was a tendency to introduce slight changes into a Mission narrative, with the view of showing that it did not refer to the Mission of the Twelve, but to the Mission of some other body. And that some corruption of this kind has here caused Luke to diverge from the correct tradition we maintain to be absolutely demonstrable by a comparison of the text of Luke and Matthew in the light of the considerations above alleged :—

LUKE x. 4, 5	MATTHEW x.
Carry no(t) purse, no(t) wallet, no(t) shoes; and salute no man on the journey. And into whatsoever house ye shall enter, first say, Peace be to this house. And if a son of peace be there, your peace shall rest upon him (*more probably* "upon it"); but if not, it shall turn to you again.	Get you no gold...in your purses, no wallet for (the) journey...nor shoes. And into whatsoever city or village ye shall enter, search out who in it is worthy...And as ye enter into the house salute it. And if the house be worthy, let your peace come upon it; but if it be not worthy, let your peace return to you.

Here we have to consider these facts :—

1. The precept "not to salute people by the way" is well fitted for Gehazi in extreme haste, but not fitted for disciples of Jesus going forth to carry a Gospel of conciliation through Galilee. There are no indications of any such precept in the Mission of the Twelve; and there seems still less reason for it in the Mission of the Seventy, who, being more numerous, may reasonably be supposed to have a less onerous task, and more time for the performance of it.

2. The precept is quite contrary to the implied precept in Matthew v. 47 : "If ye salute your brethren only, what do ye more than others?"—which implies that the disciples of Jesus were bound to "salute" strangers as well as friends.

3. Sanctus Ephraemus(ed. Moesinger, p. 92)—who is supposed to have used the early Harmony of the Gospels composed by Tatian—reads, "Into whatsoever house ye enter, first *salute the house.*" This *might* have arisen from a blending of Luke with Matthew;[1] but the quotation is valuable as showing how natural it is to interchange the expressions "Salute the house," and "Peace be to the house." Supposing that an editor found the tradition already corrupted into "Salute no one by the way, and into whatsoever house

---

[1] The Commentary of Sanctus Ephraemus contains what may be called "layers" of commentaries, written by different commentators, who used different texts; and very erroneous inferences may be easily drawn from a cursory, or even a prolonged but unintelligent perusal of this book.

ye enter, salute the house," it is obvious that he would be tempted to avoid tautology by substituting, for the latter "salute," its equivalent, " Peace be to this house."

4. The word "salute" is rare in the Gospels, occurring only twice in Matthew, viz. v. 47 and here; and only twice in Luke, viz. i. 40 and here. It is therefore extremely unlikely that, in a tradition in which the two Evangelists closely resemble each other, they should both use this rare word, but with a variation of *context which gives the passage two totally different meanings,* whereas a slight remodelling of the context would make the meanings the same.

Besides the restoration of the true Original of this particular passage, other far more important consequences may follow, if it be recognized that Matthew's Mission of the Twelve contains two distinct Traditions, one of which closely resembles Mark, and is considered by Luke to refer to the Twelve, while the other is omitted by Mark, and referred by Luke to the Mission of the Seventy.

These specimens of the Confusion of the Original Tradition in the Synoptic Gospels are but a few out of a very large collection, which the writer hopes in due course to publish in such a form as to be intelligible to the general reader without ceasing to be useful to the student of the Greek Testament. There is no ancient document in existence for the elucidation of which so little has been done, as that venerable Greek Tradition of the words and deeds of Christ which is embedded in the Synoptic Gospels. For the rest of the New Testament the days of emendation, unsupported by MSS., may possibly be past; for this portion of it they are only beginning.

EDWIN A. ABBOTT.

32, ABBEY ROAD, N.W.,
June 4, 1884.

THE COMMON TRADITION

OF THE

SYNOPTIC GOSPELS.

THE COMMON TRADITION

St. Mark. [Portions not found in Matthew or Luke.]	**St. Mark.** [Complete.]
	I. 1-8
1 The beginning of the gospel of Jesus Christ, the Son of God. 2 Even... Behold, I send my messenger before thy face, Who shall prepare thy way. (*But the words* "Behold, I send my messenger before thy face, who shall prepare thy way" *are found in Matthew* xi. 10 *and Luke* vii. 27). 4 ...came, who baptized [?]...and... 5 And...all (they of Jerusalem)... 6 And...was...and did eat (Gr. *eating*)... 7 And he preached,.. stoop down and (Gr. *stooping down*)... 8 ...but [? ?]...	1 The beginning of the gospel of Jesus Christ, [1] the Son of God. 2 Even as it is written [2] in **Isaiah the prophet,** Behold, I send my messenger before thy face, Who shall prepare thy way ; 3 **The voice of one crying in the wilderness,** **Make ye ready the way of the Lord,** **Make his paths straight ;** 4 **John** came, who baptized **in the wilderness** and **preached** the **baptism** [?] of **repentance** unto remission of sins. 5 And there **went out** unto him **all the country** of Judæa, and all they of Jerusalem ; and they were **baptized of him** in the river Jordan, confessing their sins. 6 And John was clothed with camel's hair, and *had* a leathern girdle about his loins, and did eat locusts and wild honey. 7 And he preached, saying, There **cometh** after me **he that is mightier than I,** the latchet of **whose shoes I am not** [3] **worthy** to stoop down and unloose. 8 **I baptized you** [4] **with water ;** but **he shall baptize you** [4] **with the** [5] **Holy Ghost.**
	[1] Some ancient authorities omit *the Son of God*. [2] Some ancient authorities read *in the prophets*. [3] Gr. *sufficient*. [4] Or, *in* [5] Or, *Holy Spirit*: and so throughout this book.
Mark i. 8, W. & H. omit the Greek preposition in both cases.	

St. Matthew. [*Passages parallel to Mark.*]	St. Luke. [*Passages parallel to Mark.*]
III. 1-6, 11-12. 1 And in those days cometh **John** the **Baptist**[?], **preaching in the wilderness** of Judæa, saying, 2 **Repent** ye: for the kingdom of heaven is at hand. 3 For this is he that was spoken of ¹ by **Isaiah the prophet**, saying, **The voice of one crying in the wilderness,** **Make ye ready the way of the Lord,** **Make his paths straight.** 4 Now John himself had his raiment of camel's hair, and a leathern girdle about his loins; and his food was locusts and wild honey. 5 Then **went out** unto him Jerusalem, and **all** [?] Judæa, and all [?] **the region** round about Jordan; 6 And they were **baptized of him** in the river Jordan, confessing their sins. 11 **I** indeed **baptize you** ² with **water** unto repentance: but **he that cometh** after me is **mightier than I, whose shoes I am not** ³ **worthy** to bear: **he shall baptize you** ² with **the Holy Ghost** and *with* fire: 12 Whose fan is in his hand, and he will throughly cleanse his threshing-floor; and he will gather his wheat into the garner, but the chaff he will burn up with unquenchable fire. ¹ Or, *through*. ² Or, *in*. ³ Gr. *sufficient*.	III. 1-4, 7, 15-17. 1 Now in the fifteenth year of the reign of Tiberius Cæsar, Pontius Pilate being governor of Judæa, and Herod being tetrarch of Galilee, and his brother Philip tetrarch of the region of Ituræa and Trachonitis, and Lysanias tetrarch of Abilene, 2 In the high-priesthood of Annas and Caiaphas, the word of God came unto **John** the son of Zacharias **in the wilderness.** 3 And he came into **all the region** round about Jordan, **preaching** the **baptism** [?] **of repentance** unto remission of sins; 4 As it is written in the book of the words of **Isaiah the prophet,** **The voice of one crying in the wilderness,** **Make ye ready the way of the Lord,** **Make his paths straight.** 7 He said therefore to the multitudes that **went out** to be **baptized of him,** Ye offspring of vipers, who warned you to flee from the wrath to come? 15 And as the people were in expectation, and all men reasoned in their hearts concerning John, whether haply he were the Christ; 16 John answered, saying unto them all, **I** indeed **baptize you** with **water;** but there **cometh he that is mightier than I,** the latchet **of whose shoes I am not** ¹ **worthy** to unloose: **he shall baptize you** ² with **the Holy Ghost** and *with* fire: 17 Whose fan is in his hand, throughly to cleanse his threshing-floor, and to gather the wheat into his garner; but the chaff he will burn up with unquenchable fire. ¹ Gr. *sufficient*. ² Or, *in*.

THE COMMON TRADITION

St. Mark. [*Portions not found in Matthew or Luke.*]	St. Mark. [*Complete.*]
9 And...in those days...came...Nazareth...and ..in (Gr. into)...	I. 9–11. 9 And it came to pass in those days, that **Jesus** came from Nazareth of Galilee, and was **baptized** of John [1] in the Jordan.
10 And...out of...rent asunder...	10 And straightway coming up out of the water, he saw **the heavens** rent asunder, **and** the **Spirit** as **a dove descending** upon **him:** 11 **And a voice** came **out of** the **heavens,** Thou art **my beloved Son, in** thee **I am well pleased.**
12 ...straightway...driveth him forth... 13 ...he was ..the wilderness[?] . Satan; and he was with the wild beasts ..the (angels)...	I. 12–13. 12 And straightway **the Spirit** driveth him forth into **the wilderness,** 13 **And** he was in the wilderness **forty days tempted of** Satan ; and he was with the wild beasts ; and the angels ministered unto him.
14 ...after that...came...the gospel of God, and saying (Gr. that) 15 The time is fulfilled and ..of God... and believe in the gospel.	I. 14–15. 14 Now after that John was delivered up, **Jesus** came **into Galilee,** preaching the gospel of God, and saying, 15 The time is fulfilled, and the kingdom of God is at hand : repent ye, and believe in the gospel.
16 ...passing along...of Simon...in... 17 ...to become... 18 And...	I. 16–20. 16 And passing along **by the** sea of Galilee, **he saw Simon** and Andrew the brother of Simon casting a net in the sea : for they were **fishers.** 17 **And** Jesus said unto them, Come ye after me, and I will make you to become fishers of **men.** 18 And straightway they **left** the nets, **and followed him.**

[1] Gr. *into.*

Synopticon, pages 2–4.

St. Matthew.	St. Luke.
[*Passages parallel to Mark.*]	[*Passages parallel to Mark.*]

III. 13, 16–17.
13 Then cometh Jesus from Galilee to the Jordan unto John, to be baptized of him.

16 And **Jesus**, when he was **baptized**, went up straightway from the water: and lo, **the heavens** were opened ¹ unto him, **and** he saw the **Spirit** of God **descending** as a **dove**, and coming upon **him**;
17 **And** lo, **a voice out of** the **heavens**, saying, ² This is **my beloved Son, in** whom **I am well pleased.**

III. 21–22.
21 Now it came to pass, when all the people were baptized, that, **Jesus** also having been **baptized**, and praying, **the heaven** was opened,
22 **And** the Holy **Ghost descended** in a bodily form, as **a dove**, upon **him, and a voice** came **out of heaven**, Thou art **my beloved Son; in** thee **I am well pleased.**

IV. 1–2, 11.
1 Then was Jesus led up of **the Spirit** into **the wilderness** to be **tempted of the** devil.
2 **And** when he had fasted **forty days** and forty nights, he afterward hungered.

11 Then the devil leaveth him; and behold, angels came and ministered unto him.

IV. 1–2, 13.
1 And Jesus, full of the Holy Spirit, returned from the Jordan, and was led ¹ by **the Spirit** in **the wilderness** during **forty days**, being **tempted of the** devil.
2 **And** he did eat nothing in those days: and when they were completed, he hungered.

13 And when the devil had completed every temptation, he departed from him ² for a season.

IV. 12, 17.
12 Now when he heard that John was delivered up, he withdrew **into Galilee:**

17 From that time began **Jesus** to preach, and to say, Repent ye; for the kingdom of heaven is at hand.

IV. 14–15.
14 And **Jesus** returned in the power of the Spirit **into Galilee**: and a fame went out concerning him through all the region round about.
15 And he taught in their synagogues, being glorified of all.

IV. 18–22.
18 And walking **by the** sea of Galilee, **he saw** two brethren, **Simon** who is called Peter, and Andrew his brother, casting a net into the sea; for they were **fishers.**
19 **And** he saith unto them, Come ye after me, and I will make you fishers of **men.**
20 And they straightway **left** the nets, **and followed him.**

V. 1–2, 9–11.
1 Now it came to pass, while the multitude pressed upon him and heard the word of God, that he was standing **by the** lake of Gennesaret;
2 And **he saw** two boats standing by the lake: but the **fishermen** had gone out of them, and were washing their **nets.**

9 For he was amazed, and all that were with him, at the draught of the fishes which they had taken;

¹ Some ancient authorities omit *unto him*.
² Or, *This is my Son; my beloved in whom I am well pleased.* See ch. xii. 18.

¹ Or, *in*.   ² Or, *until*.

THE COMMON TRADITION

St. Mark. [Portions not found in Matthew or Luke.]	St. Mark. [Complete.]
	I. 16–20.
19 ...a little further...who also were...	19 And going on a little further, he saw **James** the *son* **of Zebedee, and John** his brother, who also were in the boat mending the **nets**.
20 ...Zebedee in...with the hired servants and went after...	20 And straightway he called them : and they left their father Zebedee in **the boat** with the hired servants, and went after him.
	I. 21–28.
21 ... they-go-into ... straightway ... he entered into the synagogue and taught.	21 And they go **into Capernaum;** and straightway on the sabbath day he entered into the synagogue and taught. **22 And they were astonished at his teaching;** for **he taught them** as having **authority,** and not as the scribes.
23 ...straightway...their	23 And straightway there was in their synagogue a man with an unclean spirit ; and he cried out,
24 Saying...	24 Saying, What have we to do with thee, thou Jesus of Nazareth ? art thou come to destroy us ? I know thee who thou art, the Holy One of God.
25 ...out of...	25 And Jesus rebuked [1] him, saying, Hold thy peace, and come out of him.
26 ...unclean spirit tearing ..and crying...out of...	26 And the unclean spirit, [2] tearing him and crying with a loud voice, came out of him.
27 .. insomuch that they questioned among themselves .is...a new teaching! with...even ..obey him.	27 And they were all amazed, insomuch that they questioned among themselves, saying, What is this ? a new teaching ! with authority he commandeth even the unclean spirits, and they obey him.
28 ... the report ... went ... straightway everywhere...all...of Galilee.	28 And the report of him went out straightway everywhere into all the region of Galilee round about.
	I. 29–31.
29 ...straightway when they were come out of...and Andrew with James and John.	29 And straightway, [3] when they were come out of the synagogue, they **came into the house** of Simon and Andrew, with James and John.
30 ...lay...straightway they tell...	30 Now Simon's **wife's mother** lay sick of a **fever;** and straightway they tell him of her :
Mk. i. 21, Gr. *they-go-into into.*	[1] Or, *it.* [2] Or, *convulsing.* [3] Some ancient authorities read *when he was come out of the synagogue, he came, &c.*

[*Synopticon, pages* 4–6, 127 A.]

| St. Matthew. | St. Luke. |
| [*Passages parallel to Mark.*] | [*Passages parallel to Mark.*] |

IV. 18-22.
21 And going on from thence he saw other two brethren, ¹ **James** the *son* **of Zebedee, and John** his brother, in the boat with Zebedee their father, mending their **nets**; and he called them.
22 And they straightway left **the boat** and their father, and followed him.

IV. 12-13.
12 Now when he heard that John was delivered up, he withdrew into Galilee;
13 And leaving Nazareth, he came and dwelt **in Capernaum**, which is by the sea, in the borders of Zebulun and Naphtali:

VII. 28-29.
28 **And** it came to pass, when Jesus ended these words, the multitudes **were astonished at his teaching:**
29 For **he taught them** as *one* having **authority,** and not as their scribes.

V. 1-2, 9-11.
10 And so were also **James and John,** sons **of Zebedee,** which were partners with Simon. And Jesus said unto **Simon,** Fear not; from henceforth thou shalt ¹ catch **men.**
11 And when they had brought their boats to land, they left all, **and followed him.**

IV. 31-37.
31 And he came down **to Capernaum,** a city of Galilee. And **he was teaching them** on the sabbath day:
32 **And they were astonished at his teaching;** for his word was with **authority.**
33 And in the synagogue there was a man, which had a spirit of an unclean ² devil; and he cried out with a loud voice,
34 ³ Ah! what have we to do with thee, thou Jesus of Nazareth? art thou come to destroy us? I know thee who thou art, the Holy One of God.
35 And Jesus rebuked him, saying, Hold thy peace, and come out of him. And when the ² devil had thrown him down in the midst, he came out of him, having done him no hurt.
36 And amazement came upon all, and they spake together, one with another, saying, What is ⁴ this word? for with authority and power he commandeth the unclean spirits, and they come out.
37 And there went forth a rumour concerning him into every place of the region round about.

VIII. 14-15.
14 And when Jesus was **come into** Peter's **house,** he saw his **wife's mother** lying sick of a fever.

IV. 38-39.
38 And he rose up from the synagogue, and **entered into the house** of Simon. And Simon's **wife's mother** was holden with a great **fever;** and they besought him for her.

¹ Or, *Jacob:* and so elsewhere.

¹ Gr. *take alive.*
² Gr. *demon.*   ³ Or, *Let alone.*
⁴ Or, *this word, that with authority...come out?*

THE COMMON TRADITION

St. Mark. [*Portions not found in Matthew or Luke.*]	St. Mark. [*Complete.*]
31 ...he came and took...and raised her up...	I. 29–31. 31 **And** he came and took her by the hand, **a**nd raised **her** up; **and** the **fever left her,** and **she ministered** unto them.
32 ...when...they brought...all that were [?] sick and them-that-were...	I. 32–34. 32 **And** at even, when the sun did set, they brought **unto him** all that were sick, and them that were [1] possessed with devils.
33 And all the city was gathered together at the door. 34 ...many...suffered...the devils...	33 And all the city was gathered together at the door. 34 And **he healed** many that were sick with divers diseases, **and** cast **out** many [2] devils; and he suffered not the [2] devils to speak, because they knew him[3].
35 And in the morning a great while before day, he rose up and...and departed...and there prayed.	I. 35–39. 35 And in the morning, a great while before day, he rose up and went out, and departed into a desert place, and there prayed.
36 ...Simon and they that were with him followed after... 37 ...they found...and say unto him (Gr. that) all...thee. 38 And he saith...Let us go elsewhere into the next towns, that I may preach there also; for to...came I forth. 39 ...he went...throughout (Gr. into) ...casting out (Gr. the) devils.	36 And Simon and they that were with him followed after him; 37 And they found him, and say unto him, All are seeking thee. 38 And he saith unto them, Let us go elsewhere into the next towns, that I may preach there also; for to this end came I forth. 39 **And** he went into their **synagogues** throughout all **Galilee preaching** and casting out [2] devils.
40 And there cometh...him, beseeching him and kneeling down to-him and ...(Gr. that)... 41 ...being moved with compassion... and...	I. 40–45. 40 And there cometh to him a **leper,** beseeching him, [4] and kneeling down to him, and **saying** unto **him, If thou wilt, thou canst make me clean.** 41 **And** being moved with compassion, **he stretched forth his hand, and touched him,** and **saith** unto him, **I will; be thou made clean.**
Mk. 1. 40, W. & H. *beseeching him and kneeling down saying unto him.*	[1] Or, *demoniacs.* [2] Gr. *démons.* [3] Many ancient authorities add *to be Christ.* See Luke iv. 41. [4] Some ancient authorities omit *and kneeling down to him.*

Synopticon, pages 6–8.]

St. Matthew. [Passages parallel to Mark.]	St. Luke. [Passages parallel to Mark.]
VIII. 14–15. 15 **And** he touched **her** hand, **and the fever left her;** and she arose, and **ministered** unto him.	IV. 38–39. 39 **And** he stood over **her,** and rebuked the **fever; and it left her**: and immediately she rose up and **ministered** unto them.
VIII. 16–17. 16 **And** when even was come, they brought **unto him** many [1] possessed with devils : **and** he cast **out** the spirits with a word, and **healed** all that were sick : 17 That it might be fulfilled which was spoken [2] by Isaiah the prophet, saying, Himself took our infirmities, and bare our diseases.	IV. 40–41. 40 **And** when the sun was setting, all they that had any sick with divers diseases brought them **unto him;** and he laid his hands on every one of them, and **healed** them. 41 And [1] devils **also** came **out** from many, crying out, and saying, Thou art the Son of God. And rebuking them, he suffered them not to speak, because they knew that he was the Christ.
IV. 23. 23 **And** [3] Jesus went about in all **Galilee,** teaching in their **synagogues** and **preaching** the [4] gospel of the kingdom, and healing all manner of disease and all manner of sickness among the people.	IV. 42–44. 42 And when it was day, he came out and went into a desert place : and the multitudes sought after him, and came unto him, and would have stayed him, that he should not go from them. 43 But he said unto them, I must preach the [2] good tidings of the kingdom of God to the other cities also ; for therefore was I sent. 44 **And** he was **preaching** in **the synagogues** of [3] **Galilee.**
VIII. 1–4. 1 And when he was come down from the mountain, great multitudes followed him. 2 And behold, there came to him a **leper** and worshipped **him, saying,** Lord, **if thou wilt, thou canst make me clean. And he stretched forth his hand, and touched him, saying, I will; be thou made clean.**	V. 12–16. 12 And it came to pass, while he was in one of the cities, behold, a man full of **leprosy;** and when he saw Jesus, he fell on his face, and besought **him, saying, Lord, if thou wilt, thou canst make me clean.** 13 **And he stretched forth his hand, and touched him, saying, I will;** be thou made clean.

[1] Or, *demoniacs.*
[2] Or, *through.*
[3] Some ancient authorities read *he.*
[4] Or, *good tidings:* and so elsewhere.

[1] Gr *demons.*
[2] Or, *gospel*
[3] Very many ancient authorities read *Judæa.*

THE COMMON TRADITION

St. Mark. [Portions not found in Matthew or Luke.]	St. Mark. [Complete.]
	I. 40–45.
42 ...and...	42 **And straightway the leprosy** departed from **him**, and he was made clean.
43 And he strictly charged him and straightway sent him out.	43 And he [1] strictly charged him, and straightway sent him out,
44 ...nothing...the-things-which...	44 **And** saith **unto him,** See thou **say** nothing **to any man: but** go thy way, **shew thyself to the priest, and offer** for thy cleansing the things which **Moses commanded, for a testimony unto them.**
45 ...he went out and began to publish it much, and to spread abroad...insomuch that Jesus (Gr. he) could no more openly enter into a city, but... without in...places...to him from every quarter.	45 But he went out, and began to publish it much, and to spread abroad the [2] matter, insomuch that [3] Jesus could no more openly enter into [4] a city, but was without in desert places: and they came to him from every quarter.
	II. 1–12.
1 ...again...Capernaum after somedays, it was noised (Gr. it was heard) that he was in the house.	1 And when he entered again into Capernaum after some days, it was noised that he was [5] in the house.
2 And many were gathered together, so that there was no longer room *for them*, no, not even about the door: and he spake the word unto them.	2 And many were gathered together, so that there was no longer room *for them*, no, not even about the door: and he spake the word unto them.
3 ...they come...borne of four.	3 **And** they come, **bringing** unto him a man **sick of the palsy,** borne of four.
4 ...when-they-could...come-nigh unto him they uncovered the roof where he was, and when-they-had-broken-it-up, they let down the bed whereon the sick of the palsy lay.	4 And when they could not [6] come nigh unto him for the crowd, they uncovered the roof where he was: and when they had broken it up, they let down the bed whereon the sick of the palsy lay.
5 ...saith...	5 **And** Jesus **seeing their faith** saith unto the sick of the palsy, [7] Son, **thy sins are forgiven.**
6 But...there and...hearts,	6 But there were certain of the **scribes** sitting there, and reasoning in their hearts,
7 ...thus...one...	7 Why doth **this** man thus speak? he **blasphemeth**: who can forgive sins but one, *even* God?
Mark ii. 4, W. & H. *bring nigh.* Mark ii. 5, Matt. ix. 2, W. & H. *are being forgiven.*	[1] Or, *sternly.* [2] Gr. *word.* [3] Gr. *he.* [4] Or, *the city.* [5] Or, *at home.* [6] Many ancient authorities read *bring him unto him.* [7] Gr. *Child.*

Synopticon, pages 8–9.

OF THE SYNOPTIC GOSPELS. 11

St. Matthew. [*Passages parallel to Mark.*]	St. Luke. [*Passages parallel to Mark.*]
VIII. 1–4. **And straightway his leprosy** was cleansed. 4 **And** Jesus saith **unto him,** See thou **tell no man; but** go thy way, **shew thyself to the priest, and offer** the gift that **Moses commanded, for a testimony unto them.**	v. 12–16. **And straightway the leprosy** departed from **him.** 14 **And** he charged **him** to **tell no man: but** go thy way, and **shew thyself to the priest, and offer** for thy cleansing, according as **Moses commanded, for a testimony unto them.** 15 But so much the more went abroad the report concerning him: and great multitudes came together to hear, and to be healed of their infirmities. 16 But he withdrew himself in the deserts, and prayed.
IX. 1–8. 1 And he entered into a boat, and crossed over, and came into his own city. 2 **And** behold, they **brought** to him a man, **sick of the palsy,** lying on a bed: **and** Jesus **seeing their faith** said unto the sick of the palsy, [1] Son, be of good cheer; **thy sins are forgiven.** 3 And behold, certain of the **scribes** said within themselves, **This** man **blasphemeth.**	v. 17–26. 17 And it came to pass on one of those days, that he was teaching; and there were Pharisees and doctors of the law sitting by, which were come out of every village of Galilee and Judæa and Jerusalem: and the power of the Lord was with him [1] to heal. 18 **And** behold, men **bring** on a bed a man that was **palsied**: and they sought to bring him in, and to lay him before him. 19 And not finding by what *way* they might bring him in because of the multitude, they went up to the housetop, and let him down through the tiles with his couch into the midst before Jesus. 20 **And seeing their faith,** he said, Man, **thy sins are forgiven** thee. 21 And the **scribes** and the Pharisees began to reason, saying, Who is **this** that speaketh **blasphemies?** Who can forgive sins but God alone?
[1] Gr. *Child.*	[1] Gr. *that he should heal.* Many ancient authorities read *that he should heal them.*

THE COMMON TRADITION

St. Mark. [Portions not found in Matthew or Luke.]	St. Mark. [Complete.]
	II. 1–12.
8 ...straightway...in his spirit that... so...within...saith...these-things...	8 And straightway **Jesus**, perceiving in his spirit that they so reasoned within **themselves**, saith unto them, **Why reason ye these things in your hearts?**
9 to-the sick-of-the-palsy...and take-up thy bed...walk.	9 **Whether is easier, to say** to the sick of the palsy, **Thy sins are forgiven; or to say, Arise,** and take up thy bed, **and walk?** 10 **But that ye may know that the Son of man hath** [1] **power on earth to forgive sins** (he saith **to the** sick of the **palsy**),
11 ...bed (Gr. the bed)...	11 I say unto thee, **Arise, take up thy** bed, **and go unto thy house.**
12 ... and straightway ... the bed ... (went) forth before them (Gr. omits *them*) all; insomuch-that...never...on-this-fashion (Gr. thus).	12 **And** he arose, and straightway took up the bed, and **went** forth before them all; insomuch that they were all amazed, **and glorified God,** saying, We never saw it on this fashion.
	II. 13–17.
13 ...again by the sea side; and all the multitude resorted unto him, and he taught them. 14 ...the *son* of Alphæus...	13 And he went forth again by the sea side; and all the multitude resorted unto him, and he taught them. 14 **And** as he passed by, he saw Levi the *son* of Alphæus **sitting at the place of toll, and he saith unto him, Follow me. And he arose and followed him.**
15 ...for there-were many, and they-followed him.	15 **And** it came to pass, that he was sitting at meat **in** his **house, and many** [2] **publicans and** sinners sat down with Jesus and his disciples: for there were many, and they followed him.
16 ...of-the...that he was eating with the sinners and publicans...	16 **And the** scribes [3] **of the Pharisees,** when they saw that he was eating with the sinners and publicans, **said unto his disciples,** (Gr. that) [4] **He eateth** [5] **and drinketh with publicans and sinners.**

Mark ii. 9, Matt. ix. 5, W. & H. *are being forgiven.*
Mark ii. 16, W & H. *publicans and sinners.*
Mark ii. 16, Gr. *drinketh with the publicans and sinners.*

[1] Or, *authority.*
[2] See marginal note on Matt. v. 46.
[3] Some ancient authorities read *and the Pharisees.*
[4] Or, How is it *that he eateth...sinners?*
[5] Some ancient authorities omit *and drinketh.*

Synopticon, pages 10–11.

St. Matthew. [*Passages parallel to Mark.*]	St. Luke. [*Passages parallel to Mark.*]
IX. 1–8.	V. 17–26.
4 And **Jesus** [1] knowing **their** thoughts said, **Wherefore** think ye evil **in your hearts?**	22 But **Jesus** perceiving **their** reasonings, answered and said unto them, [1] **What** reason ye **in your hearts?**
5 For **whether is easier, to say, Thy sins are forgiven; or to say, Arise, and** walk?	23 **Whether is easier, to say, Thy sins are forgiven** thee; **or to say, Arise and** walk?
6 **But that ye may know that the Son of man hath** [2] **power on earth to forgive sins** (then saith he **to the** sick of the **palsy**), **Arise,** and **take up thy** bed, and go **unto thy house.** 7 **And** he arose, and **departed** to his house. 8 But when the multitudes saw it, they were afraid, **and glorified God,** which had given such [2] power unto men.	24 **But that ye may know that the Son of man hath** [2] **power on earth to forgive sins** (he said **unto him** that was **palsied**), I say unto thee, **Arise, and take up thy** couch, **and** go **unto thy house.** 25 **And** immediately he rose up before them, and took up that whereon he lay, **and departed** to his house, glorifying God. 26 And amazement took hold on all, **and** they **glorified God;** and they were filled with fear, saying, We have seen strange things to-day.
IX. 9–13.	V. 27–32.
9 **And** as Jesus passed by from thence, he saw a man, called Matthew, **sitting at the place of toll: and** he saith **unto him, Follow me. And he** arose, and followed him. 10 **And** it came to pass, as he [3] sat at meat **in the house,** behold, **many publicans and** sinners came and **sat** down with Jesus and his disciples.	27 **And** after these things he went forth, **and** beheld a publican, named Levi, **sitting at the place of toll,** and said **unto him, Follow me.** 28 **And he** forsook all, **and rose up and followed him.** 29 And Levi made him a great feast **in** his **house**: **and** there was a **great** multitude of **publicans and** of others that were **sitting** at meat with them.
11 **And** when **the Pharisees** saw it, they **said** unto **his disciples,** Why eateth your [4] **Master with the publicans and sinners?**	30 **And** [3] **the Pharisees** and their scribes murmured against **his disciples, saying,** Why do ye **eat** and drink **with the publicans and sinners?**

[1] Many ancient authorities read *seeing*.
[2] Or, *authority*
[3] Gr. *reclined*: and so always.
[4] Or, *Teacher*.

[1] Or, *Why*.
[2] Or, *authority*.
[3] Or, *the Pharisees and the scribes among them*.

St. Mark. [*Portions not found in Matthew or Luke.*]	St. Mark. [*Complete.*]
	II. 13-17.
17 ... he saith...	17 And when Jesus heard it, he saith unto them, **They that are** [1] **whole have no need of a physician, but they that are sick : I came not to call the righteous, but sinners.**
	II. 18-22.
18 And...and the Pharisees were fasting : and...and...John's disciples...disciples...	18 And **John's disciples** and the Pharisees were fasting : and they come and say unto **him,** Why do John's disciples **and the** disciples of the **Pharisees fast, but thy** disciples fast not ?
19 ...as long as they have the bridegroom with them they cannot fast.	19 And **Jesus said** unto **them, Can the sons of the bride-chamber** fast, while **the bridegroom is with them?** as long as they have the bridegroom with them they cannot fast. **20 But the days will come, when the bridegroom shall be taken away from them, and then will they fast** in that day.
21 ...seweth (Gr. seweth-on on)...	21 **No man** seweth **a piece** of undressed cloth **on an old garment :** else that which should fill it up taketh from it, the new from the old, and a worse rent is made.
	22 And **no man putteth new wine into old** [2] **wine-skins :** else the wine will **burst the skins, and** the wine **perisheth, and the skins : but** *they put* **new wine into fresh wine-skins.**
	II. 23-28.
23 And...	23 And it came to pass, that he was **going** on the **sabbath** day **through** the **cornfields ;** and **his disciples**
Luke vi. 1, Gr. *through cornfields.*	[1] Gr. *strong.* [2] That is, *skins used as bottles.*

Synopticon, pages 11-13.]

OF THE SYNOPTIC GOSPELS. 15

St. Matthew. [*Passages parallel to Mark.*]	St. Luke. [*Passages parallel to Mark.*]
IX. 9–13. 12 But when he heard it, **he said, They that are** [1] **whole have no need of a physician, but they that are sick.** 13 But go ye and learn what *this* meaneth, I desire mercy, and not sacrifice: for **I came not to call the righteous, but sinners.**	v. 27–32. 31 And Jesus answering said unto them, **They that are whole have no need of a physician; but they that are sick.** 32 I am **not come to call the righteous but sinners** to repentance.
IX. 14–17. 14 Then come to **him the disciples of John,** saying, Why do we **and the Pharisees fast** [2] **oft, but thy** disciples fast not?	v. 33–39. 33 And they said unto **him, The disciples of John fast** often, and make supplications; likewise **also the** *disciples* of the **Pharisees; but thine** eat and drink.
15 And **Jesus said** unto **them, Can the sons of the bride-chamber** mourn, as long as **the bridegroom is with them?** **but the days will come, when the bridegroom shall be taken away from them, and then will they fast.** 16 And **no man** putteth **a piece of** undressed cloth **upon an old garment;** for that which should fill it up taketh from the garment, and a worse rent is made.	34 And **Jesus said** unto **them, Can** ye make **the sons of the bride-chamber** fast, while **the bridegroom is with them?** 35 **But the days will come;** and **when the bridegroom shall be taken away from them, then will they fast** in those days. 36 And he spake also a parable unto them; **No man** rendeth **a piece** from a new garment and putteth it **upon an old garment;** else he will rend the new, and also the piece from the new will not agree with the old.
17 **Neither** do *men* **put new wine into** old [3] **wine-skins;** *else **the skins burst, and** the wine is spilled, **and the skins perish:** but they put **new wine into fresh wine-skins** and both are preserved.	37 And **no man putteth new wine into** old [1] **wine-skins;** *else **the** new wine will **burst the skins, and** itself will be spilled, **and the skins** will **perish.** 38 **But new wine** must be put **into fresh wine-skins.** 39 And no man having drunk old *wine* desireth new: for he saith, The old is [2] good.
XII. 1–8. 1 At that season Jesus **went on the sabbath** day **through** the **cornfields;** and **his disciples** were an hungred,	VI. 1–5. 1 Now it came to pass on a [3] **sabbath,** that he was **going through** the **cornfields; and his disciples plucked**

[1] Gr *strong*.
[2] Some ancient authorities omit *oft*.
[3] That is, *skins used as bottles*.

[1] That is, *skins used as bottles*.
[2] Many ancient authorities read *better*.
[3] Many ancient authorities insert *second-first*.

16 THE COMMON TRADITION

St. Mark. [*Portions not found in Matthew or Luke.*]	St. Mark. [*Complete.*]
	II. 23-28.
...as they went (Gr. to-make way)...	[1] began, as they went, to **pluck the ears of corn.**
24 And...said...	24 And the **Pharisees** said unto him, Behold, why **do** they on * the **sabbath day** that **which is not lawful?**
25 ...he saith...he had need, and...	25 And he said unto **them, Did ye** never **read** what **David did,** when he had need, and **was an hungred,** he, **and they that were with him?**
26 ...when Abiathar was high priest... that-were with (Gr. being with)...	26 How **he entered into the house of God** when [2] Abiathar was high priest, **and did eat the shewbread, which** it is **not lawful to eat save for the priests,** and gave also **to them** that were with **him?**
27 ...The sabbath was made for man, and not man for the sabbath.	27 And he **said** unto them, The sabbath was made for man, and not man for the sabbath :
28 So that...	28 So that **the Son of man is lord even of the sabbath.**
	III. 1-6.
1 ...again...	1 And he **entered** again **into the synagogue;** and there was **a man** there which had his **hand withered.**
2 ...(heal) him...	2 And they watched **him, whether** he would **heal** him on * **the sabbath day; that** they might **accuse him.**
3 And he saith...man...	3 And he saith unto the man that had his hand withered, [3] Stand forth.

Mark ii. 24, Luke vi. 2, Gr. has no preposition, Matt. xii. 2, Gr. *in sabbath* (omitting article).
Mark iii. 2, Matt. xii. 10, Gr has no preposition, Luke vi. 7, Gr. *in sabbath* (omitting article).
Mark iii. 1, W. & H. *into synagogue.*
Matt. xii. 2, Gr. *in sabbath.*
Matt. xii. 10, Gr. *If it is lawful.*
Luke vi. 6-11; compare also Luke xiv. 1-6,

[1] Gr. *began to make* their *way plucking.*
[2] Some ancient authorities read *in the days of Abiathar the high priest.*
[3] Gr. *Arise into the midst.*

Synopticon, pages 13-14.

St. Matthew. [*Passages parallel to Mark.*]	St. Luke. [*Passages parallel to Mark.*]
XII. 1–8. and began to **pluck ears of corn**, and to eat. 2 But the **Pharisees,** when they saw it, said unto him, Behold, thy disciples **do** that **which it is not lawful** to do upon the **sabbath.** 3 But he said unto **them, Have ye** not **read** what **David did,** when **he was an hungred, and they that were with him;** 4 How **he entered into the house of God, and** ¹ did **eat the shewbread, which** it was **not lawful** for him to eat, neither for them that were with him, **but only** for **the priests?** 5 Or have ye not read in the law, how that on the sabbath day the priests in the temple profane the sabbath, and are guiltless? 6 But I **say** unto you, that ² one greater than the temple is here. 7 But if ye had known what this meaneth, I desire mercy, and not sacrifice, ye would not have condemned the guiltless. 8 For **the Son of man is lord of the sabbath.**	VI. 1–5. the **ears of corn,** and did eat, rubbing them in their hands. 2 But certain of the **Pharisees** said, Why **do** ye that **which it is not lawful** to do on * the **sabbath** day? 3 And Jesus answering **them** said, **Have ye** not **read** even this, what **David did,** when **he was an hungred,** he, **and they that were with him;** 4 How **he entered into the house of God, and** did take and **eat the shewbread,** and gave also **to them** that were with **him; which** it is **not lawful to eat save** for **the priests** alone? 5 And he **said** unto them, **The Son of man is lord of the sabbath.**
XII. 9–14. 9 And he departed thence, and **went into** their **synagogue:** 10 **and** behold, **a man** having a **withered hand.** And they asked **him,** saying, **Is it lawful** [?] to **heal** on * **the sabbath** day? **that** they might **accuse him.**	VI. 6–11. 6 And it came to pass on another sabbath, that he **entered into the synagogue** and taught: **and there was a man** there, and his right **hand was withered.** 7 And the scribes and the Pharisees watched **him, whether** he would **heal** on **the sabbath; that** they might find how to **accuse him.** 8 But he knew their thoughts; and he said to the man that had his hand withered, Rise up, and stand forth in the midst. And he arose and stood forth.

¹ Some ancient authorities read *they did eat.*
² Gr. *a greater thing.*

THE COMMON TRADITION

St. Mark. [*Portions not found in Matthew or Luke.*]	St. Mark. [*Complete.*]
	III. 1–6.
4 And he saith... But they held their peace.	4 And he saith unto **them, Is it lawful** on **the sabbath** day to **do** good, or to do harm? to save a life, or to kill? But they held their peace.
5 ...with anger, being grieved at the hardening of their heart...	5 And when he had looked round about on them with anger, being grieved at the hardening of their heart, he saith unto the man, **Stretch forth thy hand.** And he stretched it forth: **and his hand was restored.**
6 And...straightway with the Herodians ..took (Gr. gave)...	6 And the Pharisees went out, and straightway with the Herodians took counsel against him, how they might destroy him.
	III. 7–12.
7 ...to the sea...from (Judæa),	7 And Jesus with his disciples withdrew to the sea: **and a great** multitude **from** Galilee followed: and from Judæa,
8 ...from...and from Idumæa...about... a great multitude,...what great things he did (Gr. does)...	8 **And** from * **Jerusalem,** and from Idumæa, and beyond Jordan, and about Tyre and Sidon, a great multitude, hearing ¹ what great things he did, came unto **him.**
9 And he spake to his disciples that a little boat should wait on him because of the crowd, lest they should throng him: 10 For...many; insomuch that as many as had plagues pressed upon him that... 11 ... the ... whensoever they beheld him, fell down before him, and cried, saying (Gr. that), Thou art the Son of God. 12 ...much...	9 And he spake to his disciples, that a little boat should wait on him because of the crowd, lest they should throng him: 10 For he had **healed** many; insomuch that as many as had ² plagues ³ pressed upon him that they might touch him. 11 And the unclean spirits, whensoever they beheld him, fell down before him, and cried, saying, Thou art the Son of God. 12 And he charged them much that they should not make him known.
	¹ Or, *all the things that he did.* ² Gr *scourges.* ³ Gr. *fell.*

[*Synopticon, pages* 14–15]

St. Matthew. [*Passages parallel to Mark.*]	St. Luke. [*Passages parallel to Mark.*]
XII. 1-14. 11 And he said unto them, What man shall there be of you, that shall have one sheep, and if this fall into a pit on the sabbath day, will he not lay hold on it, and lift it out? 12 How much then is a man of more value than a sheep! Wherefore **it is lawful** to **do** good on **the sabbath** day. 13 Then saith he to the man, **Stretch forth thy hand.** And he stretched it forth; **and it was restored** whole, as the other.	VI. 1-11. 9 And Jesus said unto **them,** I ask you, **Is it lawful** on **the sabbath** to **do** good, or to do harm? to save a life, or to destroy it? 10 And he looked round about on them all, and said unto him, **Stretch forth thy hand.** And he did *so;* **and** his hand **was restored.**
14 But the Pharisees went out, and took counsel against him, how they might destroy him.	11 But they were filled with ¹madness; and communed one with another what they might do to Jesus.
IV. 24-25. 24 And the report of him went forth into all Syria: and they brought unto **him** all that were sick, holden with divers diseases and torments, ¹possessed with devils, and epileptic, and palsied; and he **healed** them. 25 **And** there followed him **great** multitudes **from** Galilee and Decapolis **and** * **Jerusalem** and **Judæa** and *from* beyond Jordan.	VI. 17-19. 17 And he came down with them, and stood on a level place, and a great multitude of his disciples, **and a great** number of the people **from** all **Judæa and** * **Jerusalem,** and the sea coast of Tyre and Sidon, which came to hear **him,** and to be healed of their diseases:
XII. 15-17. 15 And Jesus perceiving *it* withdrew from thence: and many followed him; and he healed them all, 16 And charged them that they should not make him known: 17 That it might be fulfilled, &c.	18 And they that were troubled with unclean spirits were **healed.** 19 And all the multitude sought to touch him: for power came forth from him and healed *them* all.
¹ Or, *demoniacs*.	¹ Or, *foolishness.*

20   THE COMMON TRADITION

St. Mark. [*Portions not found in Matthew or Luke.*]	St. Mark. [*Complete.*]
	III. 13–19.
13 And he goeth up ... calleth...whom he himself would : and they went unto him.	13 And he goeth up into the mountain, and * calleth unto him whom he himself would : and they went unto him.
14 ..he appointed twelve that they might be with him, and that he might send them forth to preach.	14 And he appointed **twelve,** [1] that they might be with him, and that he might
15 And to have...devils.	15 send them forth to preach, and to have authority to cast out [2] devils :
16 ...he surnamed (Gr. he-set-upon S. the-name)...	16 [3] And **Simon** he surnamed **Peter;**
17 ..of James ; and them he surnamed (Gr. he-set-upon them the-name) Boanerges, which is, Sons of Thunder :	17 And **James** the *son* of Zebedee, **and John** the brother of James ; and them he surnamed Boanerges, which is, Sons of thunder :
	18 **And Andrew,** and **Philip, and Bartholomew, and Matthew,** and **Thomas,** and **James** the *son* **of Alphæus, and** Thaddæus, and **Simon the** [4] Cananæan,
	19 **And Judas Iscariot,** which also **betrayed** him.
	III. 20–30.
19 And he cometh into a house.	
20 And the multitude cometh together again so that they could not so much as eat bread.	20 And he cometh [5] into a house. And the multitude cometh together again, so that they could not so much as eat bread.
21 And when his friends heard it, they went out to lay hold on him : for they said, (Gr. that) He is beside himself.	21 And when his friends heard it, they went out to lay hold on him : for they said, He is beside himself.
22 And the scribes which came down from Jerusalem said (Gr. that) He hath...and (Gr. that)...	22 And the scribes which came down from Jerusalem said, He hath **Beelzebub,** and, [6]**By the prince of the** [6] **devils casteth he out the** [7] **devils.**
23 And he called them unto him and said...in parables, How can...	23 And he called them unto him, and said **unto them** in parables, How can **Satan** [?] cast out Satan ?
24 And if...that kingdom cannot stand.	24 And if a **kingdom** be * **divided against itself,** that kingdom cannot stand.
25 ...if...that house will...be able ..	25 **And** if a **house** be divided against itself, that house will not be able to stand.
26 ...Satan hath risen...and...he cannot...but hath an end.	26 **And if Satan** [?] hath risen up **against himself,** and * **is divided,** he cannot **stand,** but hath an end.
Mark iii. 14, 16, W. & H. adopt the readings of the Revisers' margin. Matt x 2, W & H. *and* James. Mark iii. 22, Matt. xii, 24, Luke xi. 15, Gr. *cast(eth) out the devils.* Luke ix. 17, 18, Gr. *completely-divided.* Mark iii 22 ; compare also Matt ix. 32-34.	[1] Some ancient authorities add *whom also he named apostles.* See Luke vi 13. [2] Gr. *demons.* [3] Some ancient authorities insert *and he appointed twelve.* [4] Or, *Zealot.* See Luke vi. 15 ; Acts i. 13. [5] Or, *home.* [6] Or, *In.* [7] Gr. *demons.*

Synopticon, pages 16–17.]

OF THE SYNOPTIC GOSPELS.

St. Matthew. [Passages parallel to Mark.]	St. Luke. [Passages parallel to Mark.]
x. 1-5..., 7..., ...8...	vi. 12-16.
1 And he * called unto him his **twelve** [?] disciples, and gave them authority over unclean spirits, to cast them out, and to heal all manner of disease and all manner of sickness.	12 And it came to pass in these days, that he went out into the mountain to pray; and he continued all night in prayer to God.
2 Now the names of the **twelve** [?] apostles are these: The first, **Simon**, who is called **Peter, and Andrew** his brother; **James** the *son* of Zebedee, **and John** his brother;	13 And when it was day, he * called his disciples: and he chose from them **twelve**, whom also he named apostles;
3 **Philip, and Bartholomew; Thomas, and Matthew** the publican; **James** the *son* **of Alphæus, and** Thaddæus;	14 **Simon**, whom he also named **Peter, and Andrew** his brother, and **James and John**, and **Philip and Bartholomew**,
4 **Simon the** ¹ Canannæan, **and Judas Iscariot**, who also ² **betrayed** him.	15 **And Matthew** and **Thomas**, and **James** *the son* **of Alphæus**, and **Simon** which was called **the Zealot**,
5 These twelve Jesus sent forth, and charged them, saying... 7 And as ye go, preach,... 8 ...cast out devils...	16 **And** Judas *the* ¹ *son of* James, **and Judas Iscariot**, which was the **traitor;**
xii. 22-32.	xi. 14-23.
22 Then was brought unto him ³ one possessed with a devil, blind and dumb: and he healed him, insomuch that the dumb man spake and saw. 23 And all the multitudes were amazed, and said, Is this the son of David?	14 And he was casting out a ² devil *which was* dumb. And it came to pass, when the ² devil was gone out, the dumb man spake; and the multitudes marvelled.
24 But when the Pharisees heard it, they said, This man **doth** not **cast out** ⁴ **devils,** but ⁵ **by Beelzebub the prince of the** ⁴ **devils.**	15 But some of them said, ³ **By Beelzebub the prince of the** ⁴ **devils casteth he out** ⁴ **devils.** 16 And others, tempting *him*, sought of him a sign from heaven.
25 And knowing their thoughts he said **unto them,** Every **kingdom** * **divided** against **itself** is brought to desolation; **and** every city or **house** divided against itself shall not stand: 26 **And if Satan** casteth out Satan, he * **is divided against himself;** how then shall his kingdom **stand?**	17 But he, knowing their thoughts, said **unto them,** Every **kingdom** * **divided** against **itself** is brought to desolation; ⁵ **and** a **house** *divided* against a house falleth. 18 **And if Satan** also * **is divided against himself,** how shall his kingdom **stand?** because ye say that I cast out ⁴ devils ³ by Beelzebub.

¹ Or, *Zealot* See Luke vi 15; Acts i. 13. ² Or, *delivered him up*: and so always ³ Or, *a demoniac.* ⁴ Gr. *demons* ⁵ Or, *in.*	¹ Or, *brother.* See Jude 1. ² Gr *demon.* ³ Or, *In.* ⁴ Gr. *demons.* ⁵ Or, *and house falleth upon house.*

22   THE COMMON TRADITION

St. Mark. [*Portions not found in Matthew or Luke*]	St. Mark. [*Complete.*]
	III. 20-30.
27 But no one (Gr. no one not)...	27 But no one can **enter** into the house of **the strong** *man*, and spoil **his** goods, except he first bind the strong *man*; and then he will spoil his house.
28 Verily...(Gr. that)...their (Gr. the) ...their (Gr. the)...wherewithsoever they shall blaspheme.	28 Verily I say unto you, All their sins **shall be forgiven unto the sons of men,** and their blasphemies wheresoever they shall blaspheme:
29 ...hath...for (the age, *see note*)...but is guilty of an eternal sin.	29 **But** whosoever shall blaspheme against **the Holy Spirit** hath never **forgiveness,** but is guilty of an eternal sin:
30 ...He hath an unclean spirit.	30 Because they said, He hath an unclean spirit.
	III. 31-35.
31 And there come his...they sent unto him calling...	31 And there come his **mother and his brethren;** and, standing without, they sent unto him, calling him.
32 And...was sitting about him; and they say...	32 And a **multitude** was sitting about him; and they say unto **him,** Behold, **thy mother and thy brethren without** seek for **thee.**
33 And he...saith...	33 And he **answereth** them, **and** saith, Who is my mother and my brethren?
34 ...looking round on...which sat round about...he saith...	34 And looking round on them which sat round about him, he saith, Behold, **my mother and my brethren!**
	35 For whosoever shall **do** the will **of** God, the same is my brother, and sister, and mother.
Mark iii. 29 *not* for *the age,* Matt xiii. 32 *not...neither* in *this age nor...* Mark iii. 33, Matt. xii. 48, Luke viii. 21, Gr. *having answered.* Mark iii 35, W. & H. omit *For.* Mark iii. 35, Gr *that one is.*	

Synopticon, pages 18-19.]

| St. Matthew. | St. Luke. |
| [*Passages parallel to Mark.*] | [*Passages parallel to Mark.*] |

XII. 22–32.	XI. 14–23.
27 And if I ¹ by Beelzebub cast out ² devils, ¹ by whom do your sons cast them out? therefore shall they be your judges. 28 But if I ¹ by the Spirit of God cast out ² devils, then is the kingdom of God come upon you. 29 Or how can one **enter** into the house of **the strong** *man*, and spoil **his** goods except he first bind the strong *man*? and then he will spoil his house.	19 And if I ¹ by Beelzebub cast out ² devils, by whom do your sons cast them out? therefore shall they be your judges. 20 But if I by the finger of God cast out ² devils, then is the kingdom of God come upon you. 21 When **the strong** *man* fully armed guardeth his own court, his goods are in peace: 22 But when a stronger than he shall **come** upon him, and overcome him, he taketh from him his whole armour wherein he trusted, and divideth **his** spoils.
30 He that is not with me is against me; and he that gathereth not with me scattereth. 31 Therefore I say unto you, Every sin and blasphemy shall be forgiven ³ unto men; but the **blasphemy** against the Spirit shall not be forgiven. 32 And whosoever shall speak a word against **the Son of man**, it **shall be forgiven** him; **but** whosoever shall speak against **the Holy Spirit** it shall **not** be **forgiven** him, neither in this ⁴ world, nor in that which is to come.	23 He that is not with me is against me; and he that gathereth not with me scattereth. XII. 10. 10 And every one who shall speak a word against **the Son of man**, it **shall be forgiven** him: **but** unto him that **blasphemeth** against **the Holy Spirit** it shall **not** be **forgiven**.
XII. 46–50. 46 While he was yet speaking to the **multitudes**, behold, his **mother and his brethren** stood without, seeking to speak to him. 47 ⁵ And one said unto **him**, Behold, **thy mother and thy brethren** stand **without**, seeking to speak to **thee**. 48 But he **answered and** said unto him that told him, Who is my mother? and who are my brethren? 49 And he stretched forth his hand towards his disciples, and said, Behold, **my mother and my brethren**! 50 For whosoever shall **do** the will **of** my Father which is in heaven, he is my brother, and sister, and mother.	VIII. 19–21. 19 And there came to him **his mother and brethren**, and they could not come at him for the **crowd**. 20 And it was told **him**, **Thy mother and thy brethren** stand **without** desiring to see **thee**. 21 But he **answered and** said unto them, **My mother and my brethren** are these which hear the word **of** God, and **do** it.

¹ Or, *In*.   ² Gr. *demons*.
3 Some ancient authorities read *unto you men*.
4 Or, *age*.
5 Some ancient authorities omit ver. 47.

¹ Or, *In*.   ² Gr. *demons*.

THE COMMON TRADITION

St. Mark. [*Portions not found in Matthew or Luke.*]	St. Mark. [*Complete.*]
IV.	IV. 1-9.
1 And again he began to teach ..there is gathered...in the sea...were by the sea...the land.	1 And again he began to teach by the sea side. And there is gathered **unto him** a very **great multitude**, so that he entered into a boat, and sat in the sea; and all the multitude were by the sea on the land.
2 ...he taught...and...unto them in his teaching.	2 And he taught them many things in **parables,** and said unto them in his teaching,
3 Hearken.	3 Hearken: Behold, **the sower went forth to sow:**
4 ...it came to pass...	4 **And** it came to pass, **as he sowed, some** *seed* **fell by the way side, and the birds** came and **devoured it.**
	5 And other **fell on the rocky** *ground*, where it had not much earth; and straightway it sprang up, because it had no deepness of earth:
6 And when the ..	6 And when the sun was risen, it was scorched; **and because it had no** root, **it withered away.**
7 ...among (Gr. into)...and it yielded no fruit.	7 And other **fell** among **the thorns, and the thorns** grew up, and *choked it,** and it yielded no fruit.
8 ...growing up and increasing, and brought forth to (thirty) and in (sixty) and in (a hundred).	8 And others **fell** into **the** good **ground, and** yielded **fruit,** growing up and increasing; and brought forth, thirtyfold, and sixtyfold, and * **a hun-** dred*fold*.
9 And...Who...	9 And he said, Who **hath ears** to hear, **let him hear.**
	IV. 10-20.
10 When he was alone...about...with the twelve ..the...	10 And when he was alone, **they that were** about him with the twelve asked of **him** the **parables.**
11 And he said unto them ..without, all things are done (Gr. become)...	11 And he said unto them, **Unto you is given the mystery of the kingdom of** God: **but** unto them that are without, all things are done **in parables:**
	12 That **seeing they** may **see,** and not perceive; **and hearing they** may hear, and not **understand;** lest haply they should turn again, and it should be forgiven them.
Luke viii 6, Gr. *fell down on.*	

Synopticon, pages 20-21.]

St. Matthew. [*Passages parallel to Mark.*]	St. Luke. [*Passages parallel to Mark.*]
XIII. 1–9. 1 On that day went Jesus out of the house, and sat by the sea side. 2 And there were gathered **unto him great multitudes,** so that he entered into a boat, and sat; and all the multitude stood on the beach. 3 And he spake to them many things in **parables,** saying, Behold, **the sower went forth** to **sow; and as he sowed, some** *seeds* **fell by the way side, and the birds** came and **devoured them:** 5 And others **fell upon the rocky** *places,* where they had not much earth: and straightway they sprang up, because they had no deepness of earth: 6 And when the sun was risen, they were scorched; **and because they had no** root, **they withered away.** 7 And others fell upon **the thorns; and the thorns** grew up, and *choked **them:** 8 And others **fell** upon **the good ground, and** yielded **fruit,** some * a **hundredfold,** some sixty, some thirty. 9 He that **hath ears**[1]**, let him hear.**	VIII. 4–8. 4 And when a **great multitude** came together, and they of every city resorted **unto him,** he spake by a **parable:** 5 **The sower went forth** to **sow** his seed: **and as he sowed, some fell by the way side;** and it was trodden under foot, **and the birds** of the heaven **devoured it.** 6 And other * **fell on the rock;** and as soon as it grew, **it withered away, because it had no** moisture. 7 And other **fell** amidst **the thorns; and the thorns** grew with it, and ***choked it.** 8 And other **fell** into **the good ground, and** grew, and brought forth **fruit** * **a hundredfold.** As he said these things, he cried, He that **hath ears** to hear, **let him hear.**
XIII. 10, 11, 13, ...15. 10 And **the** disciples came, and said unto **him,** Why speakest thou unto them in **parables?** 11 And he answered and said unto them, **Unto you it is given** to know **the mysteries of the kingdom of** heaven, **but** to them it is not given. 12 For whosoever hath, to him... 13 Therefore speak I to them **in parables;** because **seeing they see** not, **and hearing** they hear not, neither do **they understand.** 15 ...Lest haply they should... And should turn again, And I should heal them.	VIII. 9–15. 9 And his disciples asked **him,** what this **parable** might be. 10 And he said, **Unto you it is given** to know **the mysteries of the kingdom of** God **but** to the rest **in parables;** that **seeing they** may not see, **and hearing they** may not **understand.**

[1] Some ancient authorities add here, and in ver. 43, *to hear*: as in Mark iv. 9, Luke viii. 8.

26   THE COMMON TRADITION

St. Mark. [*Portions not found in Matthew or Luke.*]	St. Mark. [*Complete.*]
IV. 13 And he saith unto them, Know ye not…and how shall ye know all the parables? 14 …soweth… 15 …where the word is sown, and when …straightway…Satan…in (Gr. into)… 16 And…in like manner are… 17 …then… 18 And others are… 19 …the…the lusts of other things… (entering) in… 20 And those…accept…[Gr. in (thirty) and in (sixty) and in (a hundred).]	IV. 10–20. 13 And he saith unto them, Know ye not this **parable**? and how shall ye know all the parables? 14 The sower soweth **the word**. 15 And these **are they by the way** side, where the word is sown; and when they have heard, straightway **cometh** Satan, **and** taketh away the word which hath been sown in **them**. 16 And these in like manner are **they** that are sown **upon the rocky** *places*, who, when they have **heard the word**, straightway receive it **with joy**; 17 And they **have no root** in themselves, but endure **for a while**; then, when tribulation or persecution ariseth because of the word, straightway they stumble. 18 And others are **they** that are sown **among the thorns; these are they** that have **heard** the word, 19 **And** the **cares** of the ¹ world, **and** the deceitfulness **of riches**, and the lusts of other things entering in, **choke** the word, **and** it becometh unfruitful. 20 And those **are they** that were sown upon **the good ground;** such as **hear the word**, and accept it, and **bear fruit**, thirtyfold, and sixtyfold, and a hundredfold.
	IV. 21–25.
21 And he said unto them (Gr. that) Is the…brought (Gr. comes) to (Gr. in order that)…under the (bed) *and* not to (Gr. in order that)…,	21 And he said unto them, Is the **lamp** brought to be **put *under** the bushel, or under the bed, *and* not to be put **on** the **stand**?
Mark iv. 17, Matt. xiii. 21, *endure* (Gr. *are*), *endureth* (Gr. *is*). Mark iv. 17, Matt xiii. 21, *for a while* represents an adjective in Greek.	¹ Or, *age*.

Synopticon, pages 22–23.]

St. Matthew. [*Passages parallel to Mark.*]	St. Luke. [*Passages parallel to Mark.*]
XIII. 10–23. 18 Hear then ye **the parable** of the sower. 19 When any one heareth **the word** of the kingdom, and understandeth it not, *then* **cometh the** evil *one*, **and** snatcheth away that which hath been sown in **his** heart. This **is he** that was sown **by the way side.** 20 And **he** that was sown **upon the rocky** *places*, this is he that **heareth the word,** and straightway **with joy** receiveth it; 21 Yet **hath** he **not root** in himself, but endureth **for a while;** and when tribulation or persecution ariseth because of the word, straightway he stumbleth. 22 And **he** that was sown **among the thorns, this is he** that **heareth** the word; **and** the **care** of the ¹world, **and** the deceitfulness **of riches, choke** the word, **and** he becometh unfruitful. 23 And **he** that was sown upon **the good ground,** this **is** he that **heareth the word,** and understandeth it; who verily **beareth fruit,** and bringeth forth, some a hundredfold, some sixty, some thirty.	VIII. 9–15. 11 Now **the parable** is this: The seed is **the word** of God. 12 And **those by the way side are** they that have heard; then **cometh the** devil, **and** taketh away the word from **their** heart, that they may not believe and be saved. 13 And **those on the rock** *are* they which, when they have **heard,** receive **the word with joy;** and these **have no root,** which **for a while** believe, and in time of temptation fall away. 14 And **that** which fell **among the thorns, these are they** that have **heard, and** as they go on their way they are **choked** with **cares and riches** and pleasures of *this* life, **and** bring no fruit to perfection. 15 And that in **the good ground,** these **are** such as in an honest and good heart, having **heard the word,** hold it fast, and **bring forth fruit** with patience.
v. 14–16. 14 Ye are the light of the world. A city set on a hill cannot be hid. 15 Neither do *men* light a **lamp, and put** it *under the bushel, but **on the stand;** and it shineth unto all that are in the house. 16 Even so let your light shine before men, that they may see your good works, and glorify your Father which is in heaven.	VIII. 16–17. 16 And no man, when he hath lighted a **lamp,** covereth it with a vessel, or **putteth** it ***under** (Gr. underneath) a bed; but putteth it **on a stand,** that they which enter in may see the light. *Compare also* XI. 33:— [No man when he hath lighted a lamp, putteth it in a cellar, neither under the bushel, but on the stand, that they which enter in may see the light.]

¹ Or, *age*.

THE COMMON TRADITION

St. Mark. [*Portions not found in Matthew or Luke.*]	St. Mark. [*Complete.*]
	IV. 22–24.
22 ... save that ... was ... made ... but that...	22 **For there is** nothing hid, save that it should be manifested; neither was *anything* made **secret,** but that it should come to light.
23 If any man...	23 If any man **hath ears** to hear, **let him hear.**
24 And he said unto them...what...	24 And he said unto them, Take heed what ye hear: **with what measure ye mete, it shall be measured unto you:**
	and more shall be given unto you.
	25 **For** he that **hath, to him shall be given:** and he that **hath** not, from him shall be taken away even that which he hath.
Mark iv. 22, Luke viii. 17, *for there is not (aught) hidden.* Mark iv 24, Matt. vii 2, in *what measure;* Luke vi. 38, *with-what measure.*	

[*Synopticon, pages 23–24.*]

St. Matthew. [*Passages parallel to Mark.*]	St. Luke. [*Passages parallel to Mark.*]
x. 26. 26 Fear them not therefore: **for there is** nothing covered, that shall not be revealed; and **hid,** that shall not be known.	**VIII. 9–15.** 17 **For** nothing **is** hid, that shall not be made manifest; nor *anything* **secret,** that shall not be known and come to light. *Compare also* XII. 2 :— [But there is nothing covered up, that shall not be revealed: and hid, that shall not be known.]
XI. 15. 15 He that **hath ears** [1] to hear, **let him hear.**	**XIV. 35.** 35 …He that **hath ears** to hear, **let him hear.** **VIII. 18.** 18 Take heed therefore how ye hear:…
VII. 2. 2 For with what judgement ye judge, ye shall be judged: and **with what measure ye mete, it shall be measured unto you.**	**VI. 38.** 38 Give, and it shall be given unto you; good measure, pressed down, shaken together, running over, shall they give into your bosom. For **with what measure ye mete, it shall be measured to you** again.
VI. 33. 33 But seek ye first his kingdom, and his righteousness; **and** all these things **shall be added unto you.**	**XII. 31.** 31 Howbeit seek ye [1] his kingdom, **and** these things **shall be added unto you.**
XIII. 12. 12 **For** whosoever **hath, to him shall be given,** and he shall have abundance: but whosoever **hath** not, **from him shall be taken away even that which he hath.** *Compare also* XXV. 29 :— [For unto every one that hath shall be given, and he shall have abundance: but from him that hath not, even that which he hath shall be taken away.]	**VIII. 18.** for whosoever **hath, to him shall be given;** and whosoever **hath** not, **from him shall be taken away even that which** he [2] thinketh he **hath.** *Compare also* XIX. 26: [I say unto you, that unto every one that hath shall be given; but from him that hath not, even that which he hath shall be taken away from him.]
[1] Some ancient authorities omit *to hear.*	[1] Many ancient authorities read *the kingdom of God.* [2] Or, *seemeth to have.*

St. Mark. [*Portions not found in Matthew or Luke.*]	St. Mark. [*Complete.*]
	IV. 26-29.
26 And...so is...God, as if (Gr. *as* or *that*)...should cast (Gr. the)...upon the earth,	26 And he said, So is the kingdom of God, as if a man should cast seed upon the earth ;
27 And...and rise night and day, and the seed...and grow he knoweth not how.	27 And should sleep and rise night and day, and the seed should spring up and grow, he knoweth not how.
28 The earth beareth...of herself; first the blade, then the ear, then the full ...in the ear.	28 The earth [1] beareth fruit of herself; first the blade, then the ear, then the full corn in the ear.
29 But when the fruit is ripe, straightway he putteth forth his sickle, because...is come,	29 But when the fruit [2] is ripe, straightway he [3] putteth forth the sickle, because the harvest is come.
	IV. 30-34.
30 And...How...or in...	30 And he **said,** How shall we liken **the kingdom of** God ? or in what parable shall we set it forth ?
31 It is like (Gr. as)...when it is sown upon the earth, though it be (Gr. being) ...that are upon the earth.	31 [4] It is like **a grain of mustard seed, which,** when it is sown upon the earth, though it be less than all the seeds that are upon the earth,
32 ...sown, groweth up,...all...putteth out (Gr. maketh) great...can...under the shadow thereof.	32 Yet when it is sown, groweth up, **and becometh** greater than all the herbs, and putteth out great **branches;** so that **the birds of the heaven** can **lodge** under the shadow thereof.
33 And with many such...the word unto them, as they were able to hear it.	33 And with many such parables spake he the word unto them, as they were able to hear it :
34 And...but privately to his own disciples he expounded all things.	34 And without a parable spake he not unto them : but privately to his own disciples he expounded all things.

[1] Or, *yieldeth.*
[2] Or, *alloweth.*
[3] Or, *sendeth forth.*
[4] Gr. *As unto.*

Synopticon, pages 25-26]

St. Matthew.
[Passage parallel to Mark.]

XIII. 24–30.

24 Another parable set he before them, saying, The kingdom of heaven is likened unto a man that sowed good seed in his field :
25 But while men slept, his enemy came and sowed [1] tares also among the wheat, and went away.
26 But when the blade sprang up, and brought forth fruit, then appeared the tares also.
27 And the [2] servants of the householder came and said unto him, Sir, didst thou not sow good seed in thy field ? whence then hath it tares ?
28 And he said unto them, [3] An enemy hath done this. And the [2] servants say unto him, Wilt thou then that we go and gather them up ?
29 But he saith, Nay ; lest haply while ye gather up the tares, ye root up the wheat with them.
30 Let both grow together until the harvest: and in the time of the harvest I will say to the reapers, Gather up first the tares, and bind them in bundles to burn them : but gather the wheat into my barn.

[1] Or, *darnel.*   [2] Gr. *bondservants.*   [3] Gr. *a man* that is *an enemy.*

St. Matthew.
[Passages parallel to Mark.]

XIII. 31–32.

31 Another parable set he before them, **saying, The kingdom of** heaven is like **unto a grain of mustard seed which** a man took, and sowed in his field :
32 Which indeed is less than all seeds ; but when it is grown, it is greater than the herbs, **and becometh** a tree, so that **the birds of the heaven** come and **lodge** in the **branches** thereof.

XIII. 34–35.

34 All these things spake Jesus in parables unto the multitudes ; and without a parable spake he nothing unto them :
35 That it might be fulfilled which was spoken [1] by the prophet, saying, I will open my mouth in parables ; I will utter things hidden from the foundation [2] of the world.

[1] Or, *through.*
[2] Many ancient authorities omit *of the world.*

St. Luke.
[Passages parallel to Mark.]

XIII. 18–19.

18 He **said** therefore, Unto what is **the kingdom of** God like ? and whereunto shall I liken it ?
19 It is like **unto a grain of mustard seed, which** a man took, and cast into his own garden ; and it grew, **and became** a tree ; and **the birds of the heaven lodged** in the **branches** thereof.

St. Mark. [*Portions not found in Matthew or Luke.*]	St. Mark. [*Complete.*]
	IV. 35–41.
35 ...that...when even was come, he saith...	35 And on that day, when even was come, he saith unto them, Let us **go over unto the other side.**
36 ...leaving the...they take...with them even as he was in...And other boats were with him.	36 And leaving the multitude, they take **him** with them, even as he was, in the **boat.** And other boats were with him.
37 ...beat into the boat...was now filling.	37 **And** there ariseth a great storm of wind, and the waves beat into the boat, insomuch that the boat was now filling.
38 And...was in the stern...on the cushion...and (say) unto him, Master, carest thou not that...	38 And he himself was in the stern, asleep on the cushion : and they **awake him,** and **say** unto him, [1] Master, carest thou not that **we perish?**
39 And...said...Peace, be still...the wind ceased...	39 And he **awoke, and rebuked the wind, and** said unto the sea, Peace, be still. And the wind ceased, **and there was a** great **calm.**
40 ...have ye not yet...	40 And he said **unto them,** Why are ye fearful? have ye not yet **faith?**
41 And...exceedingly (Gr. a great fear), and...	41 And they feared exceedingly, and **said** one to another, Who then **is this, that even the wind and** the sea **obey him?**
	V. 1–20.
1 ...they came...of the sea...	1 **And** they came to the **other side** of the sea, **into the country of the** Gerasenes.
2 And [?]...out of the boat, straightway ...the tombs [?] a man with (Gr. in) an unclean spirit,	2 And when he was **come** out of the boat, straightway there **met him out of the tombs** a man with an unclean spirit,
3 Who had his dwelling...[?] : and no man could any more bind him, no, not with a chain ;	3 Who had his dwelling in the tombs : and no man could any more bind him, no, not with a chain ;
4 Because that he had been...bound... the chains had been rent asunder [?] by him and the fetters broken in pieces, and no man...to tame him.	4 Because that he had been often bound with fetters and chains, and the chains had been rent asunder by him, and the fetters broken in pieces : and no man had strength to tame him.
5 And always, night and day, in the tombs and in the mountains, he was crying out, and cutting himself with stones.	5 And always, night and day, in the tombs and in the mountains, he was crying out, and cutting himself with stones.
	[1] Gr. *Teacher.*

Synopticon, pages 27–28.]

St. Matthew. [Passages parallel to Mark]	St. Luke. [Passages parallel to Mark.]
VIII. 18, 23-27. 18 Now when Jesus saw great multitudes about him, he gave commandment **to depart unto the other side.** 23 And when he was entered into a **boat,** his disciples followed **him.** 24 **And** behold, there arose a great tempest in the sea, insomuch that the boat was covered with the waves; but he was asleep. 25 And they came to him, and **awoke him, saying,** Save, Lord; **we perish.** 26 And he saith **unto them,** Why are ye fearful, O ye of little **faith?** Then he **arose, and rebuked the winds and** the sea; **and there was a** great **calm.** 27 And the men marvelled, **saying,** What manner of man **is this, that even the winds and** the sea **obey him?**	VIII. 22-25. 22 Now it came to pass on one of those days, that he entered into a **boat, himself** and his disciples; and he said unto them, Let us **go** over **unto the other side** of the lake: and they launched forth. 23 But as they sailed he fell asleep: **and** there came down a storm of wind on the lake; and they were filling *with water*, and were in jeopardy. 24 And they came to him, and **awoke him, saying,** Master, master, **we perish.** And he **awoke, and rebuked the wind** and the raging of the water: and they ceased, **and there was a calm.** 25 And he said **unto them,** Where is your **faith?** And being afraid they marvelled, **saying** one to another, Who then **is this, that** he commandeth **even the winds and** the water, and they **obey him?**
VIII. 28-34. 28 **And** when he was **come** to the **other side into the country of the** Gadarenes, there **met him** two [1] possessed with devils, coming forth **out of the tombs,** exceeding fierce, so that no man could pass by that way.	VIII. 26-39. 26 **And** they arrived **at the country of the** [1] Gerasenes, which is **over** against Galilee. 27 And when he was **come** forth upon the land, there **met him** a certain man **out of** the city, who had [2] devils; and for a long time he had worn no clothes, and abode not in *any* house, but in **the tombs.**

[1] Or, *demoniacs.*

[1] Many ancient authorities read *Gergesenes:* others, *Gadarenes:* so in 37.
[2] Gr. *demons.*

THE COMMON TRADITION

St. Mark. [*Portions not found in Matthew or Luke*]	St. Mark. [*Complete.*]
	v. 1–20.
6 And [?]...from afar he ran and worshipped [?]... 7 ...I adjure...by God...	6 And when he saw Jesus from afar, he ran and worshipped him; 7 **And crying out** with a loud voice, he saith, **What** have I to do **with thee, Jesus, thou Son of** the Most High **God?** I adjure thee by God, **torment** me not.
8 ...he said unto him...out of...	8 For he said unto him, Come forth, thou unclean spirit, out of the man.
9 And...And he saith unto him, My name is...we are...	9 And he asked him, What is thy name? And he saith unto him, My name is Legion; for we are many.
10 ...much... he would ... send them away out of the country.	10 And he besought him much that he would not send them away out of the country.
11 ...on...great...	11 **Now** there **was** there on the mountain side a great **herd of swine feeding.**
12 ...Send...that...into them.	12 And they **besought him,** saying, Send us **into** the swine, that we may enter into them.
13 ...And the [?] unclean spirits... about two thousand...sea.	13 **And** he gave **them** leave. And the unclean spirits **came out, and entered into** the **swine: and the herd rushed down the steep into the** sea, *in number* about two thousand; and they were choked in the sea.
14 And ..them...what it was (Gr. is)...	14 And **they that fed** them **fled, and told it in the city,** and in the country. And they **came** to see what it was that had come to pass.
15 ...they come...behold...him that had the legion...	15 And they come [?] to **Jesus,** and behold [1] him that was possessed with devils sitting, clothed and in his right mind, *even* him that had the legion: and they were afraid.
16 And...declared...it befell...and concerning the swine.	16 And they that saw it declared unto them how it befell [1] him that was **possessed with devils,** and concerning the swine.
Mark v. 7, Luke viii. 28, Gr. *to me and thee;* Matt viii. 29, Gr. *to us and thee.* Matt. viii. 33, Gr. omits *them* (fled): Luke viii. 34, Gr. omits *them*.	[1] Or, *the demoniac.*

Synopticon, pages 28–30.

St. Matthew. [Passages parallel to Mark.]	St. Luke. [Passages parallel to Mark.]
VIII. 28-34. 29 **And** behold, they * **cried out,** saying, **What** have we to do **with thee, thou Son of God?** art thou come hither to **torment** us before the time?	VIII. 26-39. 28 And when he saw Jesus, he :* **cried out,** and fell down before him, **and** with a loud voice said, **What** have I to do **with thee,** Jesus, **thou Son of** the Most High **God?** I beseech thee **torment** me not.
	29 For he commanded the unclean spirit to come out from the man. For ¹ oftentimes it had seized him :- and he was kept under guard, and bound with chains and fetters; and breaking the bands asunder, he was driven of the ² devil into the deserts.
	30 And Jesus asked him, What is thy name? And he said, Legion; for many ³ devils were entered into him.
	31 And they intreated him that he would not command them to depart into the abyss.
30 **Now there was** afar off from them **a herd of** many **swine feeding.** 31 And the ¹ devils **besought him,** saying, if thou cast us out, send us away **into** the herd of swine. 32 **And** he said **unto them,** Go. And they **came out, and went into the swine :** and behold, the whole **herd rushed down the steep into the** sea, and perished in the waters. 33 And **they that fed** them **fled, and** went away **into the city,** and **told** everything, and what was befallen to them that were ² **possessed with devils.** 34 And behold, all the city **came** out to meet **Jesus ;** ...	32 **Now there was** there **a herd of** many **swine feeding** on the mountain: and they **intreated him** that he would give them leave to enter **into** them. **And** he gave **them** leave. 33 And the ³ devils **came out** from the man, **and' entered into the swine : and the herd rushed down the steep into the** lake, and were choked. 34 And when **they that fed** them saw what had come to pass, **they fled, and told it in the city** and in the country. 35 And they **went** [?] out to see what had come to pass; and they came [?] to **Jesus,** and found the man, from whom the ³ devils were gone out, sitting, clothed and in his right mind, at the feet of Jesus; and they were afraid. 36 And they that saw it told them how he that was **possessed with ³ devils** was ⁴ made whole.
¹ Gr. *demons.* ² Or, *demoniacs.*	¹ Or, *of a long time.* ² Gr *demon.* ³ Gr. *demons* ⁴ Or, *saved.*

THE COMMON TRADITION

St. Mark. [Portions not found in Matthew or Luke.]	St. Mark. [Complete.]
	v. 1-20.
17 ...they began...	17 **And** they began to beseech **him** to depart **from their** borders.
18 And ... the ... besought ... that he might be with...	18 And as he was entering into the boat, he that had been possessed with ¹devils besought him that he might be with him.
19 And he suffered...not, but...unto him, Go...unto thy friends,...tell them ... Lord ... and ... he had mercy on thee.	19 And he suffered him not, but saith unto him, Go to thy house unto thy friends, and tell them how great things the Lord hath done for thee, and *how* he had mercy on thee.
20 ...and began...in (*see Introduction*) ...and all men did marvel.	20 And he went his way, and began to publish in *Decapolis how great things Jesus had done for him : and all men did marvel.
	v. 21-24.
21 And when...had crossed over again in the boat unto the other side, a great ...was gathered unto...and he was by the sea.	21 And when Jesus had crossed over again in the boat unto the other side, a great multitude was gathered unto him : and he was by the sea.
22 ...there cometh...of the...seeing him ...his [?]...	22 And there cometh one of the **rulers** of the synagogue, Jaïrus by name ; and seeing him, he falleth at his feet,
23 And...much...[Gr. The (of me)]... is at the point of death : that ..lay ...that she may be made whole...	23 And beseecheth **him** much, saying, (Gr. **that**) My little **daughter** is at the point of death : *I pray thee*, that thou **come** and lay thy hands on her, that she may be ²made whole, and live.
24 ...he went (Gr. went away) with him. And a great ... and they thronged (Gr. crushed)...	24 And he went with him ; and a great multitude followed him, and they * thronged him.
	v. 25-34.
	25 **And a woman**, which had **an issue** [?] of **blood twelve years,**
26 And had suffered many things of many physicians, and had spent all that she had, and was nothing bettered, but rather grew worse,	26 And had suffered many things of many physicians, and had spent all that she had, and was nothing bettered, but rather grew worse,
27 Having heard the things concerning Jesus ..in the crowd...	27 Having heard the things concerning Jesus, * **came** in the crowd **behind, and touched his garment.**
That, in Mk. v 23, Matt. ix. 18, corresponds to *for* in Luke viii. 42. Matt. ix. 20, Lu. viii. 44, Gr. omits *him*.	¹ Gr. *demons*. ² Or, *saved*.

Synopticon, pages 30-31.

OF THE SYNOPTIC GOSPELS.   37

St. Matthew. [Passages parallel to Mark.]	St. Luke. [Passages parallel to Mark.]
viii. 28-34. 34...**and** when they saw **him**, they besought *him* that he would depart **from their** borders.	VIII. 26-39. 37 **And** all the people of the country of the Gerasenes round about asked **him** to depart **from them**; for they were holden with great fear: and he entered into a boat, and returned. 38 But the man from whom the [1] **devils** were gone out prayed him that he might be with him: but he sent him away, saying, 39 Return to thy house, and declare how great things God hath done for thee. And he went his way, publishing throughout the whole * city how great things Jesus had done for him.
IX. 18-19. 18 While he spake these things unto them, behold, there came [1] **a ruler**, and worshipped **him**, saying, (Gr. **that**) My **daughter** is even now dead: but **come** and lay thy hand upon her, and she shall live. 19 And Jesus arose, and followed him, and *so did* his disciples.	VIII. 40-42. 40 And as Jesus returned, the multitude welcomed him; for they were all waiting for him. 41 And behold, there came a man named Jaïrus, and he was **a ruler** of the synagogue; and he fell down at Jesus' feet, and besought **him** to **come** into his house; 42 **For** he had an only **daughter**, about twelve years of age, and she lay a dying. But as he went the multitudes * thronged him.
ix. 20-22. 20 **And** behold, **a woman**, who had **an issue** [?] of **blood twelve years**, * **came behind** him, **and touched** the border of **his garment:**	viii. 43-48. 43 **And a woman** having **an issue** [?] of **blood twelve years**, which [2] had spent all her living upon physicians, and could not be healed of any, 44 * **Came behind** him, **and touched** the border of **his garment**; and immediately the issue of her blood stanched.
[1] Gr. *one ruler*.	[1] Gr. *demons*. [2] Some ancient authorities omit *had spent all her living upon physicians and*.

THE COMMON TRADITION

St. Mark. [Portions not found in Matthew or Luke.]	St. Mark. [Complete.]
28 ...(Gr. that)...but (Gr. even if)...	v. 25–34. 28 For she said, If I touch but his garments, I shall be ¹ made whole.
29. ...straightway...fountain...was dried up; and she felt in her body that she was healed of her plague.	29 And straightway the fountain of her blood was dried up; and she felt in her body that she was healed of her ² plague.
30. ...straightway...in himself that the ...from him...about in the crowd, and said...(Gr. the) garments?	30 And straightway Jesus, perceiving in himself that the power *proceeding* from him had gone forth, turned him about in the crowd, and said, Who touched my garments?
31 And his disciples said unto him, Thou seest...and sayest thou...	31 And his disciples said unto him, Thou seest the multitude thronging thee, and sayest thou, Who touched me?
32 And he looked round about...her that had done this thing.	32 And he looked round about to see her that had done this thing.
33 ...fearing and...knowing what had been done (Gr. has happened) to her, ...and told him all the truth.	33 But the woman fearing and trembling, knowing what had been done to her, came and fell down before him, and told him all the truth.
34 ...go...and be whole of thy plague.	34 **And he said** unto **her, Daughter, thy faith hath ³ made thee whole;** go in peace, and be whole of thy ² plague.
	v. 35–43.
35 ...from...why...	35 While he yet spake, they come from **the *ruler** of the synagogue's *house*, saying, Thy daughter is dead: why troublest thou the ⁴ Master any further?
36 ...the word spoken, saith unto the ruler of the synagogue...	36 But **Jesus** ⁵ not * heeding the word spoken, saith unto the ruler of the synagogue, Fear not, only believe.
37 And...no man to follow with...the brother of James.	37 And he suffered no man to follow with him, save Peter, and James, and John the brother of James.
38 ...they come...of the ruler of the synagogue,...he beholdeth...and...and wailing greatly.	38 And they come **to the house** of the ruler of the synagogue; and he beholdeth a tumult, and *many* weeping and wailing greatly.
39 And...unto them, Why make ye a tumult and...child...	39 And when he was entered in, he saith unto them, Why make ye a

¹ Or, *saved*. ² Gr. *scourge*.
³ Or, *saved thee*. ⁴ Or, *Teacher*.
⁵ Or, *overhearing*.

Matt. ix. 22, W. & H. *But he.*

Synopticon, *pages* 31–33.

OF THE SYNOPTIC GOSPELS. 39

St. Matthew. [Passages parallel to Mark.]	St. Luke. [Passages parallel to Mark.]
IX. 20-22. 21 For she said within herself, If I do but touch his garment, I shall be ¹made whole.	**VIII. 43-48.**
	45 And Jesus said, Who is it that touched me? And when all denied, Peter said, ¹and they that were with him, Master, the multitudes press thee and crush *thee*. 46 But Jesus said, Some one did touch me; for I perceived that power had gone forth from me. 47 And when the woman saw that she was not hid, she came trembling, and falling down before him declared in the presence of all the people for what cause she touched him, and how she was healed immediately.
22 **But** Jesus turning and seeing **her said, Daughter,** be of good cheer; **thy faith hath ²made thee whole.** And the woman was ¹made whole from that hour.	48 **And he said** unto **her, Daughter, thy faith hath ²made thee whole;** go in peace.
IX. 23-26. 23 And when **Jesus** came **into the *ruler's house,** and saw the flute-players, and the crowd making a tumult,	**VIII. 49-56.** 49 While he yet spake, there cometh one from **the *ruler** of the synagogue's *house*, saying, Thy daughter is dead; trouble not the ³Master. 50 But **Jesus ***hearing it, answered him, Fear not: only believe, and she shall be ⁴made whole.
	51 And when he came **to the house,** he suffered not any man to enter in with him, save Peter, and John, and James, and the father of the maiden and her mother. 52 And all were weeping, and bewailing her: but he said, Weep not; for
¹ Or, *saved*. ² Or, *saved thee*.	¹ Some ancient authorities omit *and they that were with him*. ² Or, *saved thee*. ³ Or, *Teacher*. ⁴ Or, *saved*.

THE COMMON TRADITION

St. Mark. [*Portions not found in Matthew or Luke.*]	St. Mark. [*Complete.*]
	v. 35–43.
29 ..tumult, and...child...	tumult, and weep? the child **is not dead, but sleepeth.**
40 ...all...taketh...and them that were with him, and goeth in where the child was.	40 **And they laughed him to scorn. But** he, having put them all forth, taketh the father of the child and her mother and them that were with him, and goeth in where the child was.
41 And [?]...the child...unto her, Talitha cumi; which is, being interpreted, Damsel, I say unto thee...	41 And **taking** the child **by the hand,** he saith unto her, Talitha cumi; which is, being interpreted, Damsel, I say unto thee, **Arise.**
42 ...straightway...and walked; for she was...straightway with a great amazement.	42 **And** straightway the damsel rose up, and walked; for she was twelve years old. And they were amazed straightway with a great amazement.
43 And he charged...much that... should know...he commanded that...	43 And he charged them much that no man should know this: and he commanded that *something* should be given her to eat.
	VI. 1–6...
1 ...from thence...cometh...and his disciples follow him.	1 And he **went** out from thence; **and** he cometh **into** his own country; and his disciples follow him.
2 ...when ... was come ... many.. and what. .that is given...such...wrought by his hands?	2 And when the sabbath was come, he began to teach in **the synagogue:** and [1] many hearing him were astonished, **saying,** Whence hath this man these things? and, What is the wisdom that is given unto this man, and *what mean* such [2] mighty works wrought by his hands?
3 ...the (son)...here...	3 **Is not this** the carpenter, **the son** of Mary, and brother of James, and Joses, and Judas, and Simon? and are not his sisters here with us? And they were [3] offended in him.
4 ...said...and among his own kin...	4 And Jesus said unto **them,** (Gr. that) **A prophet is not** without honour, save **in his own country,** and among his own kin, and in his own house.
5 .. he could...no...save that he laid his hands upon a few sick folk, and healed them.	5 And he could there do no [4] mighty work, save that he laid his hands upon a few sick folk, and healed them.
6 And he marvelled...	6 And he marvelled because of their unbelief...

Mark vi 2, W. and H. read *the many*, i.e *most*.

[1] Some ancient authorities insert *the*.
[2] Gr. *powers*
[3] Gr *caused to stumble.*
[4] Gr. *power.*

Synopticon, pages 33–34.

OF THE SYNOPTIC GOSPELS. 41

St. Matthew. [*Passages parallel to Mark.*]	St. Luke. [*Passages parallel to Mark.*]
IX. 23–26. 24 He said, Give place: for the damsel **is not dead, but sleepeth. And they laughed him to scorn.** 25 **But** when the crowd was put forth, he entered in, and **took** her **by the hand;** and the damsel **arose.**	VIII. 49–56. **she is not dead, but sleepeth.** 53 **And they laughed him to scorn,** knowing that she was dead. 54 **But** he, **taking** her **by the hand,** called, saying, Maiden, **arise.**
26 And [1] the fame hereof went forth into all that land.	55 And [?] her spirit returned, **and** [?] she rose up immediately: and he commanded that *something* be given her to eat. 56 And her parents were amazed: but he charged them to tell no man what had been done.
XIII. 53–58. 53 And it came to pass, when Jesus had finished these parables, he departed thence. 54 **And coming into** his own country he taught them in their **synagogue,** insomuch that they were astonished, and **said,** Whence hath this man this wisdom, and these [2] mighty works? 55 **Is not this** the carpenter's **son?** is not his mother called Mary? and his brethren, James, and Joseph, and Simon, and Judas? 56 And his sisters, are they not all with us? Whence then hath this man all these things? 57 And they were [3] offended in him. But Jesus said unto **them,** (Gr. that) **A prophet is not** without honour, save **in his own country,** and in his own house. 58 And he did not many [4] mighty works there because of their unbelief.	IV. 16–17..., 21–24, 28. 16 **And** he **came to** Nazareth, where he had been brought up: and he entered, as his custom was, into **the synagogue** on the sabbath day, and stood up to read. 17 And there was delivered unto him [1] the book of the prophet Isaiah... 21 And he began to say unto them, To-day hath this scripture been fulfilled in your ears. 22 And all bare him witness, and wondered at the words of grace which proceeded out of his mouth: and they **said, Is not this** Joseph's **son?** 23 And he said unto **them,** Doubtless ye will say unto me this parable,. Physician, heal thyself: whatsoever we have heard done at Capernaum, do also here in thine own country. 24 And he said, Verily I say unto you, **No prophet is** acceptable **in his own country.** 28 And they were all filled with wrath in the synagogue, as they heard these things;
[1] Gr. *this fame.* [2] Gr. *powers.* [3] Gr. *caused to stumble.* [4] Gr. *powers.*	[1] Or. *a roll.*

THE COMMON TRADITION

St. Mark. [Portions not found in Matthew or Luke.]	St. Mark. [Complete.]
6 ..about (Gr. in a circle)...	vi. 6. 6 ....And he went round about the villages teaching.
7 ...began...by two and two (Gr. two two), and...over the...	vi. 7–13. 7 And he called unto him the twelve, and began to send them forth by two and two ; and he gave them authority over the unclean spirits ;
8 ...that...save...only...	8 And he charged them that they should take nothing for *their* journey, save a staff only ; no bread, no wallet, no ¹money in their ²purse ;
9 But...sandals...and put not on...	9 But *to go* shod with sandals : and, *said he,* put not on two coats.
10 And he said unto them, Where......	10 And he said unto them, Wheresoever ye enter into a house, there abide till ye depart [?] thence.
11 ...place ... as ye go ...thence.... dust that is under...	11 And whatsoever place shall not receive you, and they hear you not, as ye * go forth thence, shake off the dust that is under your feet for a testimony unto them.
Mark vi. 9, W. & H. *to put not on.*	¹ Gr. *brass.* ² Gr. *girdle.*

Compare also LUKE x. 1–12.

1 Now after these things the Lord appointed seventy ¹others, and sent them two and two before his face into every city and place whither he himself was about to come.
2 And he said unto them, The harvest is plenteous, but the labourers are few : pray ye therefore the Lord of the harvest, that he send forth labourers into his harvest.
3 Go your ways : behold, I send you forth as lambs in the midst of wolves.
4 Carry no purse, no wallet, no shoes : and salute no man on the way.
5 And into whatsoever house ye shall ²enter, first say, Peace *be* to this house.
6 And if a son of peace be there, your peace shall rest upon ³him : but if not, it shall turn to you again.
7 And in that same house remain, eating and drinking such things as they give : for the labourer is worthy of his hire. 8 And into whatsoever city ye enter, and they receive you, eat such things as are set before you :
9 And heal the sick that are therein, and say unto them, The kingdom of God is come nigh unto you. 10 But into whatsoever city ye shall enter, and they receive you not, go out into the streets thereof and say, 11 Even the dust from your city, that cleaveth to our feet, we do wipe off against you : howbeit know this, that the kingdom of God is come nigh. 12 I say unto you, It shall be more tolerable in that day for Sodom, than for that city.

¹ Many ancient authorities add *and two:* and so in v. 17.   ² Or, *enter first, say...*
³ Or, *it.*

St. Matthew. [Passages parallel to Mark.]	St. Luke. [Passages parallel to Mark.]
ix. 35:— 35 **And** Jesus went about all the cities and the **villages, teaching** in their synagogues, and preaching the gospel of the kingdom, and healing all manner of disease and all manner of sickness.	**xiii. 22.** 22 **And** he went on his way through cities and **villages, teaching,** and journeying on unto Jerusalem.
x. 1, 5–15. 1 And he **called** unto him his **twelve** disciples, **and gave them authority** over unclean spirits, to cast them out, and to heal all manner of disease, and all manner of sickness. 5 These twelve Jesus **sent forth,** and charged **them,** saying, Go not into *any* way of the Gentiles, and enter not into any city of the Samaritans: 6 But go rather to the lost sheep of the house of Israel. 7 And as ye go, preach, saying, The kingdom of heaven is at hand. 8 Heal the sick, raise the dead, cleanse the lepers, cast out ¹ devils: freely ye received, freely give. 9. Get you no gold, nor silver, nor brass in your ² purses; 10 No **wallet for** *your* **journey,** neither **two coats, nor shoes,** nor **staff**: for the labourer is worthy of his food. 11 And **into** whatsoever city or village **ye shall enter,** search out who in it is worthy; and **there abide** till ye go **forth.** 12 And as ye enter into the **house,** salute it. 13 And if the house be worthy, let your peace come upon it: but if it be not worthy, let your peace return to you. 14 **And** whosoever shall **not receive you,** nor hear your words, as ye * go **forth** out of that house or that city, shake off **the** dust **of your feet.** 15 Verily I say unto you, It shall be more tolerable for the land of Sodom and Gomorrah in the day of judgement, than for that city.	**ix. 1–5.** 1 And he **called the twelve** together, **and gave them** power and **authority** over all ¹ devils, and to cure diseases. 2 And he **sent** them **forth** to preach the kingdom of God, and to heal ² the sick. 3 And he said unto **them,** Take nothing **for** your **journey,** neither **staff,** nor **wallet,** nor bread, nor money; neither have **two coats.** **x. 4.** Carry no purse, no wallet, no **shoes;** and salute no man on the way. **ix. 4.** 4 And **into** whatsoever house **ye enter, there abide,** and thence [depart. 5 **And** as many as **receive you not,** when ye depart (Gr.* go **forth**) from that city, **shake** off **the** dust from **your feet** for a testimony against them.
¹ Gr. *demons.* ² Gr. *girdles.*	¹ Gr. *demons.* ² Some ancient authorities omit *the sick.*

St. Mark. [*Portions not found in Matthew or Luke.*]	St. Mark. [*Complete.*]
	vi. 7–13.
12 And they went...and preached that *men*-should-repent.	12 And they went out, and preached that *men* should repent.
13 And they cast out many devils, and anointed with oil many that were sick...	13 And they cast out many [1] devils, and anointed with oil many that were sick, and healed them.
	VI. 14–29.
14 And king...for his name had become known :...is risen...	14 And king **Herod heard** *thereof*; for his name had become known : and [2] he said, **John** [3] the Baptist is risen from **the dead**, and therefore do these powers work in him.
15 ...others said, It is...said,...as one of...prophets.	15 But others said, It is Elijah. And others said, *It is* a prophet, *even* as one of the prophets.
16 ...when-he-heard, said...whom ..	16 But Herod, when he heard *thereof*, said, John, whom I beheaded, **he** (Gr. **this) is risen.**
17 ...himself had sent forth and...and ...him...for he had married her.	17 For **Herod** himself had sent forth and laid hold upon **John,** and bound him **in prison** for the sake of **Herodias, his brother** Philip's **wife :** for he had married her.
18 ... unto Herod (Gr. that) ... thy brother's wife.	18 For John said unto Herod, It is not lawful for thee to have thy brother's wife.
19 And Herodias set herself against him and...and she could not.	19 And Herodias set herself against him, and desired to kill him ; and she could not ;
20 For Herod...John, knowing that he was a righteous man and a holy, and kept him safe. And when he heard him, he was much perplexed ; and he heard him gladly.	20 For Herod feared John, knowing that he was a righteous man and a holy, and kept him safe. And when he heard him he [4] was much perplexed ; and he heard him gladly.
Mark vi. 17, Gr, *having sent forth.*	[1] Gr. *demons.* [2] Some ancient authorities read *they.* [3] Gr. *the Baptizer.* [4] Many ancient authorities read *did many things.*

Synopticon, pages 37 38

St. Matthew. [*Passages parallel to Mark.*]	St. Luke. [*Passages parallel to Mark.*]
	IX. 6 6 And they departed, and went throughout the villages, preaching the gospel, and healing everywhere.
XIV. 1–12. 1 At that season **Herod the** tetrarch **heard** the report concerning Jesus, 2 And said unto his servants, **This is John** the Baptist; he (Gr. himself) **is risen** from **the dead**; and therefore do these powers work in him.	IX. 7–9. 7. Now **Herod the** tetrarch **heard** of all that was done: and he was much perplexed, because that it was said by some, that **John was risen** from **the dead;** 8 And by some, that Elijah had appeared; and by others, that one of the old prophets was risen again. 9 And Herod said, John I beheaded: but who is **this,** about whom I hear such things? And he sought to see him.
	III. 18–20. 18 With many other exhortations therefore preached he [1] good tidings unto the people; 19 But **Herod** the tetrarch being reproved by him for **Herodias his brother's wife,** and for all the evil things which Herod had done, 20 Added yet this above all, that he shut up **John in prison.**
3 For **Herod** had laid hold on **John,** and bound him, and put him **in prison** for the sake of **Herodias, his brother** Philip's **wife.**	
4 For John said unto him, It is not lawful for thee to have her. 5 And when he would have put him to death, he feared the multitude, because they counted him as a prophet.	[LUKE WANTING.]
	[1] Gr. *the Gospel.*

St. Mark. [Portions not found in Matthew or Luke.]	St. Mark. [Complete.]
	VI. 14-29.
21 And...a convenient day...when...his ...made a supper to his lords, and the high captains, and the chief men of Galilee ;	21 And when a convenient day was come, that Herod on his birthday made a supper to his lords, and the [1] high captains, and the chief men of Galilee ;
22 And when...herself came in and... and them that sat at meat with him ; and the king said unto the damsel,... of me...thou wilt, and...thee.	22 And when [2] the daughter of Herodias herself came in and danced, [3] she pleased Herod and them that sat at meat with him; and the king said unto the damsel, Ask of me whatsoever thou wilt, and I will give it thee.
23 And he sware...(Gr. that) Whatsoever thou shalt ask of me, I will give it thee, unto the half of my kingdom. 24 And she went out and said...What shall I ask? And she said, The head of John the Baptist.	23 And he sware unto her, Whatsoever thou shalt ask of me, I will give it thee, unto the half of my kingdom. 24 And she went out, and said unto her mother, What shall I ask? And she said, The head of John [4] the Baptist.
25 And she came in straightway with haste unto the king, and asked, saying, I will that thou forthwith...	25 And she came in straightway with haste unto the king, and asked, saying, I will that thou forthwith give me in a charger the head of John [4] the Baptist.
26 ...was exceeding...but...he would not reject her.	26 And the king was exceeding sorry ; but for the sake of his oaths, and of them that sat at meat, he would not reject her.
27 ...straightway the king sent forth a soldier of his guard, and commanded to bring his head : and he went and... him... 28 ...it...the damsel gave it...	27 And straightway the king sent forth a soldier of his guard, and commanded to bring his head : and he went and beheaded him in the prison, 28 And brought his head in a charger, and gave it to the damsel ; and the damsel gave it to her mother.
29 ...when...heard, they came and.. his ...laid...in a tomb.	29 And when his disciples heard *thereof*, they came and took up his corpse, and laid it in a tomb.
	[1] Or, *military tribunes*, Gr. *chiliarchs*. [2] Some ancient authorities read *his daughter Herodias*. [3] Or, *it*. [4] Gr. *the Baptizer*.
Mark vi. 22, W. and H. read, *his daughter Herodias*.	

Synopticon, pages 38-39.

OF THE SYNOPTIC GOSPELS. 47

St. Matthew. [Passages parallel to Mark.]	St. Luke. [Passages parallel to Mark.]
XIV. 1–12. 6 But when Herod's birthday came, the daughter of Herodias danced in the midst, and pleased Herod.	[LUKE WANTING.]
7 Whereupon he promised with an oath to give her whatsoever she should ask.	
8 And she, being put forward by her mother, saith, Give me here in a charger the head of John the Baptist.	
9 And the king was grieved; but for the sake of his oaths, and of them which sat at meat with him, he commanded it to be given; 10 And he sent, and beheaded John in the prison. 11 And his head was brought in a charger, and given to the damsel; and she brought it to her mother.	
12 And his disciples came, and took up the corpse, and buried him; and they went and told Jesus.	

48　　　　　THE COMMON TRADITION

St. Mark. [*Portions not found in Matthew or Luke.*]	St. Mark. [*Complete.*]
	VI. 30–44.
30 ...gather themselves together unto ,..and they told...all things, ..and whatsoever they had taught.	30 And the apostles gather themselves together unto Jesus; and they told him all things, whatsoever they had done, and whatsoever they had taught.
31 ...he saith unto them, Come ye yourselves apart into a desert place, and rest a while. For there were many coming and going, and they had no leisure so much as to eat. 32 And they went away...the...	31 And he saith unto them, Come ye yourselves apart into a desert place, and rest a while. For there were many coming and going, and they had no leisure so much as to eat. 32 And they went away in the boat **to** a desert place **apart.**
33 ...saw them going, and many... and they ran there together...all... and outwent them.	33 And *the people* saw them going, and many knew *them*, and they ran there together [1] on foot from all the cities, and outwent them.
34 ...he began to teach them many things.	34 And he came forth and saw a great multitude, and he had compassion on them, because they were as sheep not having a shepherd; **and** he began to teach them many things.
35 And when the day...now far spent, his...far spent :	35 And when the day was now far spent, his disciples **came unto him,** and said, The **place is desert,** and the day is now far spent :
36 ...them...the...somewhat to eat.	36 **Send** them **away, that** they may go **into** the country and **villages** round about, and **buy** themselves somewhat to eat.
37 ...answered and...and...Shall we go and buy [?] two hundred pennyworth of bread, and give them to eat ?	37. **But** he answered and **said** unto **them, Give ye them to eat.** And they say unto him, Shall we go and buy two hundred [2] pennyworth of bread, and give them to eat ?
38 And he saith unto them, How many ...have ye? Go see. And when they knew, they say,...	38 And he saith unto them, How many **loaves** have ye? go *and* see. And when they knew, they say, **Five, and two fishes.**
39 ...he commanded them...by companies (Gr. companies companies)... green...	39 And he commanded them that all should [3] **sit** down by companies upon the green grass.
40 And they sat down in ranks (Gr. ranks ranks), by hundreds and by...	40 And they sat down in ranks, by hundreds, and by fifties.
Mark vi. 30–44. Compare the account of the Feeding of the Five Thousand in John vi. 1–14, and especially the phrase *Two hundred pennyworth of bread* in verse 7.	[1] Or, *by land.* [2] See marginal note on Matt. xviii. 28. [3] Gr. *recline.*

Synopticon, pages 40–41.

St. Matthew. [*Passages parallel to Mark.*]	St. Luke. [*Passages parallel to Mark.*]
XIV. 13-14. 13 Now when Jesus heard *it*, he withdrew from thence in a boat, **to** a desert place **apart;** and when the multitudes heard *thereof*, they followed him [1] on foot from the cities.	IX. 10-17. 10 And the apostles, when they were returned, declared unto him what things they had done. And he took them, and withdrew **apart to** a city called Bethsaida. 11 But the multitudes perceiving it followed him: and he welcomed them, and spake to them of the kingdom of God, **and** them that had need of healing he healed.
14 And he came forth, and saw a great multitude, and he had compassion on them, **and** healed their sick.	
IX. 36. But when he saw the multitudes, he was moved with compassion for them, because they were distressed and scattered, as sheep not having a shepherd.	
XIV. 15-21. 15 And when even was come, **the disciples came to him,** saying, The **place is desert,** and the time is already past; **send** the multitudes **away, that** they may go **into** the **villages,** and **buy** themselves food.	12 And the day began to wear away; and **the twelve came,** and said **unto him, Send** the multitude **away, that** they may go **into** the **villages** and country round about, and lodge, and get victuals: for we **are** [?] here in a **desert place.**
16 **But** Jesus **said** unto **them,** They have no need to go away; **give ye them to eat.** 17 And they say unto him, We have here but **five loaves, and two fishes.** 18 And he said, Bring them hither to me. 19 And he commanded the multitudes to [2] **sit** down on the grass;...	13 **But** he **said** unto **them, Give ye them to eat.** And they said, We have no more than **five loaves and two fishes;** except we should go and **buy** food for all this people. 14 For they **were** about **five thousand men.** And he said unto his disciples, Make them [1] **sit** down in companies, about fifty each. 15 And they did so, and made them all [1] sit down.

[1] Or, *by land.*   [2] Gr. *recline.*

[1] Gr *recline.*

THE COMMON TRADITION

St. Mark. [*Portions not found in Matthew or Luke.*]	St. Mark. [*Complete.*]
	VI. 30–44.
41 And...the loaves ..to...them ; and the two fishes divided he among them all.	41 And **he took the five loaves and the two fishes, and looking up to heaven, he blessed, and * brake** the loaves ; and he **gave to the disciples** to set before them ; and the two fishes divided he among them all. 42 **And they did all eat, and were filled.**
43 ...and also of the fishes.	43 **And** they **took up broken pieces, twelve** basketfuls (Gr. fillings of **baskets**), and also of the fishes.
44 And...that ate the loaves...	44 And they that ate the loaves **were five thousand men.**
	VI. 45–52.
45 ...the (boat)...to Bethsaida...himself.	45 **And** straightway he constrained his **disciples to enter into** the **boat,** and to go before *him* unto the **other side** to Bethsaida, while he himself sendeth the multitude away.
46 ...after-he-had-taken-leave-of them, he departed...	46 And after he had taken leave of them, he departed **into the mountain** to pray.
47 And...was in the midst of the sea, and he...on the land.	47 And when **even was come,** the boat was in the midst of the sea, and he **alone** on the land.
48 And seeing them...in rowing...unto them, about...he cometh...and he would have passed by them :	48 And seeing them distressed in rowing, for the **wind** was contrary unto them, about the fourth watch of the night he cometh unto them, walking on the sea ; and he would have passed by them :
49 ...supposed...	49 But they, when they saw him **walking on the sea,** supposed that it was an apparition, **and** cried out :
50 For they all saw him and...with them, and...	50 For they all saw him, and were troubled. **But he** straightway spake with them, and saith unto them, Be of good cheer : **it is I ; be not afraid.**
Matt. xiv. 22, W. and H. *into a boat.*	

Synopticon, pages 41–42.

St. Matthew. [*Passages parallel to Mark.*]	**St. Luke.** [*Passages parallel to Mark.*]
XIV. 15-21. 19 ...and **he took the five loaves, and the two fishes, and looking up to heaven, he blessed, and * brake, and gave** the loaves **to the disciples,** and the disciples to the multitudes. 20 **And they did all eat, and were filled: and** they **took up** that which remained over of the **broken pieces, twelve baskets** full. 21 And they that did eat **were** about **five thousand men,** beside women and children.	IX. 10-17. 16 And **he took the five loaves and the two fishes, and looking up to heaven, he blessed** them, **and * brake;** and **gave to the disciples** to set before the multitude. 17 **And they did eat, and were all filled: and** there was **taken up** that which remained over to them of **broken pieces, twelve baskets.**
	[LUKE WANTING.]
XIV. 22-33. 22 **And** straightway he constrained **the disciples** to **enter into** the **boat,** and to go before him unto the **other side,** till he should send the multitudes away. 23 And after he had sent the multitudes away, he went up **into the mountain** apart to pray: and when **even was come,** he was there **alone.** 24 But the boat ¹was now in the midst of the sea, distressed by the waves; for the **wind** was contrary. 25 And in the fourth watch of the night he came unto them, **walking upon the sea.** 26 And when the disciples saw him walking on the sea, they were troubled, saying, It is an apparition; **and** they cried out for fear. 27 **But** straightway Jesus spake unto them, saying, Be of good cheer; **it is I; be not afraid.** 28 And Peter answered him and said, Lord, if it be thou, bid me come unto thee upon the waters. 29 And he said, Come. And Peter went down from the boat, and walked upon the waters, ²to come to Jesus. ¹ Some ancient authorities read *was many furlongs distant from the land.* ² Some ancient authorities read *and came.*	JOHN VI. 15-21. 15 Jesus therefore perceiving that they were about to come and take him by force, to make him king, withdrew again **into the mountain** himself **alone.** 16 And when **evening came,** his **disciples** went down unto the sea; 17 **And** they **entered into a boat,** and were going **over** the sea unto Capernaum. And it was now dark, and Jesus had not yet come to them. 18 And the sea was rising by reason of a great **wind** that blew. 19 When therefore they had rowed about five and twenty or thirty furlongs, they behold Jesus **walking on the sea,** and drawing nigh unto the boat: **and** they were afraid. 20 **But he** saith unto them, **It is I; be not afraid.**

THE COMMON TRADITION

St. Mark. [*Portions not found in Matthew or Luke.*]	St. Mark. [*Complete.*]
	VI. 45–52.
51 ...unto...and they were sore amazed in themselves ;	51 And he went up unto them **into the boat**; and the wind ceased : and they were sore amazed in themselves ;
52 For they understood not concerning the loaves, but their heart was hardened.	52 For they understood not concerning the loaves, but their heart was hardened.
	VI. 53–56.
53 ...and moored to the shore.	53 And when they had [1] crossed over, they came to the land unto Gennesaret, and moored to the shore.
54 ...when they were come out of the boat straightway...	54 And when they were come out of the boat, straightway *the people* knew him,
55 And - ran - round - about ... began to carry about on their beds...where they heard he was.	55 And ran round about that whole region, and began to carry about on their beds those that were sick, where they heard he was.
56 And wheresover he entered, into villages, or into cities, or into the country, they laid the sick in the marketplaces...if-it-were-but...him...	56 And wheresoever he entered, into villages, or into cities, or into the country, they laid the sick in the marketplaces, and besought him that they might touch if it were but the border of his garment: and* as many as touched [2] him were made whole.
	VII. 1–23.
1 And there are gathered together unto him the...certain of the ..which had come...	1 And there are gathered together unto him the Pharisees, and certain of the scribes, which had come from Jerusalem,
2 And had seen that some of his disciples ate their bread with defiled, that is, unwashen, hands.	2 And had seen that some of his disciples ate their bread with [3] defiled, that is, unwashen, hands.
3 For the Pharisees, and all the Jews, except they wash their hands diligently, eat not, holding the tradition of the elders :	3 For the Pharisees, and all the Jews, except they wash their hands [4] diligently, eat not, holding the tradition of the elders :

[1] Or, *crossed over to the land, they came unto Gennesaret.*
[2] Or, *it.*
[3] Or, *common.*
[4] Or, *up to the elbow,* Gr. *with the fist.*

Mark vi 55, Gr. *that he is.*

Synopticon, pages 42-44.

St. Matthew. [*Passages parallel to Mark.*]	St. Luke. [*Passages parallel to Mark.*]
XIV. 22–33. 30 But when he saw the wind[1] he was afraid; and beginning to sink, he cried out, saying, Lord, save me. 31 And immediately Jesus stretched forth his hand, and took hold of him, and saith unto him, O thou of little faith, wherefore didst thou doubt? 32 And when they were gone up **into the boat,** the wind ceased. 33 And they that were in the boat worshipped him, saying, Of a truth thou art the Son of God.	21 They were willing therefore to receive him **into the boat:** and straightway the boat was at the land whither they were going.
XIV. 34–36. 34 And when they had crossed over, they came to the land, unto Gennesaret. 35 And when the men of that place knew him, they sent into all that region round about, and brought unto him all that were sick; 36 And they besought him that they might only touch the border of his garment: and * as many as touched were made whole.	[LUKE WANTING.]
XV. 1–20. 1 Then there come to Jesus from Jerusalem Pharisees and scribes, saying,	[LUKE WANTING.]

[1] Many ancient authorities add *strong*.

THE COMMON TRADITION

St. Mark. [*Portions not found in Matthew or Luke.*]	St. Mark. [*Complete.*]
	VII. 1–23.
4 And from the marketplace, except they wash themselves, they eat not: and many other things there be, which they have received to hold, washings of cups, and pots, and brasen vessels.	4 And *when they come* from the marketplace, except they [1] wash themselves, they eat not: and many other things there be, which they have received to hold, [2] washings of cups, and pots, and brasen vessels.[3]
5 And the Pharisees and the scribes ask him...walk not...according to...but... their...with defiled...	5 And the Pharisees and the scribes ask him, Why walk not thy disciples according to the tradition of the elders, but eat their bread with [4] defiled hands?
6 ...[Gr. you, the (hypocrites)]...as it is written (Gr. that) ... [Gr. you, the (hypocrites)].	6 And he said unto them, Well did Isaiah prophesy of you hypocrites, as it is written, This people honoureth me with their lips, But their heart is far from me. 7 But in vain do they worship me, Teaching *as their* doctrines the precepts of men.
8 Ye leave the commandment of God, and hold fast the tradition of men.	8 Ye leave the commandment of God, and hold fast the tradition of men
9 And he said unto them, Full well do ye reject...that ye may keep...	9 And he said unto them, Full well do ye reject the commandment of God, that ye may keep your tradition.
10 ...Moses...thy...thy...	10 For Moses said, Honour thy father and thy mother; and, He that speaketh evil of father or mother, let him [5] die the death:
	11 But ye say, If a man shall say to his father or his mother, That wherewith thou mightest have been profited by me is Corban, that is to say, Given to God;
11 ...a man...Korban, that is to say...	
12 Ye...longer suffer him to do aught...	12 Ye no longer suffer him to do aught for his father or his mother;
13 ...which ye have delivered: and many such like things ye do.	13 Making void the word of God by your tradition, which ye have delivered: and many such like things ye do.

[1] Gr. *baptize* Some ancient authorities read *sprinkle themselves.*
[2] Gr. *baptizings.*
[3] Many ancient authorities add *and couches.*
[4] Or, *common.*   [5] Or, *surely die.*

St. Matthew. [*Passages parallel to Mark.*]	St. Luke. [*Passages parallel to Mark.*]
xv. 1–20.	[Luke wanting.]
2 Why do thy disciples transgress the tradition of the elders? for they wash not their hands when they eat bread. 7 Ye hypocrites, well did Isaiah prophesy of you, saying, 8 This people honoureth me with their lips; But their heart is far from me. 9 But in vain do they worship me, Teaching *as their* doctrines the precepts of men. 3 And he answered and said unto them, Why do ye also transgress the commandment of God because of your tradition? 4 For God said, Honour thy father and thy mother: and, He that speaketh evil of father or mother, let him [1] die the death. 5 But ye say, Whosoever shall say to his father or his mother, That wherewith thou mightest have been profited by me is given *to God*; 6 He shall not honour his father [2]. And ye have made void the [3] word of God because of your tradition.	

[1] Or, *surely die*.
[2] Some ancient authorities add *or his mother*.
[3] Some ancient authorities read *law*.

St. Mark. [*Portions not found in Matthew or Luke.*]	St. Mark. [*Complete.*]
	VII. 1–23.
14 ...again and-said...me all-of-you..	14 And he called to him the multitude again, and said unto them, Hear me all of you, and understand:
15 There is nothing from without.. that going...him can...him: ...man are those-that...	15 There is nothing from without the man, that going into him can defile him: but the things which proceed out of the man are those that defile the man.[1]
17 And when he was entered into the house from the multitude, his.. asked...	17. And when he was entered into the house from the multitude, his disciples asked of him the parable.
18 And he saith unto them,...so.. from without...man, cannot defile him;	18 And he saith unto them, Are ye so without understanding also? Perceive ye not, that whatsoever from without goeth into the man, *it* cannot defile him;
19 Because it goeth not into his heart, but...the...making all meats clean.	19 Because it goeth not into his heart, but into his belly, and goeth out into the draught? *This he said*, making all meats clean.
20 ...he said (Gr. that)...man, ...	20 And he said, That which proceedeth out of the man, that defileth the man.
21 ... from within ... of men evil .. proceed...	21 For from within, out of the heart of men, [2] evil thoughts proceed, fornications,
22 ... covetings,... deceit, ... lasciviousness, an evil eye,...pride, foolishness :	22 Thefts, murders, adulteries, covetings, wickednesses, deceit, lasciviousness, an evil eye, railing, pride, foolishness:
23 All...evil things proceed from within and...	23 All these evil things proceed from within, and defile the man.
	VII. 24–30.
24 And ..he-arose-and...away...borders ...And he entered into a house, and would have no man know it: and he could not be hid.	24 And from thence he arose, and went away into the borders of Tyre [3] and Sidon. And he entered into a house, and would have no man know it: and he could not be hid.

[1] Many ancient authorities insert ver. 16, *If any man hath ears to hear, let him hear.*
[2] Gr. *thoughts that are evil.*
[3] Some ancient authorities omit *and Sidon*

Synopticon, pages 45–47.

St. Matthew. [*Passages parallel to Mark.*]	St. Luke. [*Passages parallel to Mark.*]
xv. 1-20. 10 And he called to him the multitude, and said unto them, Hear, and understand: 11 Not that which entereth into the mouth defileth the man; but that which proceedeth out of the mouth, this defileth the man. 12 Then came the disciples, and said unto him, Knowest thou that the Pharisees were ¹offended, when they heard this saying? 13 But he answered and said, Every ²plant which my heavenly Father planted not, shall be rooted up. 14 Let them alone: they are blind guides. And if the blind guide the blind, both shall fall into a pit. 15 And Peter answered and said unto him, Declare unto us the parable. 16 And he said, Are ye also even yet without understanding? 17 Perceive ye not, that whatsoever goeth into the mouth passeth into the belly, and is cast out into the draught? 18 But the things which proceed out of the mouth come forth out of the heart; and they defile the man. 19 For out of the heart come forth evil thoughts, murders, adulteries, fornications, thefts, false witness, railings: 20 These are the things which defile the man: but to eat with unwashen hands defileth not the man. xv. 21-28. 21 And Jesus went out thence, and withdrew into the parts of Tyre and Sidon.	[LUKE WANTING.]

¹ Gr. *caused to stumble.*
² Gr. *planting.*

THE COMMON TRADITION

St. Mark. [*Portions not found in Matthew or Luke.*]	St. Mark. [*Complete.*]
	VII. 24–30.
25 But straightway … whose little daughter had an unclean spirit, having heard of him, … fell down at his feet.	25 But straightway a woman, whose little daughter had an unclean spirit, having heard of him, came and fell down at his feet.
26 Now the woman was a Greek, a Syrophœnician by race. And she besought him that he would cast forth the … out of her …	26 Now the woman was a [1] Greek, a Syrophœnician by race. And she besought him that he would cast forth the [2] devil out of her daughter.
27 And he said unto her, Let the children first be filled: for …	27 And he said unto her, Let the children first be filled: for it is not meet to take the children's [3] bread and cast it to the dogs.
28 … answered and saith unto him, … under … children's …	28 But she answered and saith unto him, Yea, Lord: even the dogs under the table eat of the children's crumbs.
29 And … For this saying go thy way; the devil is gone out of thy …	29 And he said unto her, For this saying go thy way; the [2] devil is gone out of thy daughter.
30 And she went away unto her house, and found the child laid upon the bed, and the devil gone out.	30 And she went away unto her house, and found the child laid upon the bed, and the [2] devil gone out.
	VII. 31–37.
31 … again he went out from the borders of Tyre and … through Sidon unto … through the midst of the borders of Decapolis.	31 And again he went out from the borders of Tyre, and came through Sidon unto the sea of Galilee, through the midst of the borders of Decapolis.
32 … they bring … one that was … and had-an-impediment-in-his-speech, and they beseech him to lay his hand upon him.	32 And they bring unto him one that was * deaf, and had an impediment in his speech; and they beseech him to lay his hand upon him.
33 And he took him aside from the … privately, and put his fingers into his ears, and he spat, and touched his tongue;	33 And he took him aside from the multitude privately, and put his fingers into his ears, and he spat, and touched his tongue;
34 And looking up to heaven, he sighed, and saith unto him, Ephphatha, that is, Be opened.	34 And looking up to heaven, he sighed, and saith unto him, Ephphatha, that is, Be opened.
35 And his ears were opened, and the bond of his tongue was loosed, and he spake plain.	35 And his ears were opened, and the bond of his tongue was loosed, and he spake plain.
36 And he charged them that they should tell no man: but the more he charged them, so much the more a great deal they published it.	36 And he charged them that they should tell no man: but the more he charged them, so much the more a great deal they published it.
Mark vii. 32, Matt. xv. 30, the same Greek word means either *deaf* or *dumb*.	[1] Or, *Gentile*. [2] Gr. *demon*. [3] Or, *loaf*.

Synopticon, pages 47–49.

OF THE SYNOPTIC GOSPELS.

St. Matthew. [*Passages parallel to Mark.*]	St. Luke. [*Passages parallel to Mark.*]
xv. 21-28. 22 And behold, a Canaanitish woman came out from those borders, and cried, saying, Have mercy on me, O Lord, thou son of David; my daughter is grievously vexed with a ¹ devil. 23 But he answered her not a word. And his disciples came and besought him, saying, Send her away; for she crieth after us. 24 But he answered and said, I was not sent but unto the lost sheep of the house of Israel. 25 But she came and worshipped him, saying, Lord, help me. 26 And he answered and said, It is not meet to take the children's ² bread and cast it to the dogs. 27 But she said, Yea, Lord: for even the dogs eat of the crumbs which fall from their masters' table. 28 Then Jesus answered and said unto her, O woman, great is thy faith: be it done unto thee even as thou wilt. And her daughter was healed from that hour.	[LUKE WANTING.]
xv. 29-31. 29 And Jesus departed thence, and came nigh unto the sea of Galilee; and he went up into the mountain, and sat there. 30 And there came unto him great multitudes, having with them the lame, blind, * dumb, maimed, and many others; and they cast them down at his feet; and he healed them:	[LUKE WANTING.]
¹ Gr, *demon.* ² Or, *loaf.*	

THE COMMON TRADITION

St. Mark. [*Portions not found in Matthew or Luke.*]	St. Mark. [*Complete.*]
	VII. 31-37.
37 And they were beyond measure astonished, saying, He hath done all things well: he maketh even the...to hear and the dumb (Gr. and dumb)..	37 And they were beyond measure astonished, saying, He hath done all things well: he maketh even the * deaf to hear, and the dumb to speak.
	VIII. 1-10.
1 In those days when there was again a great multitude and they had nothing to eat,...saith unto them,	1 In those days, when there was again a great multitude, and they had nothing to eat, he called unto him his disciples, and saith unto them, 2 I have compassion on the multitude, because they continue with me now three days, and have nothing to eat:
3 ...if...to their home,...and some of them are come from far.	3 And if I send them away fasting to their home, they will faint in the way; and some of them are come from far.
4 ...his...answered...(Gr. that)...shall one be able...these-men...here in...	4 And his disciples answered him, Whence shall one be able to fill these men with ¹ bread here in a desert place?
5 ...he asked...	5 And he asked them, How many loaves have ye? And they said, Seven.
6 ...and (he took).. his.. to set before them; and they set them before...	6 And he commandeth the multitude to sit down on the ground: and he took the seven loaves, and having given thanks, he brake, and gave to his disciples, to set before them; and they set them before the multitude.
7 ...they had...and having blessed them, he commanded to set these also before them.	7 And they had a few small fishes: and having blessed them, he commanded to set these also before them. 8 And they did eat, and were filled: and they took up, of broken pieces that remained over, seven baskets.
9 ...about...them...	9 And they were about four thousand: and he sent them away.
10 ...straightway...with his disciples ...parts of Dalmanutha.	10 And straightway he entered into the boat with his disciples, and came into the parts of Dalmanutha.
	VIII. 11-13.
11 ...forth, and began to question with him...from...him.	11 And the Pharisees came forth, and began to question with him, seeking of **him a sign** from **heaven, tempting** him.
Mark vii. 37, Matt. xv. 31, the same Gr. word means either *deaf* or *dumb*. Matt. xv. 32, Gr. *I am not willing*.	¹ Gr. *loaves*.

Synopticon, pages 49-51.

OF THE SYNOPTIC GOSPELS.

St. Matthew. [*Passages parallel to Mark.*]	St. Luke. [*Passages parallel to Mark.*]
xv. 29–31. 31 Insomuch that the multitude wondered, when they saw the * dumb speaking, the maimed whole, and the lame walking, and the blind seeing: and they glorified the God of Israel. xv. 32–39. 32 And Jesus called unto him his disciples, and said, I have compassion on the multitude, because they continue with me now three days and have nothing to eat: and I would not send them away fasting, lest haply they faint in the way. 33 And the disciples say unto him, Whence should we have so many loaves in a desert place, as to fill so great a multitude? 34 And Jesus saith unto them, How many loaves have ye? And they said, Seven, and a few small fishes. 35 And he commanded the multitude to sit down on the ground; 36 And he took the seven loaves and the fishes; and he gave thanks and brake, and gave to the disciples, and the disciples to the multitudes. 37 And they did all eat, and were filled: and they took up that which remained over of the broken pieces, seven baskets full. 38 And they that did eat were four thousand men, beside women and children. 39 And he sent away the multitudes, and entered into the boat, and came into the borders of Magadan. xvi. 1–4. 1 And the Pharisees and Sadducees came, and **tempting** him asked **him** to shew them **a sign** from **heaven**.	[LUKE WANTING.] xi. 16; 29, 30. 16 And others, **tempting** *him*, sought of **him a sign** from **heaven**.

62   THE COMMON TRADITION

St. Mark. [*Portions not found in Matthew or Luke.*]	St. Mark. [*Complete.*]
	VIII. 11–13.
12 And he sighed deeply in his spirit and…Why…Verily I say unto you, no (Gr. if)…to this generation.	12 And he sighed deeply in his spirit, and saith, Why **doth** this **generation seek a sign?** verily I say unto you, **There shall** no **sign be given** unto this generation.
13 …he left…and again entering into…	13 And he left them, and again entering into *the boat* departed to the other side.
	VIII. 14–21.
14 …and they had not in the boat with them more than one loaf.	14 And they forgot to take bread; and they had not in the boat with them more than one loaf.
15 And he charged…beware…the leaven of Herod.	15 And he charged them, saying, Take heed, beware **of the leaven of the Pharisees** and the leaven of Herod.
16 And…one with another, saying, We have…	16 And they reasoned one with another, [1] saying, [2] We have no bread.
17 And…saith unto them…understand? have ye your heart hardened?	17 And Jesus perceiving it saith unto them, Why reason ye, because ye have no bread? do ye not yet perceive, neither understand? have ye your heart hardened?
18 Having eyes, see ye not? and having ears, hear ye not? and …not…	18 Having eyes, see ye not? and having ears, hear ye not? and do ye not remember?
19 When I brake…among…full of broken pieces took ye up? They say unto him, Twelve.	19 When I brake the five loaves among the five thousand, how many [3] baskets full of broken pieces took ye up? They say unto him, Twelve.

Mark viii. 12, W. and H. omit *unto you.*
Mark viii. 12, Gr. *if a sign shall be given.*
Mark viii. 16, W. and H. read *because they had* (Gr. *have*) *no bread.*
Mark viii. 17, W. and H. read *And perceiving it he-saith.*
Luke xi. 29, Gr. *seeketh a sign.*

[1] Some ancient authorities read *because they had no bread.*
[2] Or, It is *because we have no bread.*
[3] *Basket* in verses 19 and 20 represents different Greek words.

Synopticon, pages 51–52.

| St. Matthew. | St. Luke. |
| [Passages parallel to Mark.] | [Passages parallel to Mark.] |

XVI. 1-4.

2 But he answered and said unto them, [1] When it is evening, ye say, *It will be* fair weather: for the heaven is red. 3 And in the morning, *It will be* foul weather to-day: for the heaven is red and lowring. Ye know how to discern the face of the heaven; but ye cannot *discern* the signs of the times.
4 An evil and adulterous **generation seeketh** after **a sign;** and **there shall** no **sign be given** unto it, but the sign of Jonah. And he left them, and departed.
Compare also XII. 38, 39 :—
[38 Then certain of the scribes and Pharisees answered him, saying, [2] Master, we would see **a sign** from thee.
39 But he answered and said unto them, An evil and adulterous **generation seeketh** after **a sign;** and **there shall** no **sign be given** to it but the sign of Jonah the prophet:
40 For as Jonah was three days and three nights in the belly of the whale; so shall the Son of man be three days and three nights in the heart of the earth.]

xi. 29-30.

29 And when the Sadducees were gathering together unto him, he began to say, This **generation** is an evil generation: it **seeketh** after **a sign;** and **there shall** no **sign be given** to it but the sign of Jonah.
30 For even as Jonah became a sign unto the Ninevites, so shall also the Son of man be to this generation.

XVI. 5-12.

5 And the disciples came to the other side and forgot to take [3] bread.

6 And Jesus said unto them, Take heed and beware **of the leaven of the Pharisees** and Sadducees.

7 And they reasoned among themselves, saying, [4]We took no [3] bread.
8 And Jesus perceiving it, said, O ye of little faith, why reason ye among yourselves, because ye have no [3] bread?

9 Do ye not yet perceive, neither remember the five loaves of the five thousand, and how many [5] baskets ye took up?

[1] The following words, to the end of verse 3, are omitted by some of the most ancient and other important authorities.
[2] Or, *Teacher.*
[3] Gr. *loaves.*
[4] Or, It is *because we took no bread.*
[5] *Basket* in verses 9 and 10 represents different Greek words.

XII. 1.

1 In the mean time, when [1]the many thousands of the multitude were gathered together, insomuch that they trode one upon another, he began to [2]say unto his disciples first of all, Beware ye **of the leaven of the Pharisees,** which is hypocrisy.

[1] Gr. *the myriads of.*
[2] Or, *say unto his disciples, First of all beware ye.*

THE COMMON TRADITION

St. **Mark.** [*Portions not found in Matthew or Luke.*]	St. **Mark.** [*Complete.*]
	VIII. 14-21.
20 And when ... among ... (basket)fuls (Gr. fillings of how many baskets) took ye up ? And they say unto him, Seven.	20 And when the seven among the four thousand, how many ¹ basketfuls of broken pieces took ye up ? And they say unto him, Seven.
21 And he said unto them, Do ye... yet understand ?	21 And he said unto them, Do ye not yet understand ?
	viii. 22-26.
22 And they come unto Bethsaida. And they bring to him a blind man, and beseech him to touch him.	22 And they come unto Bethsaida. And they bring to him a blind man, and beseech him to touch him.
23 And he took hold of the blind man by the hand, and brought him out of the village; and when he had spit on his eyes, and laid his hands upon him, he asked him, Seest thou aught ?	23 And he took hold of the blind man by the hand, and brought him out of the village; and when he had spit on his eyes, and laid his hands upon him, he asked him, Seest thou aught ?
24 And he looked up, and said, I see men; for I behold *them* as trees, walking.	24 And he looked up, and said, I see men; for I behold *them* as trees, walking.
25 Then again he laid his hands upon his eyes; and he looked stedfastly, and was restored, and saw all things clearly.	25 Then again he laid his hands upon his eyes; and he looked stedfastly, and was restored, and saw all things clearly.
26 And he sent him away to his home, saying, Do not even enter into the village.	26 And he sent him away to his home, saying, Do not even enter into the village.
	VIII. 27-IX. 1.
27 ...forth, and his disciples [?]...the villages...and in the way...unto them...	27 And Jesus went forth, and his disciples, into the villages of Cæsarea Philippi: and in the way **he *asked his disciples, saying** unto them, **Who** do men **say** that I **am?**
28 ...him saying (Gr. that)...and ..	28 **And they told** him, saying, **John the Baptist:** and **others, Elijah; but** others, One **of the prophets.**
Mark viii. 20, W. and H read *When the.* Luke ix. 19; *a prophet of the old (prophets).*	¹ *Basket* in verses 19 and 20 represents different Greek words.

Synopticon, pages 52-53.

OF THE SYNOPTIC GOSPELS.

St. Matthew. [*Passages parallel to Mark.*]	St. Luke. [*Passages parallel to Mark.*]
XVI. 5–12. 10 Neither the seven loaves of the four thousand, and how many ¹ baskets ye took up? 11 How is it that ye do not perceive that I spake not to you concerning ² bread? But beware of the leaven of the Pharisees and Sadducees. 12 Then understood they how that he bade them not beware of the leaven of ² bread, but of the teaching of the Pharisees and Sadducees.	[LUKE WANTING.]
[MATTHEW WANTING.]	[LUKE WANTING.]
XVI. 13–16. 13 Now when Jesus came into the parts of Cæsarea Philippi, **he * asked** his **disciples, saying, Who** do men **say** ³ that the Son of man **is**? 14 **And they said**, Some *say* **John the Baptist; some, Elijah:** and others, Jeremiah, or one **of the prophets.**	IX. 18–27. 18 And it came to pass, as he was praying alone, **the disciples** were with him: and **he * asked** them, **saying, Who** do **the** multitudes **say** that I am? 19 **And they** answering **said, John the Baptist**; but **others** *say*, **Elijah**; **and** others, that one **of the** old **prophets** is risen again.

¹ *Basket* in verses 9 and 10 represents different Greek words.
² Gr. *loaves*.
³ Many ancient authorities read *that I the Son of man am.* See Mark viii. 27; Luke ix. 18.

St. Mark. [*Portions not found in Matthew or Luke.*]	St. Mark. [*Complete.*]
	VIII. 27–ix. 1.
29 And he asked...saith unto him...	29 And he asked **them, But who say ye that I am?** Peter answereth and saith unto him, Thou art **the Christ.**
30 And...of...	30 And **he charged** them that they should tell **no man** of him.
31 And...to teach them...by...the (chief priests)...the...after...rise again.	31 And he began to teach them, **that** the Son of man **must suffer many things,** and be rejected by **the elders, and** the **chief priests, and** the **scribes, and be killed, and** after **three days** rise again.
32 And he spake the saying openly.	32 And he spake the saying openly. And Peter took him, and began to rebuke him.
33 ...and seeing his disciples, rebuked ...and saith...	33 But he turning about, and seeing his disciples, rebuked Peter, and saith, Get thee behind me, Satan: for thou mindest not the things of God, but the things of men.
34 And he called unto him the multitude with...unto them...	34 And he called unto him the multitude with his disciples, and said unto them, **If any man would** come **after me, let him *deny himself, and take up his cross, and follow me.**
35 ...and the gospel's...	35 For * **whosoever would save his** ¹**life shall lose it; and** whosoever shall **lose his** ¹**life for my sake** and the gospel's shall save **it.**
36 ...and...	36 **For what** doth it **profit a man, to gain the whole world, and forfeit his** ¹life?
37 For...	37 For what should a man give in exchange for his ¹ life?
38 ...in this adulterous and sinful generation,...also...him...	38 **For** whosoever shall be ashamed of me and of my words in this adulterous and sinful generation, **the Son of man** also shall be ashamed of him, when he cometh **in the glory of** his **Father** with **the** holy **angels.**
Mark viii. 35, compare also Matt. x. 39, Luke xvii. 33. Mark viii. 38, compare also Matt. x. 33, Luke xii. 9.	¹ Or, *soul.*

Synopticon, pages 53–55.

OF THE SYNOPTIC GOSPELS.

St. Matthew. [Passages parallel to Mark.]	St. Luke. [Passages parallel to Mark.]
XVI. 13-16. 15 He saith unto them, **But who say ye that I am?** 16 And Simon **Peter answered and** said, Thou art **the Christ**, the Son of the living God.	IX. 18-27. 20 And he said unto **them, But who say ye that I am?** And **Peter answering** said, **The Christ** of God.
XVI. 20-28. 20 Then **charged he** the disciples that they should tell **no man** that he was the Christ. 21 From that time began [1]Jesus to shew unto his disciples, **how that he must** go unto Jerusalem, and **suffer many things of the elders and chief priests and scribes, and be killed, and the third day** be raised up. 22 And Peter took him, and began to rebuke him, saying, [2]Be it far from thee, Lord: this shall never be unto thee 23 But he turned, and said unto Peter, Get thee behind me, Satan: thou art a stumblingblock unto me: for thou mindest not the things of God, but the things of men. 24 Then said Jesus unto his disciples, **If any man would** come **after me, let him *deny himself, and take up his cross, and follow me.** 25 For * **whosoever would save his** [3]**life shall lose it**: **and whosoever** shall **lose his** [3]**life for my sake** shall find **it**. 26 **For what** shall **a man be profited, if** he shall **gain the whole world,** and **forfeit his** [3]life? or what shall a man give in exchange for his [3]life? 27 **For the Son of man** shall come **in the glory of** his **Father** with his **angels;** and then shall he render unto every man according to his [4]deeds.	21 But **he charged** them, and commanded *them* to tell this **to no man;** 22 Saying, (Gr. that) The Son of man **must suffer many things,** and be rejected **of the elders and chief priests and scribes, and be killed,** and the third day be raised up. 23 And he said unto all, **If any man would** come **after me, let him *deny** himself, **and take up his cross** daily, **and follow me.** 24 **For * whosoever would save** his [1] **life shall lose it;** but **whosoever** shall **lose his** [1]**life for my sake,** the same shall save **it.** 25 **For what is a man profited,** if he **gain the whole world,** and lose or **forfeit his** own **self?** 26 **For** whosoever shall be ashamed of me and of my words, of him shall **the Son of man** be ashamed, when he cometh **in his own glory,** and *the glory of* **the Father,** and **of** the **holy angels.**
[1] Some ancient authorities read *Jesus Christ.* [2] Or, God *have mercy on thee.* [3] Or, *soul.* [4] Gr. *doing.*	[1] Or, *soul.*

St. Mark. [Portions not found in Matthew or Luke.]	St. Mark. [Complete.]
	VIII. 27–IX. 1.
1 And he said unto them...come with (Gr. in) power.	1 And he said unto them, Verily **I say unto you, There be some** here **of them** that **stand** by, which shall in no wise taste of death, till they see the kingdom of God come with power.
	IX. 2–8.
2 ...by themselves (Gr. alone)..	2 And **after** six **days** Jesus **taketh with him Peter, and James, and John,** and bringeth them **up into a** high **mountain** apart by themselves: and he was transfigured before them:
3 ...glistering, exceeding...so as no fuller on earth can whiten them.	3 **And his garments** became glistering, exceeding **white**; so as no fuller on earth can whiten them.
4 ...with...and...Jesus.	4 **And** there **appeared** unto them **Elijah** with **Moses**: and they were **talking with** Jesus.
5 ...saith...Rabbi,...	5 And **Peter** answereth and saith **to Jesus,** Rabbi, **it is good for us to be here**: and let us **make three** ¹**tabernacles;** one for thee, and one for Moses, and one for Elijah.
6 For he wist not what to answer, for they became sore (afraid).	6 For he wist not what to answer; for they became sore * **afraid.**
7 And...	7 And there came **a cloud overshadowing them**: and there came a **voice out of the cloud, This is my** beloved **Son: hear ye him.**
8 And suddenly looking round about ...any more (Gr. no more)...with themselves.	8 And suddenly looking round about, they saw no one any more, save **Jesus only** with themselves.
Mark ix. 1, Matt xvi. 28, Gr. *I say unto you that.*	¹ Or, *booths.*

Synopticon, pages 55–57.

OF THE SYNOPTIC GOSPELS.

St. Matthew. [Passages parallel to Mark.]	St. Luke. [Passages parallel to Mark.]
XVI. 20-28. 28 Verily **I say unto you, There be some of them that stand here, which *shall in no wise taste of death, till they see** the Son of man coming in his **kingdom.**	IX. 18-27. 27 But **I tell you** of a truth, **There be some of them that stand here, which shall in no wise taste of death, till they see the kingdom** of God.
XVII. 1-8. 1 And **after** six **days** Jesus **taketh with him Peter, and James, and John** his brother, and bringeth them **up into a high mountain** apart : 2 And he was transfigured before them : **and** [?] his face did shine as the sun, and **his garments** became **white** as the light. 3 **And** behold, there **appeared** unto them **Moses** and **Elijah talking with** him.	IX. 28-36. 28 And it came to pass about eight **days after** these sayings, he **took with him Peter and John and James,** and went **up into** the **mountain** to pray. 29 And as he was praying, the fashion of his countenance was altered, **and his raiment** *became* **white** *and* dazzling. 30 **And** behold, there **talked with** him two men, which were **Moses** and **Elijah ;** 31 Who **appeared** in glory, and spake of his ¹ decease which he was about to accomplish at Jerusalem. 32 Now Peter and they that were with him were heavy with sleep : but ² when they were fully awake, they saw his glory, and the two men that stood with him.
4 And **Peter** answered, and said **unto Jesus,** Lord, **it is good for us to be here:** if thou wilt, I will **make** here **three** ¹ **tabernacles; one for thee, and one for Moses, and one for Elijah.** 5 While he was yet speaking, behold, a bright **cloud overshadowed them: and** behold, **a voice out of the cloud,** saying, **This is my** beloved **Son,** in whom I am well pleased : **hear ye him.** 6 And when the disciples heard it, they fell on their face, and were sore * **afraid.** 7 And Jesus came and touched them and said, Arise, and be not afraid. 8 And lifting up their eyes, they saw no one, save **Jesus only.**	33 And it came to pass, as they were parting from him, **Peter** said unto **Jesus,** Master, **it is good for us to be here:** and let us **make three** ³ **tabernacles; one for thee, and one for Moses, and one for Elijah :** not knowing what he said. 34 And while he said these things, there came **a cloud,** and **overshadowed them:** and they * **feared** as they entered into the cloud. 35 **And a voice** came **out of the cloud,** saying, **This is** ⁴ **my Son,** my chosen : **hear ye him.** 36 And when the voice ⁵ came, **Jesus** was found **alone**...
¹ Or, *booths.*	¹ Or, *departure.* ² Or, *having remained awake.* ³ Or, *booths.* ⁴ Many ancient authorities read *my beloved Son.* See Matt ii. 5, Mark ix. 7. ⁵ Or, *was past.*

THE COMMON TRADITION

St. Mark. [Portions not found in Matthew or Luke.]	St. Mark. [Complete.]
	IX. 9–13.
9 ...he charged ..that they should tell ...what things they had seen, save when ...should have risen.	9 And **as they** were coming **down from the mountain,** he charged them that they should tell *no man what things they had seen, save when the Son of man should have risen again from the dead.
10 And they kept the saying, questioning among themselves what the rising again from the dead should mean. 11 ...the Pharisees and...	10 And they kept the saying, questioning among themselves what the rising again from the dead should mean. 11 And they asked him, saying, [1] The scribes say that Elijah must first come.
12 ...said unto them,...cometh first, and ..and how is it written of (Gr. on) ...that he should...many things and be set at nought? 13 But...and....even as it is written of (Gr. on) him.	12 And he said unto them, Elijah indeed cometh first, and restoreth all things : and how is it written of the Son of man, that he should suffer many things and be set at nought? 13 But I say unto you, that Elijah is come, and they have also done unto him whatsoever they listed, even as it is written of him.
	IX. 14–29.
14 ...the disciples, they saw...about them and scribes questioning with them.	14 And **when they came** to the disciples, they saw a great **multitude** about them, and scribes questioning with them.
15 And straightway all the multitude, when they saw him, were greatly amazed, and running to him saluted him. 16 And he asked them, What question ye with them? 17 And one of...answered him,...unto thee...which hath a dumb... 18 ...wheresoever...and grindeth his teeth and pineth away : ..I spake.. they were...able.	15 And straightway all the multitude, when they saw him, were greatly amazed, and running to him saluted him. 16 And he asked them, What question ye with them? 17 And one of the multitude answered him, [2] Master, I brought unto thee **my son,** which hath a dumb spirit ; 18 And wheresoever it taketh him, it [3] dasheth him down : and he foameth, and grindeth his teeth, and pineth away : **and** I spake to **thy disciples** that they should cast it out ; **and** they were **not** able.
Mark ix. 11, Gr. *saying that* (or, *How is it that*) *the scribes say.* Mark ix. 13, Gr. *both Elijah is come.*	[1] Or, How is it *that the scribes say ... come?* [2] Or, Teacher. [3] Or, *rendeth him.*

Synopticon, pages 58–59.

| St. Matthew. | St. Luke. |
[*Passages parallel to Mark.*]	[*Passages parallel to Mark.*]
XVII. 9-13. 9 And **as they** were coming **down** from **the mountain,** Jesus commanded them, saying, Tell the vision *****to no man,** until the Son of man be risen from the dead.	IX. ...36-37. 36...And they held their peace and told *****no man** in those days any of the things which they had seen. 37 And it came to pass, on the next day, **when they** were come **down** from **the mountain,** a great multitude met him.
10 And his disciples asked him, saying, Why then say the scribes that Elijah must first come? 11 And he answered and said, Elijah indeed cometh, and shall restore all things: 12 But I say unto you, that Elijah is come already, and they knew him not, but did unto him whatsoever they listed. Even so shall the Son of man also suffer of them. 13 Then understood the disciples that he spake unto them of John the Baptist.	*Compare also* I. 17:— [And he shall go before his face in the spirit and power of Elijah...]
XVII. 14-21. 14 And **when they were come** to the **multitude,** there came to him a man, kneeling to him, and saying,	IX. 37-43, XVII. 6. 37 And it came to pass, on the next day, **when** they **were come** down from the mountain, a great **multitude** met him.
	38. And behold, a man from the multitude cried, saying, ¹ Master, I beseech thee to look upon **my son;** for he is mine only child:
15 Lord, have mercy on **my son:** for he is epileptic, and suffereth grievously: for oft-times he falleth into the fire, and oft-times into the water.	39 And behold, a spirit taketh him, and he suddenly crieth out; and it ² teareth him that he foameth, and it hardly departeth from him, bruising him sorely.
16 **And** I brought him to **thy disciples, and** they could **not** cure him.	40 **And** I besought **thy disciples** to cast it out; **and** they could **not.**
	¹ Or, *Teacher.* ² Or, *convulseth.*

St. Mark. [Portions not found in Matthew or Luke.]	St. Mark. [Complete.]
	ix. 14-29.
19 ...them...saith	19 **And he answereth** them **and** saith, **O faithless generation, how long shall I be** with **you?** how long **shall I bear with you?** bring him unto me.
20 And they brought him unto him: and when he saw him straightway... spirit...him...and he fell on the ground, and wallowed foaming.	20 And they brought him unto him: and when he saw him, straightway the spirit [1] tare him grievously; and he fell on the ground, and wallowed foaming.
21 And he asked his father, How long time is it since this hath come unto him? And he said, From a child.	21 And he asked his father, How long time is it since this hath come unto him? And he said, From a child.
22 And...it hath cast him both.. to destroy him: but if thou canst do anything, have compassion on us and help us.	22 And oft-times it hath cast him both into the fire and into the waters, to destroy him: but if thou canst do anything, have compassion on us, and help us.
23 And Jesus said unto him, If thou canst! All things are possible to him that believeth.	23 And Jesus said unto him, If thou canst! All things are possible to him that believeth.
24 Straightway the father of the child cried out, and said, I believe; help thou mine unbelief.	24 Straightway the father of the child cried out, and said,[2] I believe; help thou mine unbelief.
25 ...when...saw that a multitude came running together,.. saying unto him, Thou dumb and deaf spirit, I command thee, come out of him, and enter no more into him.	25 And when **Jesus** saw that a multitude came running together, **he rebuked** the unclean spirit, saying unto him, Thou dumb and deaf spirit, I command thee, come out of him, and enter no more into him.
26 ...having cried out and torn him much...and *the child* became as one dead; insomuch that the more part said, He is dead.	26 And having cried out, and [1] torn him much, he came out: and *the child* became as one dead; insomuch that the more part said, He is dead.
27 But Jesus took him by the hand and raised him up; and he arose.	27 But Jesus took him by the hand, and raised him up; and he arose.
28 And when he was come into the house, his...asked him...	28 And when he was come into the house, his disciples asked him privately, [3] *saying*, We could not cast it out.
29 And he said...This kind can come out by nothing, save by prayer.	29 And he said unto them, This kind can come out by nothing, save by prayer.[4]

Mark ix. 28, Gr. *that* (or, *How is it that*) *we could not.*

[1] Or, *convulsed.*
[2] Many ancient authorities add *with tears.*
[3] Or, How is it *that we could not cast it out?*
[4] Many ancient authorities add *and fasting.*

Synopticon, pages 60-61.

St. Matthew. [Passages parallel to Mark.]	St. Luke. [Passages parallel to Mark.]
XVII. 14–21. 17 **And** Jesus **answered and** said, **O faithless** and perverse **generation, how long shall I be** with **you?** how long **shall I bear with you?** bring him hither to me.	IX. 37–43..., xvii. 6. 41 **And** Jesus **answered and** said, **O faithless** and perverse **generation, how long shall I be** with **you,** and **bear with you?** bring hither thy son. 42 And as he was yet a coming, the [1] devil [2] dashed him down, and [3] tare *him* grievously.
[*Repeated from page 71.*] [15 ...for oft-times he falleth into the fire and oft-times into the water.]	
18 And **Jesus rebuked** him; and the [1] devil went out from him: and the boy was cured from that hour.	But **Jesus rebuked** the unclean spirit, and healed the boy, and gave him back to his father. 43 And they were all astonished at the majesty of God...
19 Then came the disciples to Jesus apart, and said, Why could not we cast it out? 20 And he saith unto them, Because of your little faith: for verily I say unto you, If ye have faith as a grain of mustard seed, ye shall say unto this mountain, Remove hence to yonder place; and it shall remove; and nothing shall be impossible unto you.[2]	XVII. 6. 6 And the Lord said, If ye have faith as a grain of mustard seed, ye would say unto this sycamine tree, Be thou rooted up, and be thou planted in the sea; and it would have obeyed you.
[1] Gr. *demon.* [2] Many authorities, some ancient, insert ver. 21, *But this kind goeth not out save by prayer and fasting.* See Mark ix. 29.	[1] Gr. *demon.* [2] Or, *rent him.* [3] Or, *convulsed.*

74 THE COMMON TRADITION

St. Mark. [*Portions not found in Matthew or Luke.*]	St. Mark. [*Complete.*]
	IX. 30–32.
30 And they went forth from thence and passed through...and he would not that any man should know it.	30 And they went forth from thence, and passed through Galilee; and he would not that any man should know it.
31 For he taught...and said...(Gr. that) ...when he is killed, after...he shall rise again.	31 For he taught his disciples, and said unto them, **The Son of man is delivered up into the hands of men,** and they shall kill him; and when he is killed, after three days he shall rise again. 32 But they understood not the saying, and were afraid to ask him.
	IX. 33–37.
33 And ..when he was in...he asked them, What...in the way?	33 And they came to Capernaum: and when he was in the house he asked them, What were ye reasoning in the way?
34 But they held their peace: for they had disputed with one another in the way...	34 But they held their peace: for they had disputed one with another in the way, **who** *was* the [1] **greatest.**
35 And he sat down and called the twelve; and he saith unto them, If any man would be first...last...and...of all.	35 And he sat down, and called the twelve; and he saith unto them, If any man would be first, he shall be last of all, and minister of all.
36 ..taking him in his arms ..	36 And he took **a little child,** and **set him** in the midst of them: **and** taking him in his arms, **he said** unto them,

[1] Gr. *greater.*

Synopticon, pages 62–63.

OF THE SYNOPTIC GOSPELS. 75

St. Matthew. [Passages parallel to Mark.]	St. Luke. [Passages parallel to Mark.]
XVII. 22–23. 22 And while they [1] abode in Galilee, Jesus said unto them, **The Son of man** shall be **delivered up into the hands of men;** 23 And they shall kill him, and the third day he shall be raised up. And they were exceeding sorry.	IX. ...43–45. 43 ...But while all were marvelling at all the things which he did, he said unto his disciples, 44 Let these words sink into your ears: for **the Son of man** shall be **delivered up into the hands of men.** 45 But they understood not this saying, and it was concealed from them, that they should not perceive it: and they were afraid to ask him about this saying.
XVII. 24–25... 24 And when they were come to Capernaum, they that received the [2] half-shekel came to Peter, and said, Doth not your [3] master pay the [2] half-shekel? He saith, Yea. 25 And when he came into the house,...	IX. 46,...48.
XVIII. 1. 1 In that hour came the disciples unto Jesus, saying, **Who** then is [4] **greatest** in the kingdom of heaven?	46 And there arose a reasoning among them, **which** of them should be [1] **greatest.**
XXIII. 11. 11 But he that is [4] greatest among you shall be your [5] servant.	48 ...for he that is [2] least among you all, the same is great. XXII. 26. 26 But ye *shall* not *be* so; but he that is the greater among you, let him become as the younger; and he that is chief, as he that doth serve.
XVIII. 2–5. 2 And he called to him **a little child,** and **set him** in the midst of them, 3 **And said,** Verily I say unto you, Except ye turn, and become as little children, ye shall in no wise enter into the kingdom of heaven.	IX. 47–48. 47 But when Jesus saw the reasoning of their heart, he took **a little child,** and **set him** by his side,

[1] Some ancient authorities read *were gathering themselves together.*
[2] Gr. *didrachma.*
[3] Or, *teacher.*
[4] Gr. *greater.*
[5] Or, *minister*

[1] Gr. *greater.*
[2] Gr. *lesser.*

THE COMMON TRADITION

St. Mark. [*Portions not found in Matthew or Luke.*]	St. Mark. [*Complete.*]
	IX. 33–37.
37 ...not me, but...	37 * **Whosoever shall receive** one of such **little children in my name, receiveth me;** and whosoever **receiveth me, receiveth** not me, but **him that sent me.**
	IX. 38–50.
38 ...said unto him, Master...	38 John said unto him, [1] Master, we saw one casting out [2] devils in thy name: and we forbade him, because he followed not us.
39 ...him...For there is no man which shall do a mighty work in my name and be able quickly to speak evil of me.	39 But Jesus said, Forbid him not: for there is no man which shall do a [3] mighty work in my name, and be able quickly to speak evil of me.
40 ...us...us.	40 For he that is not against us is for us.
41 For...you...of water in (name) that ye are Christ's...that...	41 For whosoever shall give you a cup of water to drink, [4] because ye are Christ's, verily I say unto you, (Gr. that) he shall in no wise lose his reward.
42 And...it were (Gr. is) better...he were cast (Gr. is cast)...	42 And whosoever **shall cause one of these little ones** that believe [5] on me **to stumble**, it were better **for him** if [6] a great * **millstone** were hanged **about his neck, and** he were cast into **the sea.**
	[1] Or, *Teacher.*
	[2] Gr. *demons.*
	[3] Gr. *power.*
	[4] Gr. *in name that ye are.*
	[5] Many ancient authorities omit *on me*
	[6] Gr. *a millstone turned by an ass.*
Luke xvii. 2, *millstone*, Gr. *stone pertaining-to-a-mill.*	

Synopticon, pages 63–64.

St. Matthew. [*Passages parallel to Mark.*]	St. Luke. [*Passages parallel to Mark.*]
XVIII. 4–5. 4 Whosoever therefore shall humble himself as this little child, the same is the ¹ greatest in the kingdom of heaven. 5 And * **whoso shall receive** one such **little child in my name receiveth me.**	IX. 47–48. [*Partly repeated from page 75.*] 47 But when Jesus saw the reasoning of their heart, he took **a little child,** and **set him** by his side, 48 **And said** unto them, * **Whosoever shall receive** this **little child in my name receiveth me;** and whosoever shall **receive me receiveth him that sent me:** for he that is ¹ least among you all, the same is great.
X. 40. 40 He that receiveth you receiveth me, **and he that receiveth me receiveth him that sent me.**	
	IX. 49–50. 49 And John answered and said, Master, we saw one casting out ² devils in thy name; and we forbade him, because he followeth not with us. 50 But Jesus said unto him, Forbid *him* not: for he that is not against you is for you.
X. 42. 42 And whosoever shall give to drink unto one of these little ones a cup of cold water in the name of a disciple, verily I say unto you, he shall in no wise lose his reward.	
XVIII. 6–9. 6 But whoso **shall cause one of these little ones** which believe on me **to stumble,** it is profitable **for him** that ² a great * **millstone** should be hanged **about his neck, and** *that* he should be sunk in the depth of **the sea.** 7 Woe unto the world because of occasions of stumbling! for it must needs be that the occasions come; but woe to that man through whom the occasion cometh!	XVII. 1–2. 1 And he said unto his disciples, It is impossible but that occasions of stumbling should come; but woe unto him, through whom they come! 2 It were well for him if **a * millstone** were hanged **about his neck, and** he were thrown into **the sea,** rather than that **he should cause one of these little ones to stumble.**
¹ Gr *greater*. ² Gr *a millstone turned by an ass*.	¹ Gr *lesser*. ² Gr. *demons*.

78   THE COMMON TRADITION

St. Mark. [Portions not found in Matthew or Luke]	St. Mark. [Complete]
	IX 43–50.
43 And...off...(thy two) [Gr. the (two)] ...to go into hell,...unquenchable...	43 And if thy hand cause thee to stumble, cut it off: it is good for thee to enter into life maimed, rather than having thy two hands to go into [1] hell, into the unquenchable fire.[2]
45 And if.. cause thee to stumble, cut it off: it is good for thee to enter into life...rather-than having thy (Gr. the) ...into hell.	45 And if thy foot cause thee to stumble, cut it off: it is good for thee to enter into life halt, rather than having thy two feet to be cast into [1] hell.
47 :. kingdom of God...	47 And if thine eye cause thee to stumble, cast it out: it is good for thee to enter into the kingdom of God with one eye, rather than having two eyes to be cast into [1] hell;
48 Where their worm dieth not, and the fire [?] is not quenched.	48 Where their worm dieth not, and the fire is not quenched.
49 For every one shall be salted with fire.	49 For every one shall be salted with fire [3].
50 ...have lost its saltness,...it. Have salt in yourselves, and be at peace one with another.	50 **Salt** is good : **but if the salt** have lost its saltness, **wherewith** will ye season it? Have salt in yourselves, and be at peace one with another.
	X. 1–12.
1 ...he arose from thence and cometh ...and (beyond)...together unto...again ...as he was wont, he taught...again.	1 **And** he arose from thence, and cometh into the borders of Judæa and beyond Jordan: and multitudes come together unto him again; and, as he was wont, he taught them again.
2 ...asked...for a man...	2 And there came unto him Pharisees, and asked him, Is it lawful for a man to put away *his* wife? tempting him.
3 ...unto them...you ?	3 And he answered and said unto them, What did Moses command you?
4 And they said,...suffered to write...	4 And they said, Moses suffered to write a bill of divorcement, and to put her away.
	[1] Gr *Gehenna*. [2] Ver 44 and 46 (which are identical with ver. 48) are omitted by the best ancient authorities. [3] Many ancient authorities add *and every sacrifice shall be salted with salt*. See Lev. ii. 13.
Mark x 2, W. and H. read *asked him if it is lawful*, without note of interrogation.	

Synopticon, pages 64–66.

St. Matthew. [*Passages parallel to Mark.*]	St. Luke. [*Passages parallel to Mark.*]
XVIII. 8-9. 8 And if thy hand or thy foot causeth thee to stumble, cut it off, and cast it from thee: it is good for thee to enter into life maimed or halt, rather than having two hands or two feet to be cast into the eternal fire. 9 And if thine eye causeth thee to stumble, pluck it out, and cast it from thee: it is good for thee to enter into life with one eye, rather than having two eyes to be cast into the ¹hell of fire.	
v. 13. 13 Ye are **the salt** of the earth: **but if the salt** have lost its savour, **wherewith** shall it be salted? it is thenceforth good for nothing, but to be cast out and trodden under foot of men.	XIV. 34. 34 **Salt** therefore is good: **but if** even **the salt** have lost its savour, **wherewith** shall it be seasoned? 35 It is fit neither for the land nor for the dunghill: *men* cast it out.
XIX. 1-10... 1 **And** it came to pass when Jesus had finished these words, he departed from Galilee, and came into the borders of Judæa beyond Jordan; 2 And great multitudes followed him; and he healed them there. 3 And there came unto him ²Pharisees. tempting him, and saying, Is it lawful *for a man* to put away his wife for every cause? 4 And he answered and said, Have ye not read, that he… 7 They say unto him, Why then did Moses command to give a bill of divorcement, and to put *her* away?	XVII. 11. **And** it came to pass, ¹as they were on the way to Jerusalem, that he was passing ²through the midst of Samaria and Galilee.
¹ Gr. *Gehenna of fire.* ² Many authorities, some ancient, insert *the.*	¹ Or, *as he was.* ² Or, *between.*

THE COMMON TRADITION

St. Mark. [*Portions not found in Matthew or Luke.*]	St. Mark. [*Complete.*]
	x. 5–12.
5 But Jesus said…he wrote ..this commandment.	5 But Jesus said unto them, For your hardness of heart he wrote you this commandment.
6 But ..	6 But from the beginning of the creation, Male and female made he them.
7 … his (father)…	7 For this cause shall a man leave his father and mother,[1] and shall cleave to his wife.
	8 And the twain shall become one flesh; so that they are no more twain; but one flesh. 9 What therefore God hath joined together, let not man put asunder.
10 And in the house the [?] disciples [?] asked him [?] again of this matter. 11 And he-saith [?] unto them…against her.	10 And in the house the disciples asked him again of this matter. 11 And he saith unto them, Whosoever **shall put away his wife, and marry** another, committeth ***adultery** against her:
12 …she-herself…her…another…	12 **And** if she herself shall **put away** her husband, and **marry** another, she committeth **adultery**.
	x. 11–12. [*Repeated for the sake of comparison with Matt. v. 31–32.*]
11 And…unto them,…against her:	11 And he saith unto them, Whosoever shall **put away his wife**, and marry another, committeth **adultery** against her:
12 …she-herself [?] ..her…another ..	12 **And** if she herself shall **put away** her husband, and **marry** another, she committeth * **adultery**.
	[1] Some ancient authorities omit *and shall cleave to his wife*.

Mark x. 5. W. and H. read *and his mother*, omitting *and shall cleave to his wife*.
Mark x. 10, Gr. *into the house*
Matt. xix 9, W. & H. put *and he that… adultery* in the margin.

Synopticon, pages 66–67.

St. Matthew. [*Passages parallel to Mark.*]	St. Luke. [*Passages parallel to Mark.*]
XIX. 1-10... 8 He saith unto them, Moses for your hardness of heart suffered you to put away your wives: but from the beginning it hath not been so. 4 And he answered and said, Have ye not read, that he which [1]made *them* from the beginning made them male and female, 5 And said, For this cause shall a man leave his father and mother, and shall cleave to his wife; and the twain shall become one flesh? 6 So that they are no more twain, but one flesh. What therefore God hath joined together, let not man put asunder.	[LUKE WANTING.]
9 And I say unto you, Whosoever **shall put away his wife,** [2]except for fornication, **and** shall **marry** another, committeth **adultery:** [3]**and** he that **marrieth** her when she is **put away** committeth * **adultery.** 10-12 The disciples say unto him, If the case of the man...	XVI. 18. Every one that **putteth away his wife, and marrieth** another, committeth * **adultery: and** he that **marrieth** one that is **put away** from a husband committeth **adultery.**
v. 31-32.	XVI. 18. [*Repeated for the sake of comparison with Matt. v. 31-32.*]
31 It was said also, Whosoever shall put away his wife, let him give her a writing of divorcement: 32 But I say unto you, that every one that **putteth away his wife,** saving for the cause of fornication, maketh her an **adulteress: and** whosoever shall **marry** her when she is **put away** committeth * **adultery.**	Every one that **putteth away his wife,** and marrieth another, committeth **adultery: and** he that **marrieth** one that is **put away** from a husband committeth * **adultery.**

[1] Some ancient authorities read *created.*
[2] Some ancient authorities read *saving for the cause of fornication, maketh her an adulteress*: as in ch. v. 32.
[3] The following words, to the end of the verse, are omitted by some ancient authorities.

THE COMMON TRADITION

St. Mark. [*Portions not found in Matthew or Luke.*]	St. Mark. [*Complete.*]
	x. 13–16.
13 And...	13 And they * **brought unto him** little children, **that** he should touch **them; and** the disciples rebuked **them.**
14 ...he was moved with indignation, and...unto them,...	14 **But** when **Jesus** saw it, he was moved with indignation, and said unto them, **Suffer the little children** to come **unto me; forbid them not: for of such is the kingdom of** God.
	15 **Verily I say unto you,** Whosoever shall **not** receive **the kingdom of** God **as a little child, he shall in no wise enter** therein (Gr. **into it**).
16 ...he took them in his arms, and blessed them,...	16 And he took them in his arms, and blessed them, laying his hands upon them.
	x. 17–22.
17 ...as he...into the way, there ran... and kneeled to him ..	17 **And** as he was going forth [1] into the way, there ran one to him, and kneeled to **him,** and asked him, **Good** [2] **Master, what** shall I **do** that I may inherit **eternal life?**
	18 **And** Jesus **said unto him, Why** callest thou **me good?** none is good save **one,** *even* God.
19 .. Do not defraud, ..	19 Thou knowest the **commandments,** Do not **kill,** Do not **commit adultery,** Do not steal, Do not **bear false witness,** Do not defraud, **Honour thy father and mother.**
20 .. said...Master,...my...	20 And **he** said unto him, [2] Master, **all these things** have I **observed** from my youth.
	[1] Or, *on his way.* [2] Or, *Teacher.*
Mark x. 19, Matt. xix. 19, Luke xviii. 20, Gr *the father of thee, and the mother.* Matt. xix. 9, W. & H. omit *of thee.*	

Synopticon, pages 68–69.

St. Matthew. [Passages parallel to Mark.]	St. Luke. [Passages parallel to Mark.]
XIX. 13-14. 13 Then were there * **brought unto him** little children **that** he should lay his hands on **them,** and pray: **and the disciples rebuked them.** 14 **But Jesus** said, **Suffer the little children,** and **forbid them not,** to come **unto me: for of such is the kingdom of** heaven.	XVIII. 15-17. 15 And they ***brought unto him** also their babes, **that** he should touch **them: but when the disciples** saw it, they **rebuked them.** 16 **But Jesus** called them unto him, saying, **Suffer the little children** to come **unto me,** and **forbid them not: for of such is the kingdom** of God.
XVIII. 1-3. 1 In that hour ..*see p. 75.* 2 And he called...*see p.* 75. 3 And said, **Verily I say unto you,** ***Except** ye turn, and become **as little children, ye shall in no wise enter into the kingdom of** heaven.	17 **Verily I say unto you,** * **Whosoever** shall **not receive the kingdom** of God **as a little child, he shall in no wise enter** therein (Gr. **into** it).
XIX. 15. And he laid his hands on them, and departed thence.	
XIX. 16-22. 16 **And** behold, one came to **him,** and said, [1][2] **Master, what good** thing shall I **do,** that I may have **eternal life?** 17 **And he said unto him,** [3] **Why** askest thou **me** concerning that which is **good? One** there is who is **good:** but if thou wouldest enter into life, keep **the commandments.** 18 He saith unto him, Which? And Jesus said, Thou shalt not **kill,** Thou shalt not **commit adultery,** Thou shalt not **steal,** Thou shalt not **bear false witness,** 19 **Honour thy father and** thy **mother:** and, Thou shalt love thy neighbour as thyself. 20 **The** young man saith unto him, **All these things** have 1 **observed:** what lack I yet?	XVIII. 18-23. 18 **And** a certain ruler asked **him,** saying, **Good** [1] **Master, what** shall I **do** to inherit **eternal life?** 19 **And** Jesus **said unto him, Why** callest thou **me good?** none is **good,** save one, *even* God. 20 Thou knowest **the commandments,** Do not **commit** adultery, Do not **kill,** Do not **steal,** Do not **bear false witness, Honour thy father and mother.** 21 And **he** said, **All these things** have I **observed** from my youth up.
[1] Or, *Teacher.* [2] Some ancient authorities read *Good Master.* See Mark x. 17, Luke xviii. 18. [3] Some ancient authorities read *Why callest thou me good? None is good save one,* even *God.* See Mark x. 18, Luke xviii. 19.	[1] Or, *Teacher.*

THE COMMON TRADITION

St. Mark. [*Portions not found in Matthew or Luke.*]	St. Mark. [*Complete.*]
	x. 17–22.
21 ...looking upon him loved him, and...	21 And **Jesus** looking upon him loved him, and said **unto him,** One thing thou lackest : go, **sell** whatsoever thou hast, **and * give to the poor, and thou shalt have treasure in * heaven : and come, follow me.**
22 ...his countenance fell at...	22 **But** his countenance fell at the saying, and he went away * **sorrowful : for he was** one that had great possessions.
	x. 23–31.
23 And ... looked round about and saith...	23 And **Jesus** looked round about, and saith unto his disciples, How **hardly** shall they that have riches * **enter into the kingdom of** God !
24 And the disciples were amazed at his words. But Jesus answereth.. and .. unto them, Children, how hard is it for them that trust in riches to enter into the kingdom of God !	24 And the disciples were amazed at his words. But Jesus answereth again, and saith unto them, Children, how hard is it [1] for them that trust in riches to enter into the kingdom of God !
25 ...eye ..	25 **It is easier for a camel to go through** a needle's eye, **than for a rich man to enter into the kingdom of God.**
26 ...exceedingly...unto him,...	26 **And they** were astonished exceedingly saying [2] unto him, Then **who can be saved ?**
27 ...saith,...but not with God : for...	27 Jesus looking upon them saith, **With men** it is **impossible,** but not with God : for all things are **possible with God.**
28 ...began to say...	28 **Peter** began to say unto him, **Lo, we** have **left** all, and have **followed thee.**
29 ...said,...my...and for the gospel's sake,	29 Jesus said, **Verily I say unto you,** There is no man **that hath left house, or brethren,** or sisters, **or** mother, or father, **or children,** or lands, **for** my **sake,** and for the gospel's sake,
30 But ... a hundred (fold) now .. houses, and brethren, and sisters, and mothers, and children, and lands, with persecutions ;..	30 But he shall **receive** a hundredfold now in this time, houses, and brethren, and sisters, and mothers, and children, and lands, with persecutions ; **and** in the [3] world to come **eternal life.**

Mark x. 21, Luke xviii 22, Gr. *to poor*
Mark x. 21, Matt. xix. 21, Gr. *in heaven*, Luke xviii. 22, Gr. *in the heavens*, Matt. xix. 21, W. and H. *in heavens.*
Mark x. 24, W. and H. omit *for them that trust in riches.*
Mark x. 25, Matt. xix. 24, Gr *to-go-through through...to-go-into into.* Luke xviii. 25, *to-go-into through...to-go-into into.* Matt. xix. 24, W. and H. *to-go-into through,* omitting *to enter* (Gr. *to go into*).

[1] Some ancient authorities omit *for them that trust in riches.*
[2] Many ancient authorities read *among themselves.*
[3] Or, *age.*

Synopticon, pages 69–71.

OF THE SYNOPTIC GOSPELS.

St. Matthew. [*Passages parallel to Mark.*]	St. Luke. [*Passages parallel to Mark.*]
XIX. 16–22. 21 **Jesus** said **unto him**, If thou wouldest be perfect, go, **sell** that thou hast, **and * give** to the **poor, and thou shalt have treasure in * heaven: and come, follow me.** 22 **But** when **the** young man heard the saying, he went away *** sorrowful: for he was** one that had great possessions. XIX. 23–30. 23 And **Jesus** said unto his disciples, Verily I say unto you, It is **hard** for a rich man to ***enter into the kingdom of** heaven.	XVIII. 18–23. 22 And when **Jesus** heard it, he said **unto him,** One thing thou lackest yet: **sell** all that thou hast, **and * distribute** unto the **poor, and thou shalt have treasure in * heaven: and come, follow me.** 23 **But** when **he** heard these things, he became exceeding *** sorrowful: for he was** very rich. XVIII. 24–30; XIII. 30. 24 And **Jesus** seeing him said, How **hardly** shall they that have riches *** enter into the kingdom of** God!
24 And again I say unto you, **It is easier for a camel to go through a** needle's eye, **than for a rich man to enter into the kingdom of God.** 25 **And** when **the** disciples heard it, they were astonished exceedingly, saying, **Who** then **can be saved?** 26 And Jesus looking upon *them* said to them, **With men** this **is impossible; but with God** all things are **possible.** 27 Then answered **Peter** and said unto him, **Lo, we** have **left** all, and **followed thee;** what then shall we have? 28 And Jesus said unto them, **Verily I say unto you,** that ye which have followed me, in the regeneration when the Son of man shall sit on the throne of his glory, ye also shall sit upon twelve thrones, judging the twelve tribes of Israel. 29 And every one **that hath left houses, or brethren,** or sisters, **or** father, or mother,¹ **or children,** or lands, **for** my name's **sake,** shall **receive** ² a hundred**fold, and** shall inherit **eternal life.**	25 For **it is easier for a camel to enter** in **through** a needle's eye, **than for a rich man to enter into the kingdom of God.** 26 **And they that** heard it said, Then **who can be saved?** 27 But **he** said, The things which are **impossible with men** are **possible with God.** 28 And **Peter** said, **Lo, we have left** ¹ our own, **and followed thee.** 29 And **he** said unto them, **Verily I say unto you,** There is no man **that hath left house,** or **wife, or brethren, or** parents, **or children, for** the kingdom of God's sake, 30 Who shall not **receive manifold** more in this time, **and** in the ² world to come **eternal life.**
¹ Many ancient authorities add *or wife:* as in Luke xviii 29. ² Some ancient authorities read *manifold*.	¹ Or, *our own* homes. ² Or, *age*.

THE COMMON TRADITION

St. Mark. [*Portions not found in Matthew or Luke.*]	St. Mark. [*Complete.*]
31 ...the...,	x. 23–31. 31 But many *that are* **first shall be last; and the last first.**
32 And they were...and ..was going before them, and they were amazed; and they that followed were afraid.... again...began to tell . the things that were to happen unto him,	x. 32–34. 32 And they were in the way, **going up to Jerusalem** [?]; and Jesus was going before them: and they were amazed; ¹and they that followed were afraid. And he **took** again **the twelve**, and began to tell **them** the things that were to happen unto him, *saying*,
33 [Gr. That, (Behold)].	33 **Behold, we go up to *Jerusalem; and the Son of man shall be delivered** unto the chief priests and the scribes; and they shall condemn him to death, and shall deliver him **unto the Gentiles:**
34 ...him,...upon him, and ..after...	34 And they shall **mock** him, and shall spit upon him, **and shall scourge** him, and shall kill him; **and** after **three days** he shall rise again.
35 And there come ..James and John the...saying...Master, we would that thou shouldest do for us whatsoever we shall ask of thee.	x. 35–45. 35 And there come near unto him James and John, the sons of Zebedee, saying unto him, ²Master, we would that thou shouldest do for us whatsoever we shall ask of thee.
36 . .that I should do for you?	36 And he said unto them, What would ye that I should do for you?
37 And they said...Grant unto ..us... thy...left.. glory.	37 And they said unto him, Grant unto us that we may sit, one on thy right hand, and one on *thy* left hand, in thy glory.
38 ...unto them...or to be baptized with the...that I...	38 But Jesus said unto them, Ye know not what ye ask. Are ye able to drink the cup that I drink? or to be baptized with the baptism that I am baptized with?
39 And they said...And Jesus said... that I drink...and (with) the baptism that I am baptized withal shall ye be baptized:	39 And they said unto him, We are able. And Jesus said unto them, The cup that I drink ye shall drink; and with the baptism that I am baptized withal shall ye be baptized:
Mark x 32, Luke xviii. 31, Gr. *having taken unto (him),*-Matt. xx. 17, *he took unto (him), and.*	¹ Or, *but some as they followed were afraid.* ² Or, *Teacher.*

Synopticon, pages 71–73.

St. Matthew. [Passages parallel to Mark.]	St. Luke. [Passages parallel to Mark.]
XIX. 23–30. 30 But many **shall be last** *that are* **first**; and first *that are* **last**.	XIII. 30. 30 And behold, there are **last** which **shall be first, and** there are **first** which shall be **last**.
XX. 17–19. 17 And as Jesus was **going up to Jerusalem**, [?]	*Compare perhaps* Luke xix. 28; *see* p. 91. 28 And when he had thus spoken, he went on before, **going up to Jerusalem**.
he **took the twelve** disciples apart, and in the way he said unto **them**, 18 **Behold, we go up to *Jerusalem; and the Son of man shall be delivered** unto the chief priests and scribes; and they shall condemn him to death, 19 And shall deliver him **unto the Gentiles** to **mock, and to scourge**, and to crucify: **and** the **third day** he shall be raised up.	XVIII. 31–33. 31 And he **took unto him the twelve,** and said unto **them, Behold, we go up to *Jerusalem,** and all the things that are written ¹ by the prophets shall be accomplished unto **the Son of man.** 32 For he **shall be delivered up unto the Gentiles,** and shall be **mocked,** and shamefully entreated, and spit upon: 33 **And** they shall **scourge** and kill him: **and** the **third day** he shall rise again.
XX. 20–28. 20 Then came to him the mother of the sons of Zebedee with her sons, worshipping *him*, and asking a certain thing of him. 21 And he said unto her, What wouldest thou? She saith unto him, Command that these my two sons may sit, one on thy right hand, and one on thy left hand, in thy kingdom.	[LUKE WANTING.]
22 But Jesus answered and said, Ye know not what ye ask. Are ye able to drink the cup that I am about to drink? They say unto him, We are able. 23 He saith unto them, My cup indeed ye shall drink:...	*Compare* Luke xii. 50. 50 But I have a baptism to be baptized with; and how am I straitened till it be accomplished!

¹ Or, *through*.

St. Mark. [*Portions not found in Matthew or Luke.*]	St. Mark. [*Complete.*]
	x. 35-45.
40 ...or...	40 But to sit on my right hand or on *my* left hand is not mine to give : but *it is for them* for whom it hath been prepared.
41 ...began...James and John.	41 And when the ten heard it, they began to be moved with indignation concerning James and John.
42 And...saith...which are accounted ...their...	42 And Jesus called them to him, and saith unto them, Ye know that **they which** are accounted to rule **over the Gentiles *lord it** over **them;** and their great ones exercise **authority** over **them.**
	43 But it is **not so** among **you:** but whosoever would **become great among you,** shall be your [1] **minister:**
44 ...of all ..	44 **And** whosoever would be first among you, shall be [2] servant of all.
45 For verily..	45 For verily the Son of man came not to be ministered unto, but to **minister,** and to give his life a ransom for many.
	x. 46-52.
46 And they come...Jericho...with (Gr. and) his disciples and a great...the son of Timæus, Bartimæus...	46 And they come to Jericho : and as he **went** [?] out from **Jericho,** with his disciples and a great **multitude,** the son of Timæus, Bartimæus, a **blind** beggar, was **sitting by the wayside.**
47 And...it was (Gr. it is)...he began...	47 And when he **heard that** it was **Jesus** of Nazareth, he began to cry out, and **say,** Jesus, **thou son of David, have mercy on** me.
48 ...many...	48 And many **rebuked** him, **that** he should hold his peace : **but** he **cried out** the more a great deal, **Thou son of David, have mercy on** me.
49 ...said...And they call the blind man, saying unto him, Be of good cheer: rise, he calleth thee.	49 And **Jesus stood** still, **and** said, Call ye him. And they call the blind man, saying unto him, Be of good cheer : rise, he calleth thee.
50 And he, casting away his garment, sprang up, and came to Jesus.	50 And he, casting away his garment, sprang up, and came to Jesus.
Matt. xx. 25, Gr. *the great.* With Mark x. 46—52 compare also Matt. ix. 27—30 (*Synopticon.* p. 75A). That passage contains the following words common to the Common Tradition here set forth:—*blind... crying out...saying...Have mercy on...thou son of David...do...*	[1] Or, *servant.* [2] Gr. *bondservant.*

Synopticon, pages 73-75.

St. Matthew. [Passages parallel to Mark.]	St. Luke. [Passages parallel to Mark.]
xx. 20-28.	xxii. 24-27.
23 ...but to sit on my right hand, and on *my* left hand, is not mine to give, but *it is for them* for whom it hath been prepared of my Father. 24 And when the ten heard it, they were moved with indignation concerning the two brethren. 25 But Jesus called them unto him, and said, Ye know that **the** rulers **of the Gentiles *lord it** over **them, and** their great ones exercise **authority** over **them.**	24 And there arose also a contention among them, which of them is accounted to be ¹ greatest. 25 And **he** said unto them, **The** kings **of the Gentiles** have ***lordship** over **them; and they that have authority** over **them** are called Benefactors.
26 **Not so** shall it be among **you: but** whosoever would **become great among you** shall be your ¹ **minister;** 27 **And** whosoever would be first among you shall be your ² servant : 28 Even as the Son of man came not to be ministered unto, but to **minister,** and to give his life a ransom for many.	26 But **ye** shall **not** be **so: but** he that is the **greater among you,** let him **become** as the younger ; **and** he that is chief, as he that doth **serve.** 27 For whether is greater, he that ² sitteth at meat, or he that serveth? is not he that ² sitteth at meat ? but I am in the midst of you as he that **serveth.**
xx. 29-34.	xviii. 35-43.
29 And as they **went** [?] out from **Jericho,** a great **multitude** followed him. 30 And behold, two **blind** men **sitting by the way side,** when they **heard that Jesus** was passing by, cried out, **saying,** Lord, **have mercy on us, thou son of David.**	35 And it came to pass, as he drew nigh unto **Jericho,** a certain **blind** man **sat by the way side** begging : 36 And **hearing** a **multitude going** [?] by, he inquired what this meant. 37 And they told him, **that Jesus** of Nazareth passeth by. 38 And he cried, **saying,** Jesus, **thou son of David, have mercy on me.**
31 And the multitude **rebuked** them, **that** they should hold their peace : **but** they **cried out** the more, saying, Lord, **have mercy on us, thou son of David.** 32 And **Jesus stood** still, **and** called them, and said,...	39 And they that went before **rebuked** him, **that** he should hold his peace : **but** he **cried out** the more a great deal, **Thou son of David,** have **mercy on** me. 40 And **Jesus-* stood, and** commanded him to be brought unto him : and when he was come near,

¹ Or, *servant.*
² Gr. *bondservant*

¹ Or, *greater.*
² Gr. *reclineth.*

St. Mark. [Portions not found in Matthew or Luke.]	St. Mark. [Complete.]
51 ...Jesus answered and...blind...Rabboni...	x. 46–52. 51 And Jesus answered him, and said, **What wilt** thou **that I should do** unto thee? And the blind man said unto him, [1] Rabboni, **that** I may receive my sight.
52 ...Go thy way ;...him in the way.	52 And **Jesus** said unto him, Go thy way ; thy faith hath [2] made thee whole. **And** straightway he **received his sight, and followed** him in the way.
1 ...his...	xi. 1–11. 1 **And** when **they draw nigh unto Jerusalem, unto Bethphage and** Bethany, at **the mount of Olives, he sendeth two** of his **disciples,**
2 And...into it...and bring (him).	2 And **saith** unto them, Go your way **into the village** that is **over against** you : and straightway as ye enter into it, **ye shall find a colt tied,** whereon no man ever yet sat ; **loose** him, and bring him.
3 ...do ye this ? say ye,...and...back hither. 4 And...and...a colt tied at the door without in the open street ; and...him. 5 And certain of them that stood there said...do ye... 6 ...unto them,...and they let them go. 7 ...they bring...cast... 8 And... upon (Gr. into)...branches... from the fields.	3 **And if any one** say unto **you,** Why do ye this ? say ye, **The Lord hath need of** him ; and straightway he [3] will send him [4] back hither. 4 And they went away, and found a colt tied at the door without in the open street ; and they loose him. 5 And certain of them that stood there said unto them, What do ye, loosing the colt ?
	6 And they said unto them, **even as** Jesus had said : and they let them go.
Compare also John xii. 12–15 :— 12 On the morrow [1] a great multitude that had come to the feast, when they heard that Jesus was coming to Jerusalem, 13. Took the branches of the palm-trees, and went forth to meet him, and cried out Hosanna : **Blessed** is **he that cometh in the name of the Lord,** even the king of Israel. 14. And Jesus having found a young ass, sat thereon ; as it is written, 15. Fear not, daughter of Zion : behold, thy king cometh, sitting on an ass's colt. Matthew xx. 30, 31. uses the nominative for *son*. Luke xix. 28. See also page 87.	7 And they bring the colt unto Jesus, and cast **on** him their **garments;** and he sat upon him. 8 And many * **spread their garments** upon **the way ;** and others [5] **branches,** which they had cut from the fields.
[1] Some ancient authorities read, *the common people.*	[1] See John xx 16. [2] Or, *saved thee.* [3] Gr. *sendeth.* [4] Or, *again.* [5] Gr. *layers of leaves.*

Synopticon, pages 75–77.

OF THE SYNOPTIC GOSPELS.

St. Matthew. [*Passages parallel to Mark.*]	St. Luke. [*Passages parallel to Mark.*]
XX. 29-34.	XVIII. 35-43.
32 ...**What will** ye **that I should do** unto you ? 33 They say unto him, Lord, **that** our eyes may be opened.	41 He asked him, **What wilt** thou **that I should do** unto thee? And he said, Lord, **that** I may receive my sight.
34 And **Jesus**, being moved with compassion, touched their eyes: **and** straightway they **received** their **sight, and followed** him.	42 And **Jesus** said unto him, Receive thy sight: thy faith hath [1] made thee whole. 43 **And** immediately he **received** his **sight, and followed** him, glorifying God: and all the people, when they saw it, gave praise unto God.
XXI. 1-11.	XIX. 28-38.
1 **And** when they **drew nigh unto Jerusalem, and** came **unto Bethphage, unto the mount of Olives,** then Jesus **sent two disciples,**	28 And when he had thus spoken, he went on before, going up **to Jerusalem.** 29 **And** it came to pass, when he **drew nigh unto Bethphage and** Bethany, at **the mount** that is called *the mount of Olives,* **he sent two** of the **disciples,**
2 **Saying** unto them, Go **into the village** that is **over against** you, and straightway **ye shall find** an ass **tied,** and **a colt** with her: **loose** *them,* and bring *them* unto me.	30 **Saying,** Go your way **into the village over against** *you;* in the which as ye enter **ye shall find a colt tied,** whereon no man ever yet sat: **loose** him, and bring him.
3 **And if any one** say aught unto **you,** ye shall say, **The Lord hath need of** them; and straightway he will send them. 4 Now this is come to pass, that it might be fulfilled which was spoken [1] by the prophet, saying, Tell ye the daughter of Zion, Behold, thy King cometh unto thee, Meek, and riding upon an ass, And upon a colt the foal of an ass. 6 And the disciples went, and did **even as** Jesus appointed them, 7 And brought the ass, and the colt, **and** put **on** them their **garments;** and he sat thereon. 8 And the most part of the multitude *spread **their garments** in the **way;** and others cut branches from the trees, and spread them in the way.	31 **And if any one** ask **you,** Why do ye loose him? thus shall ye say, **The Lord hath need of** him. 32 And they that were sent went away, and found **even as** he had said unto them. 33 And as they were loosing the colt, the owners thereof said **unto them,** Why loose ye the colt? 34 And they said, The Lord hath need of him. 35 And they brought him to Jesus: **and** they threw their **garments upon** the colt, and set Jesus thereon. 36 And as he went, they ***spread their garments in the way.**
[1] Or, *through.*	[1] Or, *saved thee.*

THE COMMON TRADITION

St. Mark. [*Portions not found in Matthew or Luke.*]	St. Mark. [*Complete.*]
	XI. 1–11.
9 And...	9 And they that went before, and they that followed, cried, Hosanna ; **Blessed** *is* **he that cometh in the name of the Lord :**
10 Blessed is the kingdom that cometh, of our father...	10 Blessed *is* the kingdom that cometh, *the kingdom* of our father David : Hosanna **in the highest.**
11 ...into the temple ; and when he had looked round about upon all things, it being now eventide, he went out unto Bethany with the twelve.	11 And he entered into Jerusalem, into the temple ; and when he had looked round about upon all things, it being now eventide, he went out unto Bethany with the twelve.
	XI. 12–14.
12 And on the morrow, when they were come out from Bethany...	12 And on the morrow, when they were come out from Bethany, he hungered.
13 ...afar off, having leaves,...if haply he might find anything...when he came ...for it was not the season of figs.	13 And seeing a fig tree afar off having leaves, he came, if haply he might find anything thereon : and when he came to it, he found nothing but leaves ; for it was not the season of figs.
14 ...he answered and said...No man eat...And his disciples heard (it).	14 And he answered and said unto it, No man eat fruit from thee henceforward for ever. And his disciples heard it.
	XI. 15–18.
15 And they come to Jerusalem...them that (bought)...	15 And they come to Jerusalem : **and** he **entered into the temple,** and began to **cast out them that sold** and them that bought in the temple, and overthrew the tables of the moneychangers, and the seats of them that sold the doves ;
16 And he would not suffer that any man should carry a vessel through the temple.	16 And he would not suffer that any man should carry a vessel through the temple.
17 And...not...for all the nations...	17 And he taught, and **said unto them, Is it not written, My house** shall be called **a house of prayer** for all the nations ? **but ye** have **made it a den of robbers.**

Mark xi. 1-11, Compare John xii. 12-15 on page 90.
(Lu. xix. 46, Gr *ye made it*)
Luke xix. 38, W. and H *Blessed* (*is*) *he that cometh,* (*even*) *the King, in the name of the Lord.*

Synopticon, pages 77–79.

St. Matthew. [*Passages parallel to Mark.*]	St. Luke. [*Passages parallel to Mark.*]
XXI. 1-11. 9 And the multitudes that went before him, and that followed, cried, saying, Hosanna to the son of David: **Blessed** *is* **he that cometh in the name of the Lord;** Hosanna **in the highest.**	XIX. 28-38. 37 And as he was now drawing nigh, *even* at the descent of the mount of Olives, the whole multitude of the disciples began to rejoice and praise God with a loud voice for all the [1] mighty works which they had seen; 38 Saying, **Blessed** *is* the King **that cometh in the name of the Lord:** peace in heaven, and glory **in** the **highest.**
10 .And when he was come into Jerusalem, all the city was stirred, saying, Who is this? 11 And the multitudes said, This is the prophet Jesus, from Nazareth of Galilee.	
XXI. 18-19. 18 Now in the morning as he returned to the city, he hungered. 19 And seeing [1] a fig tree by the way side, he came to it, and found nothing thereon, but leaves only; and he saith unto it, Let there be no fruit from thee henceforward for ever. And immediately the fig tree withered away.	
XXI. 12-14. 12 **And** Jesus **entered into the temple** [2] of God, **and cast out all them that sold** and bought in the temple, and overthrew the tables of the moneychangers, and the seats of them that sold the doves; 13 And he **saith unto them, It is written, My house** shall be called a **house of prayer: but ye make it a den of robbers.** 14 And the blind and the lame came to him in the temple: and he healed them.	XIX. 45-48. 45 **And** he **entered into the temple,** and began to **cast out them that sold,** 46 **Saying unto them, It is written,** And **my house** shall be **a house of prayer: but ye** have **made it a den of robbers.** 47 And he was teaching daily in the temple....
[1] Or, *a single.* [2] Many ancient authorities omit *of God.*	[1] Gr. *powers.*

94   THE COMMON TRADITION

St. Mark. [*Portions not found in Matthew or Luke.*]	St. Mark. [*Complete.*]
	xi. 15–18.
18 And...heard it, and...how...for they feared him...multitude was astonished at...teaching.	18 And **the chief priests and the scribes** heard it, and sought how they might destroy him: for they feared him, for all the multitude was astonished at his teaching.
	xi. 19.
19 ...every evening...he went...	19 And [1] every evening [2] he went **forth** out of the city.
	xi. 20–25.
20 And as they passed by in the morning they saw...from the roots.	20 And as they passed by in the morning, they saw the fig tree withered away from the roots.
21 ...Peter calling to remembrance...unto him, Rabbi, behold...which thou cursedst...	21 And Peter calling to remembrance saith unto him, Rabbi, behold, the fig tree which thou cursedst is withered away.
22 And...saith...in-God (Gr. of God).	22 And Jesus answering saith unto them, **Have faith** in God.
23 ... (Gr. that) Whosoever ... in his heart, but shall believe that what he saith cometh to pass ; he shall have it.	23 Verily I say unto you, Whosoever shall say unto this mountain, Be thou taken up **and** cast into **the sea**; and shall not doubt in his heart, but shall believe that what he saith cometh to pass ; he shall have it.
24 Therefore...and...that...shall have (Gr. they-shall-be)...	24 Therefore I say unto you, All things whatsoever ye pray and **ask** for, believe that ye have received them, **and ye** shall have them.
25 And whensoever ye stand praying, ...if ye have aught against any one; that...in [Gr. the (heavens)]...	25 And whensoever ye stand praying, **forgive,** if he have aught against any one; that your Father also which is in heaven may **forgive** you your trespasses.[3]
Mark xi. 19, W and H. *they went forth.*	[1] Gr. *whenever evening came* [2] Some ancient authorities read *they.* [3] Many ancient authorities add ver 26 *But if ye do not forgive, neither will your Father which is in heaven forgive your trespasses.*

Synopticon, pages 79–80.

| St. Matthew. | St. Luke. |
| [Passages parallel to Mark.] | [Passages parallel to Mark.] |

XXI. 15-17.

15 But when **the chief priests and the scribes** saw the wonderful things that he did, and the children that were crying in the temple and saying, Hosanna to the son of David; they were moved with indignation,
16 And said unto him, Hearest thou what these are saying? And Jesus saith unto them, Yea: did ye never read, Out of the mouth of babes and sucklings thou hast perfected praise?
17 And he left them, and went **forth** out of the city to Bethany, and lodged there.

xxi....19, *repeated from page* 93.
(And immediately the fig tree withered away)

XXI. 20-22.

20 And when the disciples saw it, they marvelled, saying, How did the fig tree immediately wither away?
21 And Jesus answered and said unto them, Verily I say unto you, If ye **have faith,** and doubt not, ye shall not only do what is done to the fig tree, but even if ye shall say unto this mountain, Be thou taken up **and** cast into **the sea,** it shall be done.
22 And all things, whatsoever ye shall ask in prayer, believing, ye shall receive.

VII. 7.

7 **Ask, and** it shall be given **you;** seek, and ye shall find; knock, and it shall be opened unto you.

VI. 14-15.

14 For if ye **forgive** men their trespasses, your heavenly Father will also **forgive** you.
15 But if ye forgive not men their trespasses, neither will your Father forgive your trespasses.

XIX. 45-48.

47 ...But **the chief priests and the scribes** and the principal men of the people sought to destroy him:
48 And they could not find what they might do; for the people all hung upon him, listening.

XXI. 37-38.

37 And every day he was teaching in the temple; and every night he went **out,** and lodged in the mount that is called *the mount* of Olives.
38 And all the people came early in the morning to him in the temple, to hear him.

XVII. 5-6.

5 And the apostles said unto the Lord, Increase our faith.

6 And the Lord said, If ye **have faith** as a grain of mustard seed, ye would say unto this sycamine tree, Be thou rooted up, **and** be thou planted in **the sea;** and it would have obeyed you.

XI. 9.

9 And I say unto you, **Ask, and** it shall be given **you;** seek, and ye shall find; knock, and it shall be opened unto you.

XI. 4...

4 And **forgive** us our sins; for we ourselves also **forgive** every one that is indebted to us...

96 THE COMMON TRADITION

St. Mark. [*Portions not found in Matthew or Luke.*]	St. Mark. [*Complete.*]
	XI. 27-33.
27. And they come again to Jerusalem: .. walking...there come to...and (the scribes)...	27 And they come again to Jerusalem: **and as he was walking in the temple,** there come to him **the chief priests,** and the scribes, **and the elders ;**
28 ...to do these things.	28 And they said unto him, **By what authority doest thou these things?** or **who gave thee this authority** to do these things?
29 ...answer...	29 **And Jesus said** unto **them, I will *ask of you** one ^{1} **question,** and answer **me,** and I will tell you by what authority I do these things.
30 ...answer me.	30 **The baptism of John, was it from heaven, or from men?** answer me.
31 And...	31 And they ***reasoned** with **themselves, saying, If we shall say, From heaven; he will say, Why** then **did ye not believe him?**
32 But ..for...verily...to be (Gr. that he-was)...	32 ^{2} **But should we say, From men** —they feared the people: ^{3} for **all** verily held **John** to be **a prophet.**
33 ...they-say...saith...	33 **And** they **answered** Jesus and say, We **know** not. And Jesus saith **unto them, Neither tell I you by what authority I do these things.**
	XII. 1-12.
1 And...to speak unto them in...	1 And he began to speak unto them in **parables. A man planted a vineyard,** and set a hedge about it, and digged a pit for the winepress, and built a tower, **and let it out to husbandmen, and went into another country.**
2 ...at-the...from the husbandmen...	2 And at the **season he sent to the husbandmen** a ^{4} **servant,** that he might receive from the husbandmen **of the fruits** of the vineyard.
3 ...and (sent)...	3 And they took him, and **beat** him, and sent him away empty.

^{1} Gr. *word.*
^{2} Or, *But shall we say, From men?*
^{3} Or, *for all held John to be a prophet indeed.*
^{4} Gr. *bondservant.*

Synopticon, pages 81-82.

| St. Matthew. | St. Luke. |
| [Passages parallel to Mark.] | [Passages parallel to Mark.] |

XXI. 23-27.	XX. 1-8.
23 **And when he** was come into **the temple, the chief priests and the elders** of the people came unto him as he was teaching, and **said, By what authority doest thou these things?** and **who gave thee this authority?**	1 **And** it came to pass, on one of the days, as **he** was teaching the people **in the temple,** and preaching the gospel, there came upon him **the chief priests** and the scribes with **the elders ;** 2 And they spake, **saying** unto him, Tell us : **By what authority doest thou these things?** or **who** is he that **gave thee this authority?**
24 **And** Jesus answered and **said unto them,** I also **will *ask you** one ¹ **question,** which if ye tell **me,** I likewise will tell you by what authority I do these things.	3 **And he** answered and **said unto them,** I also **will *ask you a** ¹ **question;** and tell **me;**
25 **The baptism of John,** whence **was it? from heaven or from men?** And they ***reasoned with themselves, saying, If we shall say, From heaven ;** he will say unto us, **Why** then did ye not **believe him ?**	4 **The baptism of John, was it from heaven, or from men ?** 5 And they ***reasoned with themselves,** saying, (Gr. that) **If we shall say, From heaven ;** he will say, **Why did ye not believe him ?**
26 But if **we shall say, From men ;** we fear the multitude ; for **all** hold **John as a prophet.**	6 But if **we shall say, From men ;** all the people will stone us : for they be persuaded that **John was a prophet.**
27 **And** they **answered** Jesus, and said, We **know** not. He **also** said **unto them, Neither tell I you by what authority I do these things.**	7 **And** they **answered,** that they **knew** not whence *it was.* 8 **And** Jesus said **unto them, Neither tell I you by what authority I do these things.**

XXI. 33-46.	XX. 9-19.
33 Hear another **parable :** There was a man that was a householder, which **planted a vineyard,** and set a hedge about it, and digged a winepress in it, and built a tower, **and let it out to husbandmen, and went into another country.**	9 And he began to speak unto the people this **parable : A man planted a vineyard, and let it out to husbandmen, and went into another country** for a long time.
34 And when the **season** of the fruits drew near, **he sent** his ² **servants to the husbandmen,** to receive ³ his **fruits.**	10 And at the **season he sent unto the husbandmen a** ² **servant,** that they should give him **of the fruit** of the vineyard : but the husbandmen **beat** him, and sent him away empty.
35 And the husbandmen took his ² servants, and **beat** one, and killed another, and stoned another.	

¹ Gr. *word.*
² Gr. *bondservant's.*
³ Or, *the fruits of it.*

¹ Gr *word.*
² Gr. *bondservant.*

St. Mark. [*Portions not found in Matthew or Luke.*]	St. Mark. [*Complete.*]
	XII. 1–12.
4 ...unto them...they wounded in the head...	4 And again he sent unto them another ¹**servant; and** him they wounded in the head, and handled shamefully.
5 ...he sent another...him they killed: and many others; beating...	5 And he sent another; and him they killed: and many others; beating some, and killing some.
6 He had yet one...him last...(Gr. that)...	6 He had yet one, a beloved son: he sent him last unto them, saying, **They will reverence my son.**
7 ...those...(Gr. that)...shall be...	7 But those **husbandmen** said among themselves, **This is the heir;** come, **let us kill him,** and the inheritance shall be ours.
8 ...him (and cast)...	8 **And they** took him, and **killed** him, and **cast him forth out of the vineyard.**
	9 **What** therefore **will the lord of the vineyard do? he will** come and **destroy** the **husbandmen, and** will " **give the vineyard unto others.**
10 ...this...	10 Have ye not read even this **scripture;** **The stone which the builders rejected,** **The same was made the head of the corner:** 11 This was from the Lord, And it is marvellous in our eyes?
12 ...and they left him and went their way.	12 **And** they **sought** to lay hold on **him;** and **they feared** the multitude; for **they perceived that** he spake **the parable** against **them;** and they left him, and went away.
Mark xii. 10, Matt. xxi. 42, Luke xx. 17, *The same,* Gr. *this.*	¹ Gr. *bondservant.*

Synopticon, pages 83–84.]

St. Matthew.
[Passages parallel to Mark.]

St. Luke.
[Passages parallel to Mark.]

XXI. 33-46. 36 Again, he sent other [1] **servants** more than the first: **and** they did unto them in like manner. 37 But afterward he sent unto them his son, saying, **They will reverence my son.** 38 **But the husbandmen,** when they saw the son, said among themselves, **This is the heir;** come, **let us kill him,** and take his **inheritance.** 39 **And they** took him, and **cast him forth out of the vineyard,** and **killed** him. 40 When therefore **the lord of the vineyard** shall come, **what will he do** unto those **husbandmen?** 41 They say unto him, **He will** miserably **destroy** those miserable men, **and will** ***let** out **the vineyard unto other** husbandmen, which shall render him the fruits in their seasons. 42 Jesus saith unto them, Did ye never read in **the scriptures,** **The stone which the builders rejected,** **The same was made the head of the corner:** This was from the Lord, And it is marvellous in our eyes? 43 Therefore say I unto you, The kingdom of God shall be taken away from you, and shall be given to a nation bringing forth the fruits thereof. 44 [2] And he that falleth on this stone shall be broken to pieces: but on whomsoever it shall fall, it will scatter him as dust. 45 And when the chief priests and the Pharisees heard his **parables, they perceived that** he spake of **them.** 46 **And** when they **sought** to lay hold on **him, they feared** the multitudes, because they took him for a prophet. [1] Gr. *bondservants.* [2] Some ancient authorities omit verse 44.	XX. 9-19. 11 And he sent yet another [1] **servant.** **and** him also they beat, and handled him shamefully, and sent him away empty. 12 And he sent yet a third: and him also they wounded, and cast him forth. 13 And the lord of the vineyard said, What shall I do? I will send **my** beloved **son:** it may be **they will reverence** him. 14 **But** when **the husbandmen** saw him, they reasoned one with another, saying, **This is the heir: let us kill him,** that **the inheritance** may be ours. 15 **And they cast him forth out of the vineyard, and killed** him. **What** therefore **will the lord of the vineyard do** unto them? 16 He will come and **destroy** these **husbandmen, and will** ***give the vineyard unto others.** And when they heard it, they said, [2] God forbid. 17 But he looked upon them, and said, What then is this that is **written,** **The stone which the builders rejected,** **The same was made the head of the corner?** 18 Every one that falleth on that stone shall be broken to pieces; but on whomsoever it shall fall, it will scatter him as dust. 19 **And** the scribes and the chief priests **sought** to lay hands on **him** in that very hour; and **they feared** the people: for **they perceived that** he spake this **parable** against **them.** [1] Gr. *bondservant.* [2] Gr. *Be it not so.*

THE COMMON TRADITION

St. Mark. [*Portions not found in Matthew or Luke.*]	St. Mark. [*Complete.*]
	XII. 13-17.
13 ...unto...some of the...and...they might catch...	13 And **they send** unto him certain of the Pharisees and of the Herodians, that they might catch **him** in **talk.**
14 ...when they were come...Shall we give, or shall we not give?	14 **And** when they were come, they **say** unto him, ¹**Master, we know that** thou art true, and carest not for any one: for thou regardest **not the person** of men, but of a **truth teachest the way-of God: Is it lawful to give** tribute **unto Cæsar, or not?** Shall we give, or shall we not give?
15 ...knowing...bring...that I-may-see (it).	15 **But** he, knowing **their hypocrisy** [?]**, said** unto them, Why tempt ye me? bring **me a** ²**penny,** that I may see it.
16 ...unto him...	16 And they brought it. And he saith unto them, **Whose** is this **image and superscription?** And they said unto him, **Cæsar's.**
17 ...Jesus...	17 And Jesus said unto them, **Render unto Cæsar the things that are Cæsar's, and unto God the things that are God's. And they marvelled** greatly at him.
	XII. 18-27.
18 And there come...which...	18 And there come **unto** him **Sadducees,** which **say that there is no resurrection; and they** *asked him, saying,**
19 ...(Gr. that)...and leave-behind-him ...leave ..	19 ¹**Master, Moses** wrote unto us, **If a man's** brother die, and leave a wife behind him, and leave no **child,** that **his brother** should take **his wife, and *raise up seed unto his brother.**
	¹ Or, *Teacher.* ² See marginal note on Matt. xviii. 28.

Synopticon, pages 85-86.]

| St. Matthew. | St. Luke. |
| [Passages parallel to Mark.] | [Passages parallel to Mark.] |

XXII. 15–22.	XX. 20–26.
15 Then went the Pharisees, and took counsel how they might ensnare **him** in *his* **talk.**	20 And they watched him, and **sent forth** spies, **which feigned** [?] **themselves** to be righteous, that they might take hold of **his speech**, so as to deliver him up to the rule and to the authority of the governor.
16 **And they send** to him their disciples, with the Herodians, **saying,** ¹ **Master, we know** that thou art true, and **teachest the way of God** in **truth,** and carest not for any one: for thou regardest **not the person** of men.	21 **And** they asked him, saying, ¹ **Master, we know that** thou sayest and teachest rightly, and acceptest **not the person** of *any*, but of a **truth teachest the way of God:**
17 Tell us therefore, What thinkest thou? **Is it lawful to give** tribute **unto Cæsar, or not?**	22 **Is it lawful** for us **to give** tribute **unto Cæsar, or not?**
18 **But** Jesus perceived **their** wickedness, and **said,** Why tempt ye me, ye **hypocrites** [?]?	23 **But** he perceived **their** craftiness, and **said** unto them,
19 Shew **me** the tribute money. And they brought unto him a ² **penny.**	24 Shew me a ² **penny. Whose image and superscription** hath it? And they said, **Cæsar's.**
20 And he saith unto them, **Whose** is this **image and superscription?**	
21 They say unto him, **Cæsar's.** Then saith he unto them, **Render** therefore **unto Cæsar the things that are Cæsar's; and unto God the things that are God's.**	25 And he said unto them, Then **render unto Cæsar the things that are Cæsar's, and unto God the things that are God's.**
22 **And** when they heard it, **they marvelled,** and left him, and went their way.	26 And they were not able to take hold of the saying before the people: **and they marvelled at** his answer, and held their peace.

XXII. 23–33.	XX. 27–38.
23 On that day there came **to him Sadducees,** ³**which say that there is no resurrection; and they *asked him,**	27 And there came **to him** certain of the Sadducees, they which **say that** there is no resurrection; **and they * asked him, saying,**
24 **Saying,** ¹ **Master, Moses** said, **If a man die,** having no **children, his brother** ⁴ shall marry his **wife and** ***raise up seed unto his brother.**	28 ¹ **Master, Moses** wrote unto us, that **if a man's brother die,** having a wife, and he be **childless, his brother** should take **the wife, and *raise up seed unto his brother.**

¹ Or, *Teacher.*
² See marginal note on xviii 28.
³ Gr. *saying.*
⁴ Gr. *shall perform the duty of a husband's brother to his wife.* Compare Deut. xxv. 5.

¹ Or, *Teacher.*
² See marginal note on Matt. xviii. 28.

St. Mark. [*Portions not found in Matthew or Luke.*]	St. Mark. [*Complete.*]
	XII. 18-27.
20 ...and (dying)...no (Gr. not)...	20 **There were seven brethren: and the first** took a wife, and dying left no seed;
21 ...and died, leaving no seed behind (him)...	21 **And the second** took her, and died, leaving no seed behind him; **and the third** likewise:
22 ...left...seed. Last...	22 And the **seven** left no seed. Last of all **the woman also died.**
	23 **In the resurrection whose wife** shall she be of them? **for the seven had her** to wife.
24 ..said... Is-it-not for this-cause-that...	24 **Jesus** said **unto them,** Is it not for this cause that ye err, that ye know not the scriptures, nor the power of God?
25 ...when...	25 For when they shall **rise** from the dead, **they neither marry, nor are given in marriage;** but **are** as **angels** in heaven.
26 ...in the book...the (Bush)...how... spake to him...	26 **But** as touching the **dead,** that they are raised; have ye not read in the book of Moses, in *the place concerning* the Bush, how God spake unto him, saying, I *am* **the God of Abraham, and the God of Isaac, and the God of Jacob?**
27 ...ye do greatly err.	27 **He is not the God of the dead, but of the living:** ye do greatly err.
	XII. 28-34.
28 ...came-and...them questioning-together, knowing that he-had-answered them...is the first of all?	28 **And** [?] one of the scribes came, and heard them questioning together, and knowing that he had answered them well, asked **him,** What commandment is the first of all?
29 Jesus...(Gr. that)...Hear, O Israel, the Lord our God, the Lord is one,	29 Jesus answered, The first is, Hear, O Israel; [1] The Lord our God, the Lord is one:
Mark xii. 29, W. and H. *The Lord our God is one Lord.*	[1] Or, *The Lord* is our *God; the Lord is one.*

[*Synopticon, pages 86 -88.*]

St. Matthew. [*Passages parallel to Mark.*]	St. Luke. [*Passages parallel to Mark.*]
XXII. 23–33.	XX. 27–38.
25 Now **there were** with us **seven brethren; and the first** married and deceased, and having no seed left his wife unto his brother; 26 In like manner **the second also, and the third,** unto the ¹**seventh.** 27 And after them all **the woman died.**	29 ***There were** therefore **seven brethren: and the first** took a wife, and died childless; 30 **And the second:** 31 **And the third** took her; and likewise the **seven** also left no children, and died. 32 Afterward **the woman** also **died.**
28 **In the resurrection** therefore **whose wife** shall she be of the **seven? for they** all had her. 29 But **Jesus** answered and said **unto them,** Ye do err, not knowing the scriptures, nor the power of God.	33 **In the resurrection** therefore **whose wife** of them shall she be? **for** the **seven had her** to wife. 34 And **Jesus** said **unto them,** The sons of this ¹world marry, and are given in marriage:
30 For in the **resurrection they neither marry, nor are given in marriage,** but are as **angels**² in heaven.	35 But they that are accounted worthy to attain to that ¹world, and the **resurrection** from the dead, **neither marry, nor are given in marriage;** 36 For neither can they die any more: for they **are** equal unto the **angels;** and are sons of God, being sons of the resurrection.
31 **But** as touching the resurrection of the **dead,** have ye not read that which was spoken unto you by God, saying, 32 I am **the God of Abraham, and the God of Isaac, and the God of Jacob? God is not** *the God* **of the dead, but of the living.** 33 And when the multitudes heard it, they were astonished at his teaching.	37 **But** that the **dead** are raised, even Moses shewed, in *the place concerning* the Bush, when he calleth the Lord **the God of Abraham, and the God of Isaac, and the God of Jacob.** 38 Now **he is not the God of the dead, but of the living:** for all live unto him.
XXII. 34–40. 34 But the Pharisees, when they heard that he had put the Sadducees to silence, gathered themselves together.	XX. 39–44. 39 And certain of the scribes answering said, ²Master, thou hast well said.
35 **And**[?] one of them, a lawyer, asked him a question, tempting **him,** 36 ³Master, which is the great commandment in the law?	X. 25–28. 25 **And** [?] behold, a certain lawyer stood up and tempted **him,** saying ²Master, what shall I do to inherit eternal life?

¹ Gr. *seven.*
² Many ancient authorities add *of God.*
³ Or, *Teacher.*

¹ Or, *age.*
² Or, *Teacher.*

St. Mark. [*Portions not found in Matthew or Luke.*]	St. Mark. [*Complete.*]
	XII. 28-34.
30 And...with (all thy soul) ..with (all thy mind)...with (all thy strength).	30 And **thou shalt love the Lord thy God** [1] with **all thy heart, and** [1] with **all thy soul, and** [1] with **all thy mind,** and [1] with **all thy strength.**
31 ...(is) this. There is none other commandment greater than these.	31 The second is this, Thou shalt love **thy neighbour as thyself.** There is none other commandment greater than these.
32 And the scribe said unto him, Of a truth, master, thou hast well said that he is one; and there is none other but he:	32 And the scribe said unto him, Of a truth, [2] Master, thou hast well said that he is one; and there is none other but he:
33 And to love him with all the heart, and with all the understanding, and with all the strength, and to love his neighbour as himself, is much more than all whole burnt offerings and sacrifices.	33 And to love him with all the heart, and with all the understanding, and with all the strength, and to love his neighbour as himself, is much more than all whole burnt offerings and sacrifices.
34 And when Jesus saw that...discreetly,...unto him, Thou art not far from the kingdom of God.	34 And when Jesus saw that he answered discreetly, he said unto him, Thou art not far from the kingdom of God. And * **no man after that durst ask him any question.**
	XII. 35-37.
35 And ... answered-and...as-he-taught in the temple...the scribes that...	35 And Jesus answered and said, as he taught in the temple, How say the scribes that **the Christ** is the **son of David?**
36 ...said...the Holy...	36 **David** himself said **in** the Holy Spirit. **The Lord said unto my Lord, Sit thou on my right hand, Till I make thine enemies** [3] the footstool of **thy feet.**
37 ...himself calleth...And the common people...him gladly.	37 **David** himself calleth **him Lord;** and whence **is he his son?** And [4] the common people heard him gladly.
Mark xii. 32, Matt. xxii. 39, W. & H. omit *And* The word translated *with* is in the Greek in Mark xii. 30 and 33, always *out of,* in Matt. xxii 37, always *in,* and in Luke x. 27, the first time *out of* and afterwards *in.* Mark xii. 36, W. and H. *underneath thy feet.*	[1] Gr. *from.* [2] Or, *Teacher.* [3] Some ancient authorities read *underneath thy feet.* [4] Or, *the great multitude.*

Synopticon, pages 88-89.]

St. Matthew. [*Passages parallel to Mark.*]	St. Luke. [*Passages parallel to Mark.*]
XXII. 34–40. 37 And **he** said unto him, **Thou shalt love the Lord thy God** with **all thy heart, and** with **all thy soul, and** with **all thy mind.** 38 This is the great and first commandment. 39 ¹And a second like *unto it* is this, Thou shalt love **thy neighbour as thyself.** 40 On these two commandments hangeth the whole law, and the prophets.	x. 25–28. 26 And **he** said unto him, What is written in the law? how readest thou? 27 And he answering said, **Thou shalt love the Lord thy God** ¹ with **all thy heart, and** with **all thy soul,** and with all thy strength, **and** with **all thy mind;** and **thy neighbour as thyself.** 28 And he said unto him, Thou hast answered right: this do, and thou shalt live.
XXII. 41–46. 46 And no one was able to answer him a word, * **neither durst** any man from that day forth **ask him any more questions.**	xx. 40–44. 40 For they **durst not any more ask him *any question.**
41 Now while the Pharisees were gathered together, Jesus asked them a question, 42 Saying, What think ye of **the Christ?** whose **son** is he? They say unto him, *The son* of **David.** 43 He saith unto them, How then doth **David in** the Spirit call him Lord, saying, 44 **The Lord said unto my Lord, Sit thou on my right hand, Till I put thine enemies** underneath **thy feet?** 45 If **David** then calleth **him Lord,** how **is he his son?**	41 And he said unto them, How say they that **the Christ is David's son?** 42 For **David** himself saith **in** the book of Psalms, **The Lord said unto my Lord, Sit thou on my right hand,** 43 **Till I make thine enemies** the footstool of **thy feet.** 44 **David** therefore calleth **him Lord,** and how **is he his son?** 45 And in the hearing of all the people he said...
¹ Or, *And a second is like unto it,* Thou shalt love, &c.	¹ Gr *from.*

St. Mark. [*Portions not found in Matthew or Luke.*]	**St. Mark.** [*Complete.*]
	Repeated from p. 104; xii....37. 37 ...And the common people heard him gladly.
	XII. 38–40.
38 And in his teaching...Beware...	38 And in his teaching he said, Beware of the **scribes,** which desire to walk in long robes, **and** *to have* **salutations in the marketplaces,**
	39 **And chief seats in the synagogues,** and **chief places at feasts:**
40 They-which (Gr. the)...	40 They which devour widows' houses, [1] and for a pretence make long prayers; these shall receive greater condemnation.
	XII. 41–44.
41 And he sat down over against the treasury and beheld how the multitude ..money...and many...cast in much.	41 And he sat down over against the treasury, and beheld how the multitude cast [2] money into the treasury: and many that were rich cast in much.
42 And there came a poor ... which make a farthing.	42 And there came [3] a poor widow, and she cast in two mites, which make a farthing.
43 ...he called unto him his disciples, and...unto them, Verily...than...they which are casting into the treasury;	43 And he called unto him his disciples, and said unto them, Verily I say unto you, This poor widow cast in more than all they which are casting into the treasury;
44 ...all her living.	44 For they all did cast in of their superfluity; but she of her want did cast in all that she had, *even* all her living.
Mark xiii. 2, Matt. xxiv. 2, Luke xxi. 6, Gr. *stone upon stone.* Mark xii. 42, *make* Gr. *is.* Luke xi. 43, Gr. *the chief seat.*	[1] Or, *even while for a pretence they make.* [2] Gr. *brass.* [3] Gr. *one.*

Synopticon, pages 89–91.]

St. Matthew. [Passages parallel to Mark.]	St. Luke. [Passages parallel to Mark.]
XXIII. 1–7. 1 Then spake Jesus to the multitudes and to his disciples, saying, 2 The **scribes** and the Pharisees sit on Moses' seat: 3 All things therefore whatsoever they bid you, *these* do and observe: but do not ye after their works; for they say, and do not. 4 Yea, they bind heavy burdens [1] and grievous to be borne, and lay them on men's shoulders; but they themselves will not move them with their finger. 5 But all their works they do for to be seen of men: for they make broad their phylacteries, and enlarge the borders *of their garments*, 6 And love the **chief place at feasts, and** the **chief seats in the synagogues,** 7 **And** the **salutations in the marketplaces,** and to be called of men, Rabbi. [MATTHEW WANTING.]	**XX. 45–47.** 45 And in the hearing of all the people he said unto his disciples, 46 Beware of the **scribes**, which desire to walk in long robes, **and** love **salutations in the marketplaces, and chief seats in the synagogues,** and **chief places at feasts;** 47 Which devour widows' houses, and for a pretence make long prayers: these shall receive greater condemnation. *Compare also* Luke xi. 43. Woe unto you Pharisees! for ye love the chief seats in the synagogues, and the salutations in the marketplaces. **XXI. 1–4.** 1 And he looked up, [1] and saw the rich men that were casting their gifts into the treasury. 2 And he saw a certain poor widow, casting in thither two mites. 3 And he said, Of a truth I say unto you, This poor widow cast in more than they all: 4 For all these did of their superfluity cast in unto the gifts: but she of her want did cast in all the living that she had.
[1] Many ancient authorities omit *and grievous to be borne.*	[1] Or, *and saw them that...treasury, and they were rich.*

St. Mark. [*Portions not found in Matthew or Luke.*]	**St. Mark.** [*Complete.*]
1 ...as-he...from...one of (Gr. the)... Master, behold, what-manner-of...what-manner-of... 2 And Jesus...great buildings...	XIII. 1-2. 1 **And** as he went forth out of **the temple**, one of his disciples saith unto him, ¹ Master, behold, what manner of stones and what manner of buildings ! 2 And Jesus **said** unto him, Seest thou **these** great buildings? **there shall * not be left here one stone upon another, which shall * not be thrown down.**
3 And...on (Gr. into)...over against the temple,...Peter and James and John and Andrew... 4 ...all... 5 ...began to say unto them... 6 ...(Gr. that)... 8 ...there ...shall be...	XIII. 3-8. 3 And as he sat on the mount of Olives over against the temple, Peter and James and John and Andrew asked **him** privately, 4 Tell us, **when shall these things be?** and **what** *shall be* **the sign** when these things are all about to be accomplished ? 5 And Jesus began to say unto them, **Take heed** that **no man lead you astray.** 6 **Many shall come in my name, saying, I am** *he* ; and shall lead many astray. 7 **And** when ye shall hear **of wars** and rumours of wars, be **not** troubled: *these things* **must needs come to pass ;** but the end is **not** yet. 8 For **nation shall rise against nation, and kingdom against kingdom : there shall be earthquakes in divers places ;** there shall be **famines :** these things are the beginning of travail.
In Mark xiii. 7, Luke xxi. 9, the *is* is omitted in the Greek. Luke xxi. 9, *immediately*, Gr *straightway*	¹ Or, *Teacher.*

Synopticon, pages 92–93.]

St. Matthew. [*Passages parallel to Mark.*]	St. Luke. [*Passages parallel to Mark.*]
XXIV. 1-2. 1 And Jesus went out from **the temple**, and was going on his way; and his disciples came to him to shew him the buildings of the temple. 2 But he answered and **said** unto them, See ye not all **these** things? verily I say unto you, **There shall *not be left here one stone upon another, that shall *not be thrown down.** XXIV. 3-8. 3 And as he sat on the mount of Olives, the disciples came unto **him** privately, saying, Tell us, **when shall these things be? and what** *shall be* **the sign** of thy ¹ coming, and of ² the end of the world? 4 And Jesus answered and said unto them, **Take heed that no** man **lead you astray.** 5 For **many shall come in my name, saying, I am** the Christ; and shall lead many astray. 6 **And** ye shall **hear of wars and** rumours of wars: see that ye be **not** troubled: for *these things* **must needs come to pass; but the end is not** yet. 7 For **nation shall rise against nation, and kingdom against kingdom:** and **there shall be famines** and **earthquakes in divers places.** 8 But all these things are the beginning of travail. ¹ Gr *presence*. ² Or, *the consummation of the age.*	XXI. 5-9. 5 **And** as some spake of **the temple**, how it was adorned with goodly stones and offerings, he said, 6 As for **these** things which ye behold, the days will come, in which **there shall *not be left here one stone upon another, that shall *not be thrown down.** 7 And they asked **him**, saying, ¹ Master, **when** therefore **shall these things be? and what** *shall be* **the sign** when these are about to come to pass? 8 And **he said, Take heed that** ye be **not led astray:** for **many shall come in my name, saying, I am** *he*; and, The time is at hand: go ye not after them. 9 And when ye shall **hear of wars** and tumults, be **not** terrified: for these things **must needs come to pass** first; **but the end is not** immediately. XXI. 10-11. 10 Then said he unto them, **Nation shall rise against nation, and kingdom against kingdom:** 11 And **there shall be** great **earthquakes, and in divers places famines** and pestilences; and there shall be terrors and great signs from heaven. ¹ Or, *Teacher.*

110   THE COMMON TRADITION

St. Mark. [*Portions not found in Matthew or Luke.*]	St. Mark. [*Complete.*]
9 But take ye heed to yourselves...to councils...shall ye be beaten...and (before governors)...shall ye stand...unto them. 10 ...must first...to... 11 And when they lead you...and deliver you up, be...anxious (beforehand) what ye shall speak ..but whatsoever...in that hour, that speak ye: for it is not ye that speak, but the Holy Ghost. 12 ...brother to death, and the father his child, and children shall rise up against parents...them... 9 ...take ye heed to yourselves...shall ye be beaten...and (before governors)... shall ye stand... 10 ...the gospel must first be preached to all... 11 And...they lead...but whatsoever... that... *Compare also* Luke xii. 11—12. 11. And **when** they bring **you** before the synagogues, and the rulers, and the authorities, **be not anxious** how or **what** ye shall answer, or what ye shall say: 12 For **the** Holy **Spirit** shall teach **you in** that very **hour** what ye ought to say.	XIII. 9-13. 9 But take ye heed to yourselves: for they shall **deliver you up** to councils; and in [?] synagogues shall ye be beaten; and before governors and kings shall ye stand for my sake, for a testimony unto them. 10 And the gospel must first be preached unto all the nations. 11 And when they lead you *to judgement*, and deliver you up, be not anxious beforehand what ye shall speak: but whatsoever shall be given you in that hour, that speak ye: for it is not ye that speak, but the Holy Ghost. 12 And brother shall **deliver up** brother to death, and the father his child; and children shall rise up against parents, and ¹ cause them to be put to death. 13 **And ye shall be hated of all men for my name's sake**: but he that **endureth** [?] to the end, the same shall be saved. XIII. 9-13, *repeated.* 9 But take ye heed to yourselves: for they shall **deliver you up** to councils; and [?] in **synagogues** shall ye be beaten; **and before governors and kings** shall ye stand **for my sake, for a testimony** unto them. 10 And the gospel must first be preached unto all the nations. 11 And **when** they lead **you** *to judgement*, and deliver you up, **be not anxious** *beforehand **what** ye shall speak: but whatsoever shall be **given you in** that **hour,** that speak ye: for it is not ye that speak, but **the** Holy **Ghost.** 12 And **brother** shall **deliver up** brother to death, and the father his child; and children shall rise up against **parents, and** ¹ **cause** them **to be put to death.** 13 **And ye shall be hated of all men for my name's sake**: but he that **endureth** [?] to the end, the same shall be saved. ¹ Or, *put them to death.*

Synopticon, *pages* 94A, 94, and 127A.]

| St. Matthew. | St. Luke. |
| [Passages parallel to Mark.] | [Passages parallel to Mark.] |

XXIV. 9–14.

9 Then shall they **deliver you up unto** [?] tribulation, **and** shall kill you: **and ye shall be hated of all** the nations **for my name's sake.**
10 And then shall many stumble, and shall **deliver up** one another, and shall hate one another.
11 And many false prophets shall arise, and shall lead many astray.
12 And because iniquity shall be multiplied, the love of the many shall wax cold.
13 But he that [?] **endureth** to the end, the same shall be saved.
14 And ¹this gospel of the kingdom shall be preached in the whole ²world for a testimony unto all the nations; and then shall the end come.

Another parallel.
x. 17–22.

17 But beware of men: for they will **deliver you up** to councils, and in their **synagogues** they will scourge you;
18 **Yea** and **before governors and kings** shall ye be brought **for my sake, for a testimony** to them and to the Gentiles.
19 But **when** they deliver **you** up, **be not anxious** how or **what** ye shall speak: for it shall be **given you in** that **hour** what ye shall speak.
20 For it is not ye that speak, but **the Spirit** of your Father that speaketh in you.
21 And **brother shall deliver up** brother to death, and the father his child: **and** children shall rise up against **parents, and** ³**cause** them **to be put to death.**
22 **And ye shall be hated of all men for my name's sake**: but he that **endureth** [?] to the end, the same shall be saved.

¹ Or, *these good tidings.*
² Gr. *inhabited earth.*
³ Or, *put them to death.*

XXI. 12–19.

12 But before all these things, they shall lay their hands on **you,** and shall persecute you, **delivering you up to** the synagogues and prisons, ¹ bringing you before kings and governors for my name's sake. 13 It shall turn unto you for a testimony. 14 Settle it therefore in your hearts, not to meditate beforehand how to answer: 15 For I will give you a mouth and wisdom, which all your adversaries shall not be able to withstand or to gainsay. 16 But ye shall be **delivered up** even by parents, and brethren, and kinsfolk, and friends; and *some* of you ²shall they cause to be put to death.
17 **And ye shall be hated of all men for my name's sake.** 18 And not a hair of your head shall perish.
19 In your **patience** [?] ye shall win your ³souls.

XXI. 12–19, *repeated.*

12 But before all these things, they shall lay their hands on **you,** and shall persecute you, **delivering you up to** the **synagogues and** prisons,¹ bringing you **before kings and governors for my** name's sake.
13 It shall turn unto you **for a testimony.**
14 Settle it therefore in your hearts, **not** to meditate beforehand how to answer:
15 For I will **give you** a mouth and wisdom, which all your adversaries shall not be able to withstand or to gainsay.
16 But ye shall be **delivered up** even by **parents,** and **brethren,** and kinsfolk, and friends; **and** *some* of you ²**shall they cause to be put to death.**
17 **And ye shall be hated of all** men for my name's sake.
18 And not a hair of your head shall perish.
19 In your [?] **patience** ye shall win your ³souls.

¹ Gr *you being brought.*
² Or, *shall they put to death.*
³ Or, *lives.*

THE COMMON TRADITION

St. Mark. [*Portions not found in Matthew or Luke.*]	St. Mark. [*Complete.*]
	XIII. 14–23.
14 ...where he-ought not...	14 But **when ye see** the abomination of **desolation** standing where he ought not (let him that readeth understand), **then let them that are in Judæa flee unto the mountains :**
15 ...nor enter in...anything...	15 And let him **that is on the housetop not go down,** nor enter in, **to take** anything out of **his house :**
16 ...in (Gr. into)...	16 **And let him that is in the field not return *back** to take his cloke.
	17 But **woe unto them that are with child and to them that give suck in those days !**
	18 And pray ye that it be not in the winter.
19 ...those days...such...of-the-creation which God created...and...	19 **For** those days **shall be** tribulation, such as there hath not been the like from the beginning of the creation which God created until now, and never shall be.
20 ...the-Lord...but...whom he chose ..	20 And except the Lord had shortened the days, no flesh would have been saved : but for the elect's sake, whom he chose, he shortened the days.
	21 And then if any man shall say **unto you,* Lo, here** is the Christ ; or, Lo, there ; believe ¹ *it* **not :**
22 ...that they may (Gr. for the)...	22 For there shall arise false Christs and false prophets, and shall shew signs and wonders, that they may lead astray, if possible, the elect.
23 But take ye heed...all things...	23 But take ye heed : behold, I have told you all things beforehand.

Mark xiii. 16. Luke xvii. 31, Gr. *to the* (*things*) *behind.*
Luke xxi. 21, W. and H. *therein, For.*

¹ Or, him.

Synopticon, pages 95-96]

OF THE SYNOPTIC GOSPELS.

St. Matthew.
[Passages parallel to Mark.]

St. Luke.
[Passages parallel to Mark.]

XXIV. 15–28.
15 **When** therefore **ye see** the abomination of **desolation**, which was spoken of ¹ by Daniel the prophet, standing in ² the holy place (let him that readeth understand),
16 **Then let them that are in Judæa flee unto the mountains:**

17. **Let him that is on the housetop not go down to take** out the things that are in **his house:**
18 **And let him that** is in the **field not return *back** to take his cloke.

19 But **woe unto them that are with child and to them that give suck in those days!**
20 And pray ye that your flight be not in the winter, neither on a sabbath:
21 **For** then **shall be** great tribulation, such as hath not been from the beginning of the world until now, no, nor ever shall be.
22 And except those days had been shortened, no flesh would have been saved: but for the elect's sake those days shall be shortened.
23 Then if any man shall say **unto you,* Lo, here** is the Christ, or, Here; believe ³ *it* **not.**
24 For there shall arise false Christs, and false prophets, and shall shew great signs and wonders; so as to lead astray, if possible, even the elect.
25 Behold, I have told you beforehand.
26 If therefore they shall say unto you, Behold, he is in the wilderness; go not forth: Behold, he is in the inner chambers; believe ⁴ *it* not.
27 For as the lightning cometh forth from the east, and is seen even unto the west; so shall be the ⁵ coming of the Son of man.
28 Wheresoever the carcase is, there will the ⁶ eagles be gathered together.

¹ Or, *through.* ² Or, *a holy place*
³ Or, *him.* ⁴ Or, *them.*
⁵ Gr. *presence.* ⁶ Or, *vultures.*

XXI. 20–21.
20 But **when ye see** Jerusalem compassed with armies, then know that her **desolation** is at hand.
21 **Then let them that are in Judæa flee unto the mountains;** and let them that are in the midst of her depart out; and let not them that are in the country enter therein.

XVII. 31.
31 In that day, he which shall be **on the housetop**, and **his** goods in **the house, let him not go down to take** them away: **and let him that** is in the **field** likewise **not return *back.**

XXI. 23–24.
23 **Woe unto them that are with child and to them that give suck in those days!** for there shall be great distress upon the ¹ land, and wrath unto this people.
24 And they shall fall by the edge of the sword, and shall be led captive into all the nations: and Jerusalem shall be trodden down of the Gentiles, until the times of the Gentiles be fulfilled.

XVII. 23.
23 And they shall say **to you,** Lo, there! **Lo,* here!** go **not** away, nor follow after *them;*

¹ Or, *earth*

St. Mark. [*Portions not found in Matthew or Luke.*]	St. Mark. [*Complete.*]
24 But in...that .. 25 ...shall be...from...that are in...	XIII. 24-27. 24 But in those days, after that tribulation, the **sun** shall be darkened, **and** the **moon** shall not give her light, 25 **And** the **stars** shall be falling from heaven, and **the powers** that are in **the heavens shall be shaken.**
27 ...then...of-the-earth...	26 **And then shall they see the Son of man coming** in **clouds with great power and glory.** 27 And then shall he send forth the angels, and shall gather together his elect from the four winds, from the uttermost part of the earth to the uttermost part of heaven.
30 ...until...	XIII. 28-37. 28 Now from **the fig tree** learn her **parable: when** her branch is **now** become tender, and putteth forth its leaves, **ye know that the summer is nigh;** 29 **Even so ye also, when ye see these things** coming to pass, **know ye that** ¹**he is nigh,** *even* at the doors. 30 **Verily I say unto you,** (Gr. that) **This generation shall not pass away,** until **all these things be accomplished.** 31 **Heaven and earth shall** *pass **away: but my words shall not** *pass away.

¹ Or, *it.*

Synopticon, pages 97-98.

St. Matthew. [*Passages parallel to Mark.*]	St. Luke. [*Passages parallel to Mark.*]
xxiv. 29-31. 29 But immediately, after the tribulation of those days, the **sun** shall be darkened, **and the moon** shall not give her light, **and the stars** shall fall from heaven, and **the powers of the heavens shall be shaken:** 30 **And then** shall appear the sign of the Son of man in heaven: and then shall all the tribes of the earth mourn, and **they shall see the Son of man coming** on the **clouds** of heaven **with power and great glory.** 31 And he shall send forth his angels ¹ with ² a great sound of a trumpet, and they shall gather together his elect from the four winds, from one end of heaven to the other.	xxi. 25-28. 25 And there shall be signs in **sun and moon and stars;** and upon the earth distress of nations, in perplexity for the roaring of the sea and the billows; 26 Men ¹ fainting for fear, and for expectation of the things which are coming on ² the world · for **the powers of the heavens shall be shaken.** 27 **And then shall they see the Son of man coming** in a **cloud with power and great glory.** 28 But when these things begin to come to pass, look up, and lift up your heads; because your redemption draweth nigh.
xxiv. 32-36. 32 Now from **the fig tree** learn her **parable: when** her branch is **now** become tender, and putteth forth its leaves, **ye know that the summer is nigh;** 33 **Even so ye also, when ye see** all **these things, know ye that** ³ **he is nigh,** *even* at the doors. 34 **Verily I say unto you,** (Gr. that) **This generation shall not pass away,** till **all** these things **be accomplished.** 35 **Heaven and earth shall *pass away, but my words shall * not pass away.**	xxi. 29-36. 29 And he spake to them **a parable:** Behold **the fig tree,** and all the trees: 30 **When** they **now** shoot forth, **ye** see it and **know** of your own selves **that the summer** is now **nigh.** 31 **Even so ye also, when ye see these things** coming to pass, **know ye that** the kingdom of God **is nigh.** 32 **Verily I say unto you,** (Gr. that) **This generation shall not pass away,** till **all things be accomplished.** 33 **Heaven and earth shall *pass away:** but **my words shall * not pass away.**
¹ Many ancient authorities read *with a great trumpet, and they shall gather, &c* ² Or, *a trumpet of great sound.* ³ Or, *it.*	¹ Or, *expiring.* ² Gr. *the inhabited earth.*

THE COMMON TRADITION

St. Mark. [*Portions not found in Matthew or Luke.*]	St. Mark. [*Complete.*]
	XIII. 28–37.
32 ...or that (Gr. the)...in (heaven)...	32 But of **that day** or that hour knoweth no one, not even the angels in heaven, neither the Son, but the Father.
33 Take ye heed, ..for...when the time is.	33 Take ye heed, watch ¹ and pray: for ye know not when the time is.
34 ...having left his house...authority ...his...his work,...commanded also the porter to watch.	34 *It is as when* a man, sojourning in another country, having left his house, and given authority to his ² servants, to each one his work, commanded also the porter to watch.
35 ...for...when...of the house...whether at even, or at midnight, or at cockcrowing, or in the morning;	35 **Watch** therefore: for ye know **not** when **the lord** of the house **cometh**, whether at even, or at midnight, or at cockcrowing, or in the morning;
36 Lest coming [?] suddenly he find [?] you sleeping.	36 Lest coming suddenly he **find** you sleeping.
37 And what I say unto you ..Watch.	37 And what I say unto you I say unto all, Watch.
Mark xiii. 33, W. and H. omit *and pray*.	¹ Some ancient authorities omit *and pray*. ² Gr. *bondservants*.

Synopticon, pages 98–99, 127 A.]

OF THE SYNOPTIC GOSPELS.

St. Matthew. [*Passages parallel to Mark.*]	St. Luke. [*Passages parallel to Mark.*]
XXIV. 32-36. 36 But of **that day** and hour knoweth no one, not even the angels of heaven, ¹ neither the Son, but the Father only. XXV. 13-15. 13 **Watch** [?] therefore, for ye know **not** [?] the day nor the hour. 14 For *it is* as *when* a man, going into another country, called his own ² servants, and delivered unto them his goods. 15 And unto one he gave five talents, to another two, to another one; to each according to his several ability; and he went on his journey. XXIV. 42-46. 42 **Watch** [?] therefore: for ye know **not** [?] on what day your **Lord cometh.** 43 ³ But know this, that if the master of the house had known in what watch the thief was coming, he would have watched, and would not have suffered his house to be ⁴ broken through. 44 Therefore be ye also ready: for in an hour that ye think not the Son of man cometh. 45 Who then is the faithful and wise ⁵ servant, whom his lord hath set over his household, to give them their food in due season? 46 Blessed is that servant, whom his **lord** [?] when he cometh shall **find** so doing.	XXI. 29-36. 34 But take heed to yourselves, lest haply your hearts be overcharged with surfeiting, and drunkenness, and cares of this life, and **that day** come on you suddenly as a snare: 35 For *so* shall it come upon all them that dwell on the face of all the earth. 36 But watch ye at every season, making supplication, that ye may prevail to escape all these things that shall come to pass, and to stand before the Son of man. XII. 35-41. 35 Let your loins be girded about, and your lamps burning; 36 And be ye yourselves like unto men looking for their lord, when he shall return from the marriage feast; that, when he cometh and knocketh, they may straightway open unto him. 37 Blessed are those ¹ servants, whom **the lord** when he cometh shall **find watching**: verily I say unto you, that he shall gird himself, and make them sit down to meat, and shall come and serve them. 38 And if he shall come in the second watch, and if in the third, and find *them* so, blessed are those *servants*. 39 But ² know this, that if the master of the house had known in what hour the thief was coming, he would have watched, and not have suffered his house to be ³ broken through. 40 Be ye also ready: for in an hour that ye think **not** the Son of man **cometh.** 41 And Peter said, Lord, speakest thou this parable unto us, or even unto all?
¹ Many authorities, some ancient, omit *neither the Son.* ² Gr. *bondservants.* ³ Or, *But this ye know.* ⁴ Gr. *digged through.* ⁵ Gr. *bondservant.*	¹ Gr. *bondservants.* ² Or, *But this ye know.* ³ Gr. *digged through.*

THE COMMON TRADITION

St. Mark. [Portions not found in Matthew or Luke.]	St. Mark. [Complete.]
	XIV. 1-2.
1 ...was...and...with (Gr. in)...	1 Now after two days was *the feast of* the **passover** and the unleavened bread: and **the chief priests and the** scribes sought how they might take him with subtilty, and kill him:
2 ...haply (Gr. at-some-time) there shall be...	2 For they said, Not during the feast, lest haply there shall be a tumult of **the people.**
	XIV. 3-9.
3 And while he was .. as-he ... very-costly [?]... *and* she brake the cruse, and...	3 And while he was in Bethany **in the house** of Simon the leper, as he *sat at meat, there came **a woman** having ¹**an alabaster cruse of ointment** of ²spikenard very costly; *and* she brake the cruse, and poured it over his **head** [?].
4 ...there were some... among themselves,...hath...of the ointment been made?.	4 **But** there were some that had indignation among themselves, *saying*, To what purpose hath this waste of the ointment been made?
5 ... above ... to-the ... and they murmured against her.	5 For this ointment might have been sold for above three hundred ³pence, and given to the poor. And they murmured against her.
6 ...her?...on (Gr. in)...	6 **But Jesus** said, Let her alone; why trouble ye her? she hath wrought a good work on me.
7 ...and whensoever ye will ye can do them good...	7 For ye have the poor always with you, and whensoever ye will ye can do them good: but me ye have not always.
8 ...what she could...[she hath anointed my body beforehand, Gr. she-anticipated, (to anoint)]... 9 And...throughout (Gr. into)...	8 She hath done what she could: she hath anointed my body aforehand for the burying. 9 And verily I say unto you, Wheresoever the gospel shall be preached throughout the whole world, that also which this woman hath done shall be spoken of her for a memorial of her.
Mark xiii. 36, *compare* Luke xii. 37, *page* 117.	¹ Or, *a flask.* ² Gr. *pistic nard,* pistic being perhaps a local name. Others take it to mean *genuine;* others *liquid.* ³ The word in the Greek denotes a coin worth about eightpence halfpenny.

Synopticon, pages 100-102]

OF THE SYNOPTIC GOSPELS.   119

St. Matthew. [Passages parallel to Mark.]	St. Luke. [Passages parallel to Mark.]
XXVI. 1–5.	XXII. 1–2.
1 And it came to pass, when Jesus had finished all these words, he said unto his disciples, 2 Ye know that after two days the **passover** cometh, and the Son of man is delivered up to be crucified. 3 Then were gathered together **the chief priests, and the** elders of the people, unto the court of the high priest, who was called Caiaphas ; 4 And they took counsel together that they might take Jesus by subtilty, and kill him. 5 But they said, Not during the feast, lest a tumult arise among **the people.**	1 Now the feast of unleavened bread drew nigh, which is called the **Passover.** 2 And **the chief priests and the** scribes sought how they might put him to death; for they feared **the people.**
XXVI. 6–13.	VII. 36–40...
6 Now when Jesus was in Bethany, **in the house** of Simon the leper, 7 There came unto him **a woman** having ¹ **an alabaster cruse of** exceeding precious **ointment,** and she poured it upon his **head** [?] as he *sat at meat. 8 **But** when the disciples saw it, they had indignation, saying, To what purpose is this waste ? 9 For this *ointment* might have been sold for much, and given to the poor. 10 **But Jesus** perceiving it said unto them, Why trouble ye the woman ? for she hath wrought a good work upon me. 11 For ye have the poor always with you ; but me ye have not always. 12 For in that she ² poured this ointment upon my body, she did it to prepare me for burial. 13 Verily I say unto you, Wheresoever ³ this gospel shall be preached in the whole world, that also which this woman hath done shall be spoken of for a memorial of her.	36 And one of the Pharisees desired him that he would eat with him. And he entered into the Pharisee's house, and sat down to meat. 37 And behold, **a woman** which was in the city, a sinner ; and when she knew that he was *sitting at meat **in the** Pharisee's **house,** she brought ¹ **an alabaster cruse of ointment,** 38 And standing behind at his feet, weeping, she began to wet his feet with her tears, and wiped them with the hair of her **head** [?], and ² kissed his feet, and anointed them with the ointment. 39 **Now** when the Pharisee which had bidden him saw it, he spake within himself, saying, This man, if he were ³ a prophet, would have perceived who and what manner of woman this is which toucheth him, that she is a sinner. 40 **And Jesus** answering said unto him, Simon, I have somewhat to say unto thee...
¹ Or a *flask.* ² Gr *cast.* ³ Or, *these good tidings.*	¹ Or, a *flask.* ² Gr *kissed much.* 3 Some ancient authorities read *the prophet.* See John 1. 21, 25.

THE COMMON TRADITION

St. Mark. [Portions not found in Matthew or John.]	St. Mark. [Complete.]
	XIV. 3–9, *repeated*.
3 And while he was ... as he ... very costly [?] ... *and* she brake the cruse and...	3 And while he was in **Bethany** in the house of Simon the leper, as he *sat at meat, there came a woman having [1] an alabaster cruse **of ointment** of [2] spikenard very costly ; *and* she brake the cruse, and poured it over his head [?]
4 ...there were some ... among themselves ..hath...of the ointment been made ?	4 **But** there were some that had indignation among themselves, *saying*, To **what purpose** hath this waste of the ointment been made ?
5 .. above [*three hundred pence*] .. to the...and they murmured against her.	5 For **this** ointment might have been **sold** for above three hundred [3] **pence, and given** to the **poor.** And they murmured against her.
6 ... [*Let her alone*] ; ... her...on (Gr. in)...	6 But **Jesus said,** Let her alone ; why trouble ye her? she hath wrought a good work on me.
7 ...and whensoever ye will ye can do them good...	7 **For ye have the poor always with you,** and whensoever ye will ye can do them good : **but me ye have not always.**
8 ...what she could...[she hath anointed my body beforehand, Gr. she anticipated (anoint)] ..	8 She hath done what she could : she hath anointed **my** body aforehand for **the burying.**
9 And...throughout (Gr. into)...	9 And verily I say unto you, Wheresoever the gospel shall be preached throughout the whole world, that also which this woman hath done shall be spoken of for a memorial of her.
Verses 5, 6, the italicized words in brackets are found in John's gospel, but not in Matthew or Luke.	
[*Portions not found in Matthew or Luke.*]	XIV. 10–11.
10 And...he-that-was (Gr. the)...that...	10 And **Judas *Iscariot,** [4] he that was one **of the twelve,** went away unto **the chief priests,** that he might **deliver him** unto them.
11 ...when-they-heard-it,...promised how ..	11 And they, when they heard it, were glad, and promised **to give him money. And he sought** how he might **conveniently deliver him** *unto them.*
	[1] Or, *a flask* [2] Gr. *pistic nard*, pistic being perhaps a local name. Others take it to mean *genuine ;* others, *liquid.* [3] See marginal note on Matt. xviii 28. [4] Gr. *the one of the twelve.*

Synopticon, pages 101–103.]

OF THE SYNOPTIC GOSPELS.

St. Matthew.
[*Passages parallel to Mark.*]

St. John.
[*Passages parallel to Mark.*]

XXVI. 6–13, *repeated.*

6 Now when Jesus was in **Bethany,** in the house of Simon the leper,
7 There came unto him a woman having ¹an alabaster cruse **of** exceeding precious **ointment,** and she poured it upon his head [?] as he *****sat** at meat.

8 **But** when the disciples saw it, they had indignation, saying, To **what** purpose is this waste?

9 For **this** *ointment* might have been **sold** for much, **and given to the poor.**
10 But **Jesus** perceiving it **said** unto them, Why trouble ye the woman? for she hath wrought a good work upon me.
11 **For ye have the poor always with you; but me ye have not always.**
12 For in that she ²poured this ointment upon **my** body, she did it to prepare me for **burial.**
13 Verily I say unto you, Wheresoever ³this gospel shall be preached in the whole world, that also which this woman hath done shall be spoken of for a memorial of her.

XXVI. 14–16.

14 Then one **of the twelve,** who was called **Judas *****Iscariot,** went unto **the chief priests,**
15 And said, What are ye willing **to give** [?] **me,** and I will **deliver him** unto you? And they weighed **unto him** thirty **pieces of silver.**
16 **And** from that time he **sought opportunity** to **deliver him** *unto them.*

¹ Or, *a flask.*
² Gr. *cast.*
³ Or, *these good tidings.*

XII. 1–11.

1 Jesus therefore six days before the passover came to **Bethany,** where Lazarus was, whom Jesus raised from the dead.
2 So they made him a supper there: and Martha served; but Lazarus was one of them that *****sat** at meat with him.
3 Mary therefore took a pound **of ointment** of ¹ spikenard, very precious, and anointed the feet of Jesus, and wiped his feet with her hair: and the house was filled with the odour of the ointment.
4 **But** Judas Iscariot, one of his disciples, which should betray him, saith,
5 **Why** was not **this** ointment **sold** for three hundred ²pence, **and given to the poor?**
6 Now this he said, not because he cared for the poor; but because he was a thief, and having the ³bag ⁴took away what was put therein.
7 **Jesus** therefore **said,** ⁵Suffer her to keep it against the day of **my burying.**
8 **For the poor ye have always with you; but me ye have not always.**

St. Luke.
XXII. 3–6.

3 And Satan entered into **Judas** who was called *****Iscariot,** being of the number **of the twelve.**
4 And he went away and communed with **the chief priests** and captains, how he might **deliver him** unto them.
5 And they were glad, and covenanted **to give him money.**
6 And he consented, **and sought opportunity** to **deliver him** unto them ⁶in the absence of the multitude.

¹ See marginal note on Mark xiv. 3.
² See marginal note on Matt. xviii. 28.
³ Or, *box.*
⁴ Or, *carried what was put therein.*
⁵ Or, *Let her alone: it was that she might keep it.*
⁶ Or, *without tumult.*

THE COMMON TRADITION

St. Mark. [*Portions not found in Matthew or Luke.*]	St. Mark. [*Complete.*]
	XIV. 12–16.
12 And...when...his... unto him ... go- and...	12 And on the first day **of unleavened bread,** when they sacrificed the passover, his disciples say unto him, **Where wilt thou that we** go and **make ready** that thou mayest **eat the passover?**
13 ...two of his disciples and saith... and...	13 And he sendeth two of his disciples, and saith unto them, Go **into the city,** and there shall meet you a man bearing a pitcher of water: follow him;
14 .. wheresoever ... (Gr. that) ... my (guest-chamber)...	14 **And** wheresoever he shall enter in, say to the goodman of the house, **The** ¹**Master saith,** Where is my guest-chamber, where I shall eat **the passover with my disciples?**
15 ...he-himself...ready: and. . for us.	15 And he will himself shew you a large upper room furnished *and* ready: and there make ready for us.
16 ...and came into the city and...he had said (Gr. he said)...	16 And the disciples went forth, and came into the city, and found * as he had said **unto them; and they made ready the passover.**
	XIV. 17–21.
17 ...he cometh...	17 And when it **was** evening he cometh with the twelve.
18 ...as (they) sat and...Jesus ..he that eateth...	18 **And** as they ²sat and were eating, Jesus **said,** Verily I say unto you, One of you shall **betray me,** *even* he that eateth with me.
19 ...and...by one ..	19 **They began** to be sorrowful, and to say unto him one by one, Is it I?
20 ...unto them, One of the twelve ..in (Gr. into)...	20 And he said unto them, *It is* one of the twelve, he that dippeth with me in the dish.
	21 For **the Son of man** goeth, **even** [?] as it is written of him: but **woe unto that man through whom** the Son of man **is betrayed!** good were ³it for that man if he had not been born.
With Mark xiv. 17–21, *compare also* John xiii 21–28. The only words in this passage common to Mark and Matthew are: 21 *...and said...verily, I say unto you, that one of you shall betray me* ... 25 *...saith unto him...* 26 *...dipped* [?]... The only additional words (a) common to Mark are: 21 *...Jesus...(of those) at the table* ...(b) common to Matthew are: 25 *... Lord... answereth....Judas...saith unto him...* Mark xiv. 21, Matthew xxvi. 24, Gr. *the Son of Man indeed goeth*	¹ Or, *Teacher.* ² Gr. *reclined.* ³ Gr. *for him if that man.*

[*Synopticon, pages* 104–105.]

OF THE SYNOPTIC GOSPELS. 123

St. Matthew. [*Passages parallel to Mark.*]	St. Luke. [*Passages parallel to Mark.*]
XXVI. 17–19. 17 Now on the first *day* **of unleavened bread** the disciples came to Jesus, saying, **Where wilt thou that we make ready** for thee to **eat the passover**? 18 And he said, Go **into the city** to such a man, **and** say unto him, **The** ¹ **Master saith**, My time is at hand; I keep **the passover** at thy house **with my disciples.** 19 And the disciples did ***as** Jesus appointed **them; and they made ready the passover.**	XXII. 7–13. 7 And the day **of unleavened bread** came, on which the passover must be sacrificed. 8 And he sent Peter and John, saying, Go and make ready for us **the passover,** that we may **eat.** 9 And they said unto him, **Where wilt thou that we make ready?** 10 And he said unto them, Behold, when ye are entered **into the city,** there shall meet you a man bearing a pitcher of water; follow him into the house whereinto he goeth. 11 **And** ye shall say unto the goodman of the house, **The** ¹ **Master saith** unto thee, Where is the guest-chamber, where I shall eat **the passover with my disciples?** 12 And he will shew you a large upper room furnished: there make ready. 13 And they went, and found ***as** [?] he had said **unto them: and they made ready the passover.**
XXVI. 20–25. 20 Now when even was **come**, he was sitting at meat with the twelve ² disciples; 21 **And** as they were eating, **he said,** Verily I say unto you, that one of you shall **betray me.** 22 And they were exceeding sorrowful, and **began** to say unto him every one, Is it I, Lord? 23 And he answered and said, He that dipped his hand with me in the dish, the same shall betray me. 24 **The Son of man** goeth, **even** [?] as it is written of him: but **woe unto that man through whom the Son of man is betrayed!** good were it ³ for that man if he had not been born. 25 And Judas, which betrayed him, answered and said, Is it I, Rabbi? He saith unto him, Thou hast said.	XXII. 14, 15... ; 21–23. 14 And when the hour was **come,** he sat down, and the apostles with him. 15 **And he said** unto them, With desire... 21 But behold, the hand of him that **betrayeth me** is with me on the table. 22 For **the Son of man indeed** goeth, **as** [?] it hath been determined: but **woe unto that man through whom he is betrayed!** 23 And **they began** to question among themselves, which of them it was that should do this thing.
¹ Or, *Teacher.* ² Many authorities, some ancient, omit *disciples.* ³ Gr. *for him if that man.*	¹ Or, *Teacher.*

THE COMMON TRADITION

St. Mark. [*Portions not found in Matthew or Luke.*]	St. Mark. [*Complete.*]
22 ...and (said)...	XIV. 22–25. 22 And as they were eating, he took **¹bread, and** when he had blessed, **he brake it, and gave** to them, and said, **Take ye: this is my body.**
23 ...and (they)...	23 **And** he took **a cup,** and **when he had given thanks,** he gave to them: and they all drank of it.
24 And...unto them, This...for...	24 And he said unto them, **This is my blood** of ²the ³**covenant, which is shed** for many.
25 Verily...(Gr. that)...no more...	25 Verily **I say unto you, I will** no more **drink** of **the fruit of the vine, until** that day when I drink it new **in the kingdom** of God.

ST. PAUL, 1 CORINTHIANS XI. 23–25, *showing in black type his agreement with the Synoptic Tradition.*
23 For I received of the Lord that which I also delivered unto you, how that the Lord Jesus in the night in which he was betrayed **took bread;** 24 **And when he had given thanks, he brake it,** and said, **This is my body,** which ¹is for you: this do in remembrance of me. 25 In like manner **also** the **cup,** after supper, saying, **This** cup is **the new** ²**covenant** in **my blood**: this do, as oft as ye drink *it,* in remembrance of me.

¹ Many ancient authorities read *is broken for you.*
² Or, *testament.*

The black type below, represents words common to St. Paul and the Synoptists; the ordinary type, additional words common to St. Paul and
MARK XIV. 22–24.
22 ...***took bread, and brake it**...and said,...**This is my body.**
23 ...**And**...**a cup**...**when he had given thanks,**...

24 ...**This is my blood**...**the covenant**...**for**...

27 And...(Gr. that)...for (Gr. that or because)...

XIV. 26.
26 **And** when they had sung a hymn, they **went out unto the mount of Olives.**

Mark xiv. 27, *compare also* John xviii. 1. Luke xxii. 19, 20. The words *which is given ...poured out for you* are described by W. and H. as a "very early interpolation."

¹ Or, *a loaf.*
² Or, *the testament.*
³ Some ancient authorities insert *new.*

Synopticon, pages 106A–107.]

OF THE SYNOPTIC GOSPELS.   125

St. Matthew. [*Passages parallel to Mark.*]	St. Luke. [*Passages parallel to Mark.*]
XXVI. 26–29. 26 And as they were eating, Jesus took ¹**bread, and** blessed, **and brake it; and he gave** to the disciples, and said, **Take,** eat; **this is my body.** 27 **And** he took ² **a cup, and gave thanks,** and gave to them, saying, Drink ye all of it; 28 For **this is my blood** of ³**the** ⁴**covenant, which is shed** for many unto remission of sins. 29 But **I say unto you, I will not drink** henceforth of this **fruit of the vine, until** that day when I drink it new with you **in my Father's kingdom.**	XXII. 15–20. 15 **And he said** unto them, With desire I have desired to eat this passover with you before I suffer: [*See also p.*123.] 16 For I say unto you, I will not eat it, until it be fulfilled **in the kingdom** of God. 17 **And** he received **a cup, and when he had given thanks,** he said, **Take** this, and divide it among yourselves: 18 For **I say unto you, I will not drink** from henceforth of **the fruit of the vine, until** the kingdom of God shall come. 19 And **he took** ¹**bread, and** when he had given thanks, **he brake it, and gave** to them, saying, **This is my body** ² which is given for you: this do in remembrance of me. 20 And the cup in like manner after supper, saying, **This** cup **is the new** ³**covenant in my blood,** *even* **that which is poured out** for you.
The black type below, represents words common to St. Paul and the Synoptists; the ordinary type, additional words common to St. Paul and MATTHEW XXVI. 26-28. 26 ...Jesus **took bread.. and brake it;** and said,...**This is my body.** 27 **And** ... **a cup** ... **gave thanks,**... saying,... 28 ...**This** is **my blood**...**the covenant,**	*The black type below, represents words common to St. Paul and the Synoptists; the ordinary type, additional words common to St. Paul and* LUKE XXII. 17-20. 17 **And**...**a cup, and when he had given thanks,** 19 ...**he took bread, and**...**he brake it,**...**This is my body** which is...for you; this do in remembrance of me. 20 **And** [?] the **cup** [?] in like manner after supper, saying, **This** cup ..**the new covenant** in **my blood**...
XXVI. 30. 30 **And** when they had sung a hymn, they **went out unto the mount of Olives.**	XXII. 39. 39 **And** he **came out,** and went, as his custom was, **unto the mount of Olives**; and the disciples also followed him.

¹ Or, *a loaf.*
² Some ancient authorities read *the cup.*
³ Or, *the testament.*
⁴ Many ancient authorities insert *new.*

¹ Or, *a loaf.*
² Some ancient authorities omit *which is given for you...which is poured out for you.*
³ Or, *testament.*

St. Mark. [*Portions not found in Matthew or Luke.*]	St. Mark. [*Complete.*]
	XIV. 27–31.
27 And...(Gr. that)...for (Gr. that)...	27 And Jesus saith unto them, All ye shall be [1] offended : for it is written, I will smite the shepherd, and the sheep shall be scattered abroad.
28 But...	28 Howbeit, after I am raised up, I will go before you into Galilee.
29 ...said.. [Although Gr. (if) even] ...yet (Gr. but)...	29 **But** Peter said **unto him,** Although all shall be [1] offended, yet will not I.
30 And...saith...thou...twice... [*Compare also John xiii. 38*] [Jesus answereth...Verily, verily, **I say unto thee, The cock** shall not **crow,** till thou hast *denied me thrice.]	30 And Jesus saith unto him, Verily **I say unto thee,** that thou to-day, *even* this night, before the **cock crow** twice, **shalt deny me thrice.**
31 But...spake exceeding vehemently ...And in-like-manner...said...	31 But he spake exceeding vehemently, If I must die with thee, I will not deny thee. And in like manner also said they all.
	XIV. 32–42.
32 And...which was named (Gr. of which the name)...his...here...	32 And they came unto [2] a place which was named Gethsemane : and he saith unto his disciples, Sit ye here, while I pray.
33 .. with him...James and John, and ...to be greatly amazed...	33 And he taketh with him Peter and James and John, and began to be greatly amazed, and sore troubled.
34 And...	34 And he saith unto them, My soul is exceeding sorrowful even unto death : abide ye here, and watch.
35 ...on [?] the ground...that...the hour ...from him.	35 **And** he went forward a little, and fell on the ground, and **prayed** that, **if** it were possible, the hour might pass away from him.
36 And...Abba,...all-things (are) possible unto thee ;...howbeit (Gr. but)... what...what...	36 And he **said,** Abba, **Father,** all things are possible unto thee ; remove **this cup from me :** howbeit not what I **will, but** what **thou wilt.**
37 ...Simon...	37 **And** he cometh, and **findeth them** sleeping, **and** saith unto Peter, Simon, sleepest thou ? couldest thou not watch one hour ?
	38 [3] Watch and **pray, that ye enter not into temptation :** the spirit indeed is willing, but the flesh is weak.
Mark xiv. 38, W. and H. *that ye* come. *not into temptation.*	[1] Gr. *caused to stumble.* [2] Gr. *an enclosed piece of ground.* [3] Or, *Watch ye, and pray that ye enter not.*

Synopticon, pages 107–109.]

| St. Matthew. | St. Luke. |
| [*Passages parallel to Mark.*] | [*Passages parallel to Mark.*] |

xxvi. 31-35.	xxii. 31-34.
31 Then saith Jesus unto them, All ye shall be ¹ offended in me this night : for it is written, I will smite the shepherd, and the sheep of the flock shall be scattered abroad. 32 But after I am raised up, I will go before you into Galilee. 33 **But** Peter answered and said **unto him,** If all shall be ¹ offended in thee, I will never be ¹ offended. 34 Jesus said unto him, Verily **I say unto thee,** that this night, before **the cock crow, thou shalt deny me thrice.** 35 Peter saith unto him, Even if I must die with thee, *yet* will I not deny thee. Likewise also said all the disciples.	31 Simon, Simon, behold, Satan ¹ asked to have you, that he might sift you as wheat : 32 But I made supplication for thee, that thy faith fail not : and do thou, when once thou hast turned again, stablish thy brethren. 33 **And he** said **unto him,** Lord, with thee I am ready to go both to prison and to death. 34 And he said, **I tell thee,** Peter, **the cock** shall not **crow** this day, until **thou shalt thrice deny** that thou knowest **me.**

xxvi. 36-46.	xxii. 40-46.
36 Then cometh Jesus with them unto a ² place called Gethsemane, and saith unto his disciples, Sit ye here, while I go yonder and pray. 37 And he took with him Peter and the two sons of Zebedee, and began to be sorrowful and sore troubled. 38 Then saith he unto them, My soul is exceeding sorrowful, even unto death : abide ye here, and watch with me. 39 **And** he went forward a little, and fell on his face, and **prayed, saying,** O my **Father, if** it be possible, let **this cup** pass away **from me:** nevertheless, not as I **will, but as thou** wilt.	40 And when he was at the place, he said unto them, Pray that ye enter not into temptation. 41 **And** he was parted from them about a stone's cast ; and he kneeled down and **prayed, saying,** 42 **Father, if** thou be willing, remove **this cup from me:** nevertheless not my **will, but thine,** be done. 43 ²**And** there appeared unto him an angel from heaven, strengthening him. 44 And being in an agony he prayed more earnestly : and his sweat became as it were great drops of blood falling down upon the ground.
40 **And** he cometh unto the disciples, and **findeth them** sleeping, **and** saith unto Peter, What, could ye not watch with me one hour ? 41 ³ Watch and **pray, that ye enter not into temptation:** the spirit indeed is willing, but the flesh is weak.	45 ²**And** when he rose up from his prayer, he came unto the disciples, and **found them** sleeping for sorrow, 46 **And** said unto them, Why sleep ye ? rise and **pray, that ye enter not into temptation.**

¹ Gr. *caused to stumble.* ² Gr. *an enclosed piece of ground.* ³ Or, *Watch ye, and pray that ye enter not.*	¹ Or. *obtained you by asking.* ² Many ancient authorities omit verses 43, 44.

THE COMMON TRADITION

St. Mark. [*Portions not found in Matthew or Luke.*]	St. Mark. [*Complete.*]
	XIV. 32–42.
39 And...	39 And again he went away, and prayed, saying the same words.
40 ...and they wist not what to answer him.	40 And again he came, and found them sleeping, for their eyes were very heavy; and they wist not what to answer him.
41 ...the (third) ... [now Gr. the (remainder)]...it is enough...is come (Gr. came) ... the (hands) of the...	41 And he cometh the third time, and saith unto them, Sleep on now, and take your rest: it is enough; the hour is come; behold, the Son of man is betrayed into the hands of sinners.
	42 Arise, let us be going: behold, he that betrayeth me is at hand.
	XIV. 43–50.
43 ... straightway ... cometh ... from .. and the scribes...the...	43 And straightway, **while he yet spake**, cometh **Judas, one of the twelve**, and with him **a multitude** with swords and staves, from the chief priests and the scribes and the elders.
44 ...and lead him away safely.	44 Now he that betrayed him had given them a token, saying, Whomsoever I shall kiss, that is he; take him, and lead him away safely.
45 ...when-he-was-come,...to-him, and-saith...	45 And when he was come, straightway he came to him, and saith, Rabbi; and ¹**kissed him**.
46 And they...on him...	46 And they laid **hands on** [?] him, and took him.
47 But...that-stood-by...smote. .	47 But a certain **one** of them that stood by drew his **sword**, and smote the ²**servant of the high priest, and struck off his** ear.
[*Compare also* John xviii. 10–11. 10 Simon Peter therefore having a **sword** drew it, and struck **the high priest's servant, and** cut **off his** right ear. Now the ¹servant's name was Malchus. 11 Jesus therefore said unto Peter, Put up the sword into the sheath: the cup which the Father hath given me, shall I not drink it?]	
¹ Gr. *bondservant.*	¹ Gr *kissed him much.* ² Gr *bondservant.*

Synopticon, pages 109–110.]

St. Matthew.	St. Luke.
[*Passages parallel to Mark.*]	[*Passages parallel to Mark.*]

XXVI. 36–46.

42 Again a second time he went away, and prayed, saying, O my Father, if this cannot pass away, except I drink it, thy will be done.
43 And he came again and found them sleeping, for their eyes were heavy.
44 And he left them again, and went away, and prayed a third time, saying again the same words.
45 Then cometh he to the disciples, and saith unto them, Sleep on now, and take your rest : behold, the hour is at hand, and the Son of man is betrayed unto the hands of sinners.
46 Arise, let us be going : behold, he is at hand that betrayeth me.

[LUKE WANTING.]

XXVI. 47–56.

47 And **while he yet spake**, lo, **Judas, one of the twelve**, came, and with him a great **multitude** with swords and staves, from the chief priests and elders of the people.
48 Now, he that betrayed him gave them a sign, saying, Whomsoever I shall kiss, that is he : take him.
49 And straightway he came to Jesus, and said, Hail, Rabbi ; and ¹ **kissed him.**
50 And Jesus said unto him, Friend, *do* that for which thou art come. Then they came and laid **hands on** [?] Jesus, and took him. [*See* Luke xxii. 53, p. 133.]
51 And behold, **one** of them that were with Jesus stretched out his hand, and drew his **sword**, and smote the ² **servant of the high priest, and struck off his** ear.
52 Then saith Jesus unto him, Put up again thy sword into its place : for all they that take the sword shall perish with the **sword** [?].
53 Or thinkest thou that I cannot beseech my Father, and he shall even now send me more than twelve legions of angels ?
54 How then should the scriptures be fulfilled, that thus it must be ?

    ¹ Gr. *kissed him much.*
    ² Gr. *bondservant.*

XXII. 47–53.

47 **While he yet spake**, behold, a **multitude**, and he that was called **Judas, one of the twelve**, went before them ; and he drew near unto Jesus to **kiss him**.
  [*Compare* also John xviii. 2–3.
Now Judas also, **which betrayed him**, knew the place : for Jesus oft-times resorted thither with his disciples. 3 Judas then, having received the ¹ band *of soldiers*, and officers from **the chief priests and** the Pharisees, cometh thither **with lanterns**, and torches, and weapons.]
48 But Jesus said unto him, Judas, betrayest thou the Son of man with a kiss ?
49 And when they that were about him saw what would follow, they said, Lord, shall we smite with the **sword ?**
50 And a certain **one** of them smote the ² **servant of the high priest, and struck off his** right * ear.
51 But Jesus answered and said, Suffer ye thus far. And he touched his ear, and healed him.

    ¹ Or, *cohort.*
    ² Gr. *bondservant.*

THE COMMON TRADITION

St. Mark. [*Portions not found in Matthew or Luke.*]	St. Mark. [*Complete.*]
48 And...answered and...unto them...	XIV. 43–50. 48 And **Jesus** answered and **said** unto them, **Are ye come out, as against a robber, with swords and staves** to seize [?] me?
49 I was...with (Gr. to)..	49 I was **daily** with you **in the temple** teaching, and ye took **me not**: but *this is done* that the scriptures might be fulfilled.
50 And...	50 And they all left him, and fled.
	XIV. 51, 52.
51 And a certain young man followed with him, having a linen cloth cast about him, over *his* naked *body*: and they lay hold on him; 52 But he left the linen cloth, and fled naked.	51 And a certain young man followed with him, having a linen cloth cast about him, over *his* naked *body*: and they lay hold on him; 52 But he left the linen cloth, and fled naked.
	XIV. 53–65.
53 And ... and ' there come ... all the chief-priests and...	53 And **they led** Jesus away to **the high priest**: and there come together with him all the chief priests and the elders and the scribes.
54 And...into...he was...and warming-himself.. [*Compare also* John xviii. 12—13. 12 So the ¹ band and the ²chief captain, and the officers of the Jews, seized Jesus and bound him, 13 **And led him** to Annas first; for he was father in law to Caiaphas, which was **high priest** that year.] ¹ Or, *cohort.* ² Or, *military tribune,* Gr. *chiliarch.*	54 And **Peter** had **followed** him **afar off**, even within, into **the court** of the high priest; **and** he was **sitting** with the officers, and warming himself in the light *of the fire.*
55 ...to (Gr. for the)...	55 Now the **chief priests** and **the whole council** sought witness against Jesus to put him to death; and found it not.
56 For...against him, and their witness agreed not together.	56 For many bare false witness against him, and their witness agreed not together.
57 And there stood up certain, and bare false witness against him, saying, 58 (Gr. that) We heard him say (Gr. that) I...this...that is made with hands ...another made without hands.	57 And there stood up certain, and bare false witness against him, saying, 58 We heard him say, I will destroy this ¹ temple that is made with hands, and in three days I will build another made without hands.
59 And not even so did their witness agree together.	59 And not even so did their witness agree together.
Mark xiv. 54, Matt. xxvi. 58, Gr. *from afar off.*	¹ Or, *sanctuary*

Synopticon, pages 111–112.]

St. Matthew. [Passages parallel to Mark.]	St. Luke. [Passages parallel to Mark.]
XXVI. 47–56. 55 In that hour **said Jesus** to the multitudes, **Are ye come out, as against a robber with swords and staves** to seize [?] me ? I sat **daily in the temple** teaching, and ye took **me not**. 56 But all this is come to pass, that the scriptures of the prophets might be fulfilled. Then all the disciples left him, and fled.	XXII. 47–53. 52 And **Jesus said** unto the chief priests, and captains of the temple, and elders, which were come against him, **Are ye come out, as against a robber, with swords and staves ?** 53 When I was **daily** with you **in the temple**, ye stretched **not** forth **your hands** [?] **against** [?] **me**: but this is your hour, and the power of darkness. [*See* Mark xiv. 46, *p.* 130.]
XXVI. 57–68. 57 And they that had taken Jesus **led** him away to *the house of* Caiaphas **the high priest**, where the scribes and the elders were gathered together. 58 But **Peter followed** him **afar off**, unto **the court** of the high priest, **and** entered in, and **sat with** the officers, to see the end.	XXII. 54–56. 54 And they seized [?] him, and **led** him *away*, and brought [?] him into **the high priest's** house. But **Peter followed afar off**. 55 And when they had kindled a fire in the midst of **the court, and** had sat down together, Peter **sat** in the midst of them. 56 And a certain **maid** seeing him as he sat in the light *of the fire*, and looking stedfastly upon him, said, This man **also** was with him. [*See* Mark xiv. 66, *p.* 134.]
59 Now the **chief priests** and **the whole council** sought false witness against Jesus, that they might put him to death ; 60 And they found it not, though many false witnesses came. But afterward came two, and said,	XXII. 66–71. 66 And as soon as it was day, the assembly of the elders of the people was gathered together, both **chief priests** and scribes ; and they led him away into their **council**, saying,
61 This man said, I am able to destroy the [1] temple of God, and to build it in three days.	

[1] Or, *sanctuary:* as in ch. xxiii. 35 ; xxvii. 5.

St. Mark. [*Portions not found in Matthew or Luke.*]	St. Mark. [*Complete.*]
	XIV. 53–65.
60 ...in the midst, and asked Jesus, saying, (Gr. Answerest thou not nothing ?)...	60 And the high priest stood up in the midst, and asked Jesus, saying, Answerest thou nothing? what is it which these witness against thee ?
61 ...and answered nothing (Gr. not nothing). Again...asked him, and... Blessed ?	61 But he held his peace, and answered nothing. Again the high priest asked him, and saith unto him, **Art thou the Christ, the Son of the** Blessed ?
62 ...said,...and ...with...	62 And Jesus said, I am : and ye shall see **the Son of man sitting at the right hand of power,** and coming with the clouds of heaven.
63 ...clothes...	63 And the high priest rent his clothes, and saith, **What further need have we of witnesses ?**
64 ...think.(Gr. appears to you)...all condemned him to be...	64 **Ye have heard** the blasphemy : what think ye? And they all condemned him to be [1] worthy of death.
65 ...some began...and (to say) unto him...officers received him...	65 And some began to spit on him, and to cover his face, and to buffet him, and to say unto him, **Prophesy:** and the officers received him with [2] blows of their hands.
	XIV. 66–72.
66 ...as...was (Gr. being) beneath... there cometh ... of the ... of the high-priest. 67....Peter warming-himself, she looked-upon...Nazarene, even (Gr. the Jesus).	66 And as Peter was beneath in the court, there cometh one of the **maids** of the high priest ; 67 And seeing Peter warming himself, she looked upon him, and saith, Thou **also** wast with the Nazarene, *even* Jesus.
68 ...nor understand...thou...	68 **But he denied saying,** [3] **I neither know,** nor understand what thou sayest :...

Mark xiv. 60, Gr. *not nothing.*
Matthew xxiv. 57, Gr. *nothing.*

[1] Gr. *liable to.*
[2] Or, *strokes of rods.*
[3] Or, *I neither know, nor understand : thou, what sayest thou ?*

Synopticon, pages 113–114.]

| St. Matthew. | St. Luke. |
| [Passages parallel to Mark.] | [Passages parallel to Mark.] |

XXVI. 57–68.	XXII. 66–71.
62 And the high priest stood up, and said unto him, Answerest thou nothing? what is it which these witness against thee?	
63 But Jesus held his peace. And the high priest said unto him, I adjure thee by the living God, that thou tell us whether **thou be the Christ, the Son of** God.	67 If **thou art the Christ,** tell us. But he said unto them, If I tell you, ye will not believe:
	68 And if I ask *you*, ye will not answer.
64 Jesus saith unto him, Thou hast said: nevertheless I say unto you, Henceforth ye shall see **the Son of man sitting at the right hand of power,** and coming on the clouds of heaven.	69 But from henceforth shall **the Son of man be seated at the right hand of the power** of God.
	70 And they all said, Art thou then **the Son of God?** And he said unto them, [1] Ye say that I am.
65 Then the high priest rent his garments, saying, He hath spoken blasphemy: **what further need have we of witnesses?** behold, now **ye have heard** the blasphemy:	71 And they said, **What further need have we of witness?** for we ourselves **have heard** from his own mouth.
66 What think ye? They answered and said, He is [1] worthy of death.	
67 Then did they spit in **his** face and buffet him: and some smote him [2] with the palms of their hands, **saying,**	XXII. 63–65.
	63 And the men that held [2] *Jesus* mocked him, and beat him.
68 **Prophesy** unto us, thou Christ: who is he that struck thee?	64 And they blindfolded **him,** and asked him, **saying, Prophesy:** who is he that struck thee?
	65 And many other things spake they against him, reviling him.

XXVI. 69–75.	XXII. 56–62.
69 Now Peter was sitting without in the court: and a **maid** came unto him, saying, Thou **also** wast with Jesus the Galilæan.	56 And a certain **maid** seeing him as he sat in the light *of the fire*, and looking stedfastly upon him, said, This man **also** was with him.
	[See Mark xiv. 54, p. 132.]
70 **But he denied** before them all, **saying, I know not** what thou sayest.	57 **But he denied, saying,** Woman, **I know** him **not.**

[1] Gr. *liable to.*
[2] Or, *with rods.*

[1] Or, *Ye say it, because I am.*
[2] Gr. *him.*

St. Mark. [Portions not found in Matthew or Luke.]	St. Mark. [Complete.]
	XIV. 66–72.
68 ...and...out...the porch; and the cock crew. 69 ...the maid...began again...that-stood-by...(Gr. that)...is...	68 ...and he went out into the ¹porch; ²and the cock crew. 69 And the maid **saw him**, and began again to say to them that stood by, **This is** one **of them.**
70 ...again (they)...thou-art (a Galilæan.)	70 But he again denied it. And after a little while again they that stood by said to Peter, **Of a truth thou art** one **of them; for** thou art a Galilæan.
71 ...this...of whom...	71 But he began to curse, and to swear, **I know not** this **man** of whom ye speak.
72 ...the second time...twice...when-he-thought-thereon...	72 **And** straightway the second time **the cock crew. And Peter *called to mind the word,** how that Jesus said unto him, (Gr. that) **Before the cock crow** twice, **thou shalt deny me thrice.** ³**And** when he thought thereon, he **wept.**
	XV. 1–5.
1 ...straightway...with the...and...and the whole council held (Gr. having made)...and-carried-him-(away)...	1 And straightway in the morning the chief priests with the elders and scribes, and the whole council, held a consultation, and bound Jesus, and carried him away, and delivered him up to **Pilate.**
2 ...saith...	2 And Pilate * asked him, **Art thou the King of the Jews?** And he answering saith unto him, **Thou sayest.**
3 ...many things. 4 ...again...behold...they-accuse... 5 ...Jesus...Pilate...	3 And the **chief priests accused him** of many things. 4 And **Pilate** again asked **him,** saying, Answerest thou nothing? behold how many things they accuse thee of. 5 But Jesus no more **answered anything;** insomuch that Pilate marvelled.
Mark xiv. 68, W. and H. omit *and the cock crew*. Mark xv. 5, Gr. *no more answered nothing*.	¹ Gr. *forecourt*. ² Many ancient authorities omit *and the cock crew*. ³ Or, *And he began to weep*.

Synopticon, *pages* 115–116.]

St. Matthew. [*Passages parallel to Mark.*]	St. Luke. [*Passages parallel to Mark.*]
XXVI. 71–75. 71. And when he was gone out into the porch, another *maid* **saw him,** and saith unto them that were there, **This man** also was with Jesus the Nazarene. 72 And again he denied with an oath, I know not the man. 73 And after a little while they that stood by came and said to Peter, **Of a truth** thou also art *one* **of them; for** thy speech bewrayeth thee. 74 Then began he to curse and to swear, **I know not the man. And** straightway **the cock crew.** 75 **And Peter *remembered the word** which Jesus had said, (Gr. *that*) **Before the cock crow, thou shalt deny me thrice. And** he went out, and **wept** bitterly.	XXII. 56–62. 58 And after a little while another **saw him,** and said, Thou also **art** *one* **of them.** But Peter said, Man, I am not. 59 And after the space of about one hour another, confidently affirmed, saying, Of a **truth this man** also was with him : **for** he is a Galilæan. 60. But Peter said, **Man** [?], **I know not** what thou sayest. **And** immediately, while he yet spake, **the cock crew.** 61 And the Lord turned, and looked upon Peter. **And Peter *remembered the word** of the Lord, how that he said unto him, (Gr. *that*) **Before the cock crow** this day, **thou shalt deny me thrice.** 62 **And** he went out, and **wept** bitterly.
XXVII. 1–2, 11–14. 1 Now when morning was come, all the chief priests and the elders of the people took counsel against Jesus to put him to death : 2 And they bound him, and led him away, and delivered him up to **Pilate** the governor. 11 Now Jesus stood before the governor: and **the governor *asked him,** saying, **Art thou the King of the Jews? And** Jesus said unto him, **Thou sayest.** 12 And when he was **accused** by the **chief priests** and elders, he answered nothing. 13 Then saith **Pilate unto him,** Hearest thou not how many things they witness against thee ? 14 And he gave him no **answer, not even** to **one** word : insomuch that the governor marvelled greatly.	XXIII. 1–5..., 9–10. 1 And the whole company of them rose up, and brought him before **Pilate.** 2 And they began to accuse him, saying, We found this man perverting our nation, and forbidding to give tribute to Cæsar, and saying that he himself is [1] Christ a king. 3 And Pilate ***asked him,** saying, **Art thou the King of the Jews? And** he answered him and said, **Thou sayest.** 4 And **Pilate** said unto the chief priests and the multitudes, I find no fault in this man. 5 But they were the more urgent... 9 And he questioned him in many words ; but he **answered** him **nothing.** 10 And the **chief priests** and the scribes stood, vehemently **accusing him.** [1] Or, *an anointed king.*

THE COMMON TRADITION

St. Mark. [Portions not found in Matthew or Luke.]	St. Mark. [Complete.]
	xv. 6–15.
6 ...unto them...they-asked-of-him.	6 Now at [1] the feast he used to release unto them one prisoner, whom they asked of him.
7 ...there was one (the)...bound with them that had-made-insurrection, men-who in the...had committed...	7 And there was one called Barabbas, *lying* bound with them that had made insurrection, men who in the insurrection had committed murder.
8 And the multitude went up and began to ask him as he was wont to do unto them.	8 And the multitude went up and began to ask him *to do* as he was wont to do unto them.
9 ...answered...saying,...King of the Jews;	9 And **Pilate** answered **them,** saying, Will ye **that I release** unto you the King of the Jews?
10 ...he perceived...the chief priests...	10 For he perceived that for envy the chief priests had delivered him up.
11 ...stirred up...rather...unto them.	11 But the chief priests stirred up the multitude, that he should rather release **Barabbas** unto them.
12 ...whom ye call...King of the Jews.	12 And **Pilate** again answered and said unto them, What then shall I do unto him whom ye call the King of the Jews?
13 ...cried out again...	13 **And they** cried out again, **Crucify** him.
14 ...Pilate said...	14 And Pilate said unto them, **Why, what evil hath he done?**...
	[1] Or, *a feast.*

[Synopticon, pages 117-118.]

St. Matthew. [*Passages parallel to Mark.*]	St. Luke. [*Passages parallel to Mark.*]
xxvii. 15-26. 15 Now at ¹ the feast the governor was wont to release unto the multitude one prisoner, whom they would. 16 And they had then a notable prisoner, called Barabbas.	xxiii. 13-25.
17 When therefore they were gathered together, **Pilate** said unto **them**, Whom will ye **that I release** unto you? Barabbas, or Jesus which is called Christ? 18 For he knew that for envy they had delivered him up. 19 And while he was sitting on the judgement-seat, his wife sent unto him, saying, Have thou nothing to do with that righteous man: for I have suffered many things this day in a dream because of him.	13 And **Pilate** called together the chief priests and the rulers and the people, 14 And said unto **them**, Ye brought unto me this man, as one that perverteth the people: and behold, I, having examined him before you, found no fault in this man touching those things whereof ye accuse him: 15 No, nor yet Herod: for he sent him back unto us; and behold, nothing worthy of death hath been done by him. 16 **I will** therefore chastise him, and **release** him.¹
20 Now the chief priests and the elders persuaded the multitudes that they should ask for **Barabbas**, and destroy Jesus.	18 But they **cried out** all together, saying, Away with this man, and release unto us **Barabbas**: 19 One who for a certain insurrection made in the city, and for murder, was cast into prison.
21 But the governor answered and said unto them, Whether of the twain will ye that I release unto you? **And they** said, Barabbas. 22 **Pilate** saith unto them, What then shall I do unto Jesus which is called Christ? They all say, Let him be **crucified**. 23 And he said, **Why, what evil hath he done?**...	20 And **Pilate** spake unto them again, desiring to release Jesus; 21 **But they** shouted, saying, **Crucify,** crucify him. 22 **And he** said unto them the third time, **Why, what evil hath** this man **done?** I have found no cause of death in him: I will therefore chastise him and release him.
¹ Or, *a feast.*	¹ Many ancient authorities insert verse 17. *Now he must needs release unto them at the feast one prisoner.* Others add the same words after verse 19.

St. Mark. [Portions not found in Matthew or Luke.]	St. Mark. [Complete.]
	xv. 6-15. 14 ...**But they cried** out exceedingly, **Crucify** him.
15 ...wishing to content the multitude ...and...	15 And **Pilate**, wishing to content the multitude, **released** unto **them** Barabbas, and **delivered Jesus**, when he had scourged him, to be crucified.
	xv. 16-20.
16 And ... led him away within the court, which is ... and they call-(together)...	16 And the soldiers led him away within the court, which is the [1] Prætorium; and they call together the whole [2] band.
17 ...purple and...	17 And they clothe him with purple, and plaiting a crown of thorns, they put *it on him;
18 ...they began to salute...	18 And they began to salute him, Hail, King of the Jews!
19 ... and bowing their (Gr. the) ... worshipped...	19 And they smote his head with a reed, and did spit upon him, and bowing their knees worshipped him.
20 ... purple and ... to (Gr. in-order-that)...	20 And when they had **mocked** him, they took off from him the purple, and put on him his garments. **And** they **lead him** out to crucify him.
	xv. 21-32.
21 And ... passing by, ... the father of Alexander and Rufus,...	21 And they [3] compel one passing by, **Simon of Cyrene, coming** from the country, the father of Alexander and Rufus, to go *with them*, that he might bear his **cross**.
	[1] Or, *palace*. [2] Or, *cohort*. [3] Gr. *impress*.
Mark xv. 15, Matthew xxvii. 26, Gr. *the Barabbas...the Jesus*.	

Synopticon, pages 118-120.]

St. Matthew.
[Passages parallel to Mark.]

XXVII. 15-26.
23 ...**But they cried** out exceedingly, saying, Let him be **crucified**.

24 So when **Pilate** saw that he prevailed nothing, but rather that a tumult was arising, he took water, and washed his hands before the multitude, saying, I am innocent [1] *of the blood of this righteous man*: see ye *to it*.
25 And all the people answered and said, His blood *be* on us, and on our children.
26 Then **released he** unto **them** Barabbas: but **Jesus he** scourged and **delivered** to be crucified.

XXVII. 27-31.
27 Then the soldiers of the governor took Jesus into the [2] palace, and gathered unto him the whole [3] band.
28 And they [4] stripped him, and put * on him a scarlet robe.
29 And they plaited a crown of thorns and put it upon his head, and a reed in his right hand; and they kneeled down before him, and mocked him, saying, Hail, King of the Jews!
30 And they spat upon him, and took the reed and smote him on the head.
31 And when they had **mocked** him, they took off from him the robe, and put on him his garments, **and led him** away to crucify him.

XXVII. 32-44.
32 And **as they came** out [?], they found a man **of Cyrene, Simon** by name: him they [5] compelled to go *with them*, that he might bear his **cross**.

---

[1] Some ancient authorities read *of this blood: see ye, &c.*
[2] Gr. *Prætorium*. See Mark xv. 16.
[3] Or, *cohort*.
[4] Some ancient authorities read *clothed*.
[5] Gr. *impressed*.

St. Luke.
[Passages parallel to Mark.]

XXIII. 13-25.
23 **But they** were instant with loud voices, asking that he might be **crucified**. And their voices prevailed.
24 And **Pilate** gave sentence that what they asked for should be done.
25 And **he released him that** for insurrection and murder had been cast into prison, whom they asked for; but **Jesus he delivered up to their will**.

XXIII. 11-12.
11 And Herod with his soldiers set him at nought, and **mocked** him, and arraying * him in gorgeous apparel sent him back to Pilate.
12 And Herod and Pilate became friends with each other that very day: for before they were at enmity between themselves.

XXIII. 26.
26 **And** when they **led him** away,...

...they laid hold upon one **Simon of Cyrene, coming** from the country, and laid on him **the cross**, to bear it after Jesus.

THE COMMON TRADITION

St. Mark. [*Portions not found in Matthew or Luke.*]	St. Mark. [*Complete.*]
	xv. 21–32.
22 ...they bring him...being interpreted...	22 And they bring him unto the **place** Golgotha, which is, being interpreted, The place of a **skull**.
23 And...mingled with myrrh, but he received-it...	23 And they offered him wine mingled with myrrh : but he received it not.
24 And...and...upon them, what each should take.	24 And **they crucify him,** and **part his garments among them, casting lots** upon them, what each should take.
25 And it was the third hour, and they crucified him.	25 And it was the third hour, and they crucified him.
26 ...the...(written) over...	26 **And** the superscription of his accusation was written over, **THE KING OF THE JEWS.**
27 ...his (left).	27 And **with him** they crucify **two** robbers ; one **on his right** hand, and one **on** his left.[1]
29 And...Ha!...	29 And they that passed by railed on him, wagging their heads, **and saying,** Ha ! thou that destroyest the [2] temple, and buildest it in three days, 30 **Save thyself,** and come down from the cross.
31 ...among themselves...	31 In like manner **also the chief** priests **mocking** *him* among themselves with the scribes **said, He saved others,** [3] **himself** he cannot save.
32 ...that we may see ..	32 Let the Christ, the **King** of Israel, now come down from the cross, that we may see and believe.
	And they that were crucified with him reproached **him.**
Luke xxiii. 34, W. and H. admit, within brackets, into their text, *And Jesus...what they do,* but regard the words as an interpolation.	[1] Many ancient authorities insert ver. 28, *And the Scripture was fulfilled which saith, And he was reckoned with transgressors.* See Luke xxii. 37. [2] Or, *sanctuary.* [3] Or, *can he not save himself?*

[*Synopticon, pages* 120–121.]

St. Matthew.
[Passages parallel to Mark.]

St. Luke.
[Passages parallel to Mark.]

XXVII. 32–44.
33 **And** when they were come unto a **place** called Golgotha, that is to say, The place of a **skull**,
34. They gave him wine to drink mingled with gall: and when he had tasted it, he would not drink.
35 And when they had **crucified him, they parted his garments among them, casting lots:**
36 And they sat and watched him there.
37 **And** they set up over his head his accusation written, THIS IS JESUS **THE KING OF THE JEWS.**
38 Then are there crucified **with him two** robbers, one **on the right hand,** and one **on the left.**
39 And they that passed by railed on him, wagging their heads,
40 **And saying,** Thou that destroyest the ¹ temple, and buildest it in three days, **save thyself**: if thou art the Son of God, come down from the cross.
41 In like manner, **also the chief** priests **mocking** *him*, with the scribes and elders, **said,**
42 **He saved others;** ² **himself** he cannot **save,** He is **the King** of Israel; let him now come down from the cross, and we will believe on him.
43 He trusteth on God; let him deliver him now, if he desireth him: for he said, (Gr. that) I am the Son of God.
44 And the robbers also that were crucified with him cast upon **him** the same reproach.

XXIII. 32–43.
33 **And** when they came unto the **place** which is called ¹**The skull,** there **they crucified** him, and the malefactors, one **on the right hand** and the other **on the left.**
34 ² And Jesus said, Father, forgive them; for they know not what they do. And **parting his garments among them, they cast lots.**
32 And there were also **two** others, malefactors, led **with him** to be put to death.
35 And the people stood beholding. And **the rulers also** scoffed at him, **saying, He saved others;** let him **save himself,** if this is the Christ of God, his chosen.
36 And the soldiers also **mocked** him, coming to him, offering **him vinegar,**
(See Mark xv. 36, p. 144.)
37 **And saying,** If thou art the **King** of the Jews, **save thyself.**
38 And there was **also** a superscription over him, THIS IS **THE KING OF THE JEWS.**
39 And one of the malefactors which were hanged railed on **him,** saying, Art not thou the Christ?
40 But the other answered, and rebuking him said, Dost thou not even fear God, seeing thou art in the same condemnation?
41 And we indeed justly; for we receive the due reward of our deeds: but this man hath done nothing amiss.
42 And he said, Jesus, remember me when thou comest ³ in thy kingdom.
43 And he said unto him, Verily I say unto thee, To-day shalt thou be with me in Paradise.

---

¹ Or, *sanctuary.*
² Or, *can he not save himself?*

¹ According to the Latin, *Calvary,* which has the same meaning.
² Some ancient authorities omit *And Jesus said, Father, forgive them; for they know not what they do.*
³ Some ancient authorities read *into thy kingdom.*

142   THE COMMON TRADITION

St. Mark. [Portions not found in Matthew or Luke.]	St. Mark. [Complete.]
	xv. 33–41.
33 ...when (the sixth hour) was come (Gr. having become)...	33 And when the **sixth hour** was come, **there was darkness over the whole** [1] **land until the ninth hour.**
34 And...which...being interpreted.. for (what, Rev. *why*)...	34 And at the ninth hour Jesus cried with a loud voice, Eloi, Eloi, lama sabachthani? which is, being interpreted, My God, my God, [2] why hast thou forsaken me?
35 And...(stood) by,...Behold...	35 And some of them that stood by, when they heard it, said, Behold, he calleth Elijah.
36 And one..,filling...saying;...to-take-down,.	36 And one ran, and filling a sponge full of **vinegar**, put it on a reed, and gave **him** to drink, saying, Let be; let us see whether Elijah cometh to take him down.
37 ...uttered (Gr. uttering)...	37 **And Jesus** uttered **a loud voice**, and gave up the **ghost.** 38 And **the veil of the** [3] **temple was rent** in twain from the top to the bottom.
39 ...centurion which stood over against him,...that he so gave up the ghost, he said...	39 **And when the** centurion, which stood by over against him, **saw** that he, [4] so gave up the ghost, he said, Truly **this** man **was** [5] the Son of God.
40 ... [Gr. both (Mary)] ... less ... Salome :.	40 **And** there were also **women beholding from afar**: among whom *were* both Mary Magdalene, and Mary the mother of James the [6] less and of Joses, and Salome :
41 ...when he was in...and...unto him; and...other women...came up (with) him unto Jerusalem.	41 Who, when he was in **Galilee, followed him,** and ministered unto him; and many other women which came up with him unto Jerusalem.
	[1] Or, *earth*. [2] Or, *why didst thou forsake me?* [3] Or, *sanctuary.* [4] Many ancient authorities read *so cried out, and gave up the ghost.* [5] Or, *a son of God.* [6] Gr. *little.*
Mark xv. 39, uses the Latin word *centurion*, Matthew and Luke translate it *hecatontarch.*	

Synopticon, pages 22–123.]

OF THE SYNOPTIC GOSPELS. 143

St. Matthew. [*Passages parallel to Mark.*]	St. Luke. [*Passages parallel to Mark.*]
XXVII. 45–56. 45 Now from the **sixth hour there was darkness over** all the ¹ **land until the ninth hour.** 46 And about the ninth hour Jesus cried with a loud voice, saying, Eli, Eli, lama sabachthani? that is, My God, my God, ² why hast thou forsaken me? 47 And some of them that stood there, when they heard it, said, This man calleth Elijah. 48 And straightway one of them ran, and took a sponge, and filled it with **vinegar**, and put it on a reed, and gave **him** to drink. 49 And the rest said, Let be; let us see whether Elijah cometh to save him.³ 50 **And Jesus** cried again with a **loud voice,** and yielded up his **spirit.** 51 And behold, **the veil of the** ⁴ **temple was rent** in twain from the top to the bottom; and the earth did quake; and the rocks were rent; 52 And the tombs were opened; and many bodies of the saints that had fallen asleep were raised; 53 And coming forth out of the tombs after his resurrection they entered into the holy city and appeared unto many. 54 **Now the** centurion, and they that were with him watching Jesus, when they saw the earthquake, and the things that were done, feared exceedingly, saying, Truly this was ⁴ the of God. 55 **And** many **women** were there **beholding from afar,** which had **followed** Jesus from **Galilee,** ministering unto **him:** 56 Among whom was Mary Magdalene, and Mary the mother of James and Joses, and the mother of the sons of Zebedee. ¹ Or, *earth.* ² Or, *why didst thou forsake me?* ³ Many ancient authorities add *And another took a spear and pierced his side, and there came out water and blood.* See John xix. 34. ⁴ Or, *sanctuary.* ⁵ Or, *a son of God*	XXIII. 44–49. 44 And it was now about the **sixth hour,** and **a darkness came over** the whole ¹ **land until the ninth hour;** [36 ...offering **him vinegar** .] (*See page* 143.) 45 ² The sun's light failing: and **the veil of the** ³ **temple was rent** in the midst. 46 ⁴ And when **Jesus** had cried with **a loud voice,** he said, Father, into thy hands I commend my spirit: **and** having said this, he gave up the **ghost.** 47 **And** when the centurion saw what was done, he glorified God, saying, Certainly this was a righteous man. 48 And all the multitudes that came together to this sight, when they **beheld** the things that were done, returned smiting their breasts. 49 **And** all his acquaintance, and the **women** that **followed** with **him** from **Galilee,** stood **afar off,** seeing these things. ¹ Or, *earth.* ² Gr. *the sun failing.* ³ Or, *sanctuary.* ⁴ Or, *And Jesus, crying with a loud voice,* said.

144.   THE COMMON TRADITION

St. Mark. [Portions not found in Matthew or Luke.]	St. Mark. [Complete.]
	xv. 42–47.
42 ...now, because it was...that is, the day-before-the-(sabbath),	42 And when even was now come, because it was the Preparation, that is, the day before the sabbath,
43 ...of-honourable-estate...was...and he-boldly (Gr. having dared)...(went) in...and...	43 There came **Joseph of Arimathæa**, a councillor of honourable estate, **who** also himself was looking for the kingdom of God; and he boldly **went in unto Pilate**, and **asked for the body of Jesus**.
44 And...marvelled if he were already dead, and calling unto him the centurion, he asked him whether he had been any while dead.	44 And Pilate marvelled, if he were already dead; and calling unto him the centurion, he asked him whether he [1] had been any while dead.
45 And when-he-learned-it of the centurion, he granted the corpse to Joseph.	45 And when he learned it of the centurion, he granted the corpse to Joseph.
46 ...he bought a linen cloth (Gr. having bought),...wound...the (linen cloth) ...had been [Gr. was (hewn out)] of... against...	46 **And** he bought a linen cloth, and taking **him** down, wound him **in** the **linen cloth, and laid** him **in a tomb** which had been hewn out of a rock; and he rolled a stone against the door of the tomb.
47 ...of Joses beheld where ..	47 **And** Mary Magdalene and Mary the *mother* of Joses beheld where he was laid.
	[1] Many ancient authorities read *were already dead*.
Mark xv. 44, W. and H. *were already dead*	

Synopticon, pages 124–125.

| St. Matthew. | St. Luke. |
[*Passages parallel to Mark.*]	[*Passages parallel to Mark.*]
XXVII. 57-61.	XXIII. 50-56...
57 And when even was come, there came a rich man **from Arimathæa,** named **Joseph, who** also himself was Jesus' disciple: 58 This man **went to Pilate, and asked for the body of Jesus.** Then Pilate commanded it to be given up.	50 And behold, a man named **Joseph,** who was a councillor, a good man and a righteous 51 (He had not consented to their counsel and deed), *a man* **of Arimathæa,** a city of the Jews, **who** was looking for the kingdom of God: 52 This man **went to Pilate, and asked for the body of Jesus.**
59 **And** Joseph took the body, and wrapped it **in** a clean **linen cloth,** 60 **And laid** it **in** his own new **tomb,** which he had hewn out in the rock: and he rolled a great stone to the door of the tomb, and departed. 61 **And** Mary Magdalene was there, and the other Mary, sitting over against the sepulchre.	53 **And** he took it down, and wrapped it **in a linen cloth, and laid** him **in a tomb** that was hewn in stone, where never man had yet lain. 54 And it was the day of the Preparation, and the sabbath [1] drew on. 55 **And** the women, which had come with him out of Galilee, followed after, and beheld the tomb, and how his body was laid. 56. And they returned, and prepared spices and ointments.

[1] Gr. *began to dawn*

THE COMMON TRADITION

St. Mark. [*Portions not found in Matthew or Luke.*]	St. Mark. [*Complete.*]
	XVI. 1–8.
1 And when the...was past...of James, and Salome, bought...that they might anoint him.	1 And when the sabbath was past, **Mary Magdalene, and Mary the** *mother* of James, and Salome, bought spices, that they might **come** and anoint him.
2 And very early...they come...when the sun was risen.	2 And very early **on the first** *day* **of the week** [?] they come to the tomb when the sun was risen.
3 And they were saying among themselves, Who...us...from the door...	3 And they were saying among themselves, Who shall **roll us away the stone** from the door of the tomb?
4 And looking up...that the stone (is rolled) back; for *it* was exceeding great.	4 And looking up, they see that the stone is rolled back: for it was exceeding great.
5 ...into the tomb they saw a young man sitting on the right side arrayed in a...robe;...they were amazed.	5 And entering into the tomb, they saw a young man sitting on the right side, arrayed in a white robe; and they were amazed.
6 .. saith...Be...amazed...the Nazarene ...they laid him!	6 **And** he saith unto them, Be not amazed: **ye seek** Jesus, the Nazarene, **which** hath been crucified: **he is risen; he is not here**: behold, the place where they laid him!
7 But go,...and Peter,...	7 But go, tell his disciples and Peter, He goeth before you into **Galilee**: there shall ye see him, *****as** he said **unto you.**
8 ...fled...for trembling and astonishment had come upon them; and they said nothing to any one; for they were afraid.	8 **And** they went out, and fled **from the tomb**; for trembling and astonishment had come upon them; and they said nothing to any one; for they were afraid.

Mark xvi. 7, Gr. *even as*, as in Matthew xxviii. 6.
Luke xxiv. 3, W. and H admit, within brackets, into their text. *of the Lord Jesus*, but regard the words as an interpolation.

Synopticon, pages 125–126.]

OF THE SYNOPTIC GOSPELS.

St. Matthew. [*Passages parallel to Mark.*]	St. Luke. [*Passages parallel to Mark:*]
XXVIII. 1–10. 1 Now late on the sabbath day, as it began to dawn toward **the** [?] **first** *day* **of the week** [?], **came Mary Magdalene and the** other **Mary** to see the sepulchre. 2 And behold, there was a great earthquake ; for an angel of the Lord descended from heaven, and came and **rolled away the stone**, and sat upon it. 3 His appearance was as lightning, and his raiment white as snow : 4 And for fear of him the watchers did quake, and became as dead men. 5 **And** the angel answered and said unto the women, Fear not ye : for I know that **ye seek** Jesus, **which** hath been crucified. 6 **He is not here ;** for **he is risen,** even *as he said. Come, see the place ¹ where the Lord lay. 7 And go quickly, and tell his disciples, He is risen from the dead ; and lo, he goeth before you into **Galilee ;** there shall ye see him : lo, I have told **you.** 8 **And** they departed quickly **from the tomb** with fear and great joy, and ran to bring his disciples word. 9 And behold, Jesus met them, saying, All hail. And they came and took hold of his feet, and worshipped him. 10 Then saith Jesus unto them, Fear not : go tell my brethren that they depart into Galilee, and there shall they see me.	XXIII...56. 56 ...And on the sabbath they rested according to the commandment. XXIV. 1–11. 1 But **on the first** *day* **of the week,** at early dawn, they **came** unto the tomb, bringing the spices which they had prepared. 2 And they found **the stone rolled away** from the tomb. 3 And they entered in, and found not the body ¹ of the Lord Jesus. 4 And it came to pass, while they were perplexed thereabout, behold, two men stood by them in dazzling apparel : 5 **And** as they were affrighted, and bowed down their faces to the earth, they said unto them, Why **seek ye** ² **the** living among the dead ? 6 ³ **He is not here,** but **is risen :** remember * **how** he spake **unto you** when he was yet in **Galilee,** 7 Saying that the Son of man must be delivered up into the hands of sinful men, and be crucified, and the third day rise again. 8 And they remembered his words, 9 **And** returned ⁴ **from the tomb,** and told all these things to the eleven, and to all the rest. 10 Now they were **Mary Magdalene,** and Joanna, **and Mary the** *mother* o James : and the other women with them told these things unto the apostles. 11 And these words appeared in their sight as idle talk ; and they disbelieved them.
¹ Many ancient authorities read *where he lay.*	¹ Some ancient authorities omit *of the Lord Jesus* ² Gr. *him that liveth.* ³ Some ancient authorities omit *He is not here, but is risen.* ⁴ Some ancient authorities omit *from the tomb.*

THE LONGER APPENDIX TO ST. MARK'S GOSPEL.

[*The following verses are printed by the Revisers with an interval between them and Mark XVI. 8, to denote that they are probably not a part of the genuine Gospel.*]

9 [1] Now when he was risen early on the first day of the week, he appeared first to Mary Magdalene, from whom he had cast out seven [2] devils.
10 She went and told them that had been with him, as they mourned and wept.
11 And they, when they heard that he was alive, and had been seen of her, disbelieved.
12 And after these things he was manifested in another form unto two of them, as they walked, on their way into the country.
13 And they went away and told it unto the rest: neither believed they them.
14 And afterward he was manifested unto the eleven themselves as they sat at meat; and he upbraided them with their unbelief and hardness of heart, because they believed not them which had seen him after he was risen.
15 And he said unto them, Go ye into all the world, and preach the gospel to the whole creation.
16 He that believeth and is baptized shall be saved; but he that disbelieveth shall be condemned.
17 And these signs shall follow them that believe: in my name shall they cast out [2] devils; they shall speak with [3] new tongues;
18 They shall take up serpents, and if they drink any deadly thing, it shall in no wise hurt them; they shall lay hands on the sick, and they shall recover.
19 So then the Lord Jesus, after he had spoken unto them, was received up into heaven, and sat down at the right hand of God.
20 And they went forth, and preached everywhere, the Lord working with them, and confirming the word by the signs that followed. Amen.

THE SHORTER APPENDIX.

[*The following passage, omitted by the Revisers, is printed by Westcott and Hort as an ancient Appendix, upon the same level of authority as the Longer Appendix, but not as a part of the genuine Gospel.*]

And all that had been enjoined on them they reported briefly to the companions of Peter. And after these things Jesus himself from the East even to the West sent forth by them the holy and incorruptible preaching of eternal salvation.

---

[1] The two oldest Greek manuscripts, and some other authorities, omit from verse 9 to the end. Some other authorities have a different ending to the Gospel.
[2] Gr. *demons*.   3 Some ancient authorities omit *new*.

TABLE I.—SHOWING THE CONTENTS OF EACH PAGE.

	Mark.			Matthew.		Luke.	
Page.	Chap.	Ver.	Page.	Chap.	Ver.	Chap.	Ver.
2	i.	1–8	3	iii.	1–6	iii.	1–4
				iii.	11–12	iii.	7
						iii	15–17
4	i.	9–18	5	iii.	13	iii.	21–22
				iii.	16–17	iv.	1–2
				iv.	1–2	iv.	13–15
				iv.	11–12	v.	1–2
				iv.	17–20	v.	9
6	i.	19–30	7	iv.	12–13	v.	10–11
				iv.	21–22	iv.	31–38
				vii.	28–29		
				viii.	14		
8	i.	31–41	9	viii.	15–17	iv.	39–44
				iv.	23		
				viii.	1–2...	v.	12–13..
10	i.	42–45	11	viii.	...3–4	v.	...13–16
	ii.	1–7		ix.	1–3	v.	17–21
12	ii.	8–16	13	ix.	4–11	v.	22–30
14	ii.	17–23	15	ix.	12–17	v.	31–39
				xii.	1...	vi.	1...
16	ii.	...23–28	17	xii.	...1–10	vi.	...1–8
	iii.	1–3					
18	iii.	4–12	19	xii.	11–14	vi.	9–11
				iv.	24–25	vi.	17–19
				xii.	15–16		
20	iii.	13–26	21	x.	1–5...	vi.	12–15
				x.	7..., ...8...		
				xii.	22–26	xi.	14–18
22	iii.	27–35	23	xii.	28–32	xi.	19–23
				xii.	46–50	xii.	10
						viii.	19–21
24	iv.	1–12	25	xiii.	1–12	viii.	4–10
				xiii.	13, ...15...		
26	iv.	13–21	27	xiii.	18–23	viii.	11–16
				v.	14–16	xi.	33
28	iv.	22–25	29	x.	26	viii.	17–18
				xi.	15	xii.	2
				vii.	2	xiv.	...35
				vi.	33	vi.	38
				xiii.	12	xii.	31
				xxv.	29	xix.	26
30	iv.	26–34	31	xiii.	24–35	xiii.	18–19
32	iv.	35–41	33	viii.	18	viii.	22–27
	v.	1–5		viii.	23–28		
34	v.	6–16	35	viii.	29–34...	viii.	28–36
36	v.	17–27	37	viii.	...34	viii.	37–44
				ix.	18–20		
38	v.	28–39...	39	ix.	21–23	viii.	45–52..

The sign ... when placed before a verse, indicates that the beginning of the verse is omitted; when placed after a verse, that the end of the verse is omitted.

TABLE I.—SHOWING THE CONTENTS OF EACH PAGE.

	Mark.			Matthew.		Luke.	
Page.	Chap.	Ver.	Page.	Chap.	Ver.	Chap.	Ver.
40	v.	..39–43	41	ix.	24–26	viii.	...52–56
	vi.	1–6...		xiii.	53–58	iv.	16–17...
						iv.	21–24
						iv.	28
42	vi.	...6–11	43	ix.	35	xiii.	22
				x.	1, 5–15	ix.	1–5
	[Luke x. 1–12]		42			x.	1–12
44	vi.	12–20	45	xiv.	1–5	ix.	6–9
						iii.	18–20
46	vi.	21–29	47	xiv.	6–12		
48	vi.	30–40	49	xiv.	13–19...	ix.	10–15
				ix.	36		
50	vi.	41–50	51	xiv.	...19–29	ix.	16–17
						[John vi. 15–20]	
52	vi.	51–56	53	xiv.	30–36	[John vi. 21]	
	vii.	1–3		xv.	1		
54	vii.	4–13	55	xv.	2–9		
56	vii.	14–24	57		10–21		
58	vii.	25–36	59		22–30		
60	vii.	37	61		31–39		
	viii.	1–11		xvi.	1	xi.	16
62	viii.	12–19	63	xvi.	2–9	xi.	29–30
				xii.	38–40	xii.	1
64	viii.	20–28	65	xvi.	10–14	ix.	18–20
66	viii.	29–38	67	xvi.	15–16	ix.	20–26
				xvi.	20–27		
68	ix.	1–8	69	xvi.	28	ix.	27–36 ..
				xvii.	1–8		
70	ix.	9–18	71	xvii.	9–16	ix.	...36–40
						i.	17
72	ix.	19–29	73	xvii.	17–20	ix.	41–43...
				xvii.	...15	xvii.	6
74	ix.	30–36	75	xvii.	22–25...	ix.	...43–47
				xviii.	1–3		...48
				xxiii.	11	xxii.	26
76	ix.	37–42	77	xviii.	4–7	ix.	47–50
				x.	40, 42	xvii.	1–2
78	ix.	43–50	79	xviii.	8–9		
	x.	1–4		v.	13	xiv.	34
				xix.	1–4...	xvii.	11
				xix.	7		
80	x.	5–12	81	xix.	4–6		
				xix.	8–10...	xvi.	18
				v.	31–32		
82	x.	13–20	83	xix.	13–20	xviii.	15–21
				xviii.	3		
84	x.	21–30	85	xix.	21–29	xviii.	22–30

The sign ∴ when placed before a verse, indicates that the beginning of the verse is omitted; when placed after a verse, that the end of the verse is omitted.

TABLE I.—SHOWING THE CONTENTS OF EACH PAGE. 151

	Mark.			**Matthew.**			**Luke.**	
Page.	Chap.	Ver.	Page	Chap.	Ver.		Chap.	Ver.
86	x.	31-39	87	xix.	30		xiii.	30
				xx.	17-23...		xix.	28
							xviii.	31-33
88	x.	40-50	89	xx.	...23-32		xxii.	24-27
	[Matt. ix. 27-30]						xviii.	35-40
90	x.	51-52	91	xx.	34		xviii.	42-43
	xi.	1-8		xxi.	1-8		xix.	29 36
92	xi.	9-17	93	xxi.	9-14		xix.	37-38
				xxi.	18-19...		xix.	45-47...
94	xi.	18-25	95	xxi.	15-17		xix.	...47-48
				xxi.	20-22		xxi.	37-38
				vii.	7		xvii.	5-6
				vi.	14-15		xi.	4..., 9
96	xi.	27-33	97	xxi.	23-27		xx.	1-10
	xii.	1-3		xxi.	33-35			
98	xii.	4-12	99	xxi.	36-46		xx.	11-19
100	xii.	13-19	101	xxii.	15-24		xx.	20-28
102	xii.	20-29	103	xxii.	25-36		xx.	29-39
							x.	25
104	xii.	30-37...	105	xxii.	37-46		x.	26-28
							x.	40-45...
106	xii.	...37-44	107	xxiii.	1-7		xx.	45-47
							xi.	43
							xxi.	1-4
108	xiii.	1-8	109	xxiv.	1-8		xxi.	5-11
110	xiii.	9-13	111	xxiv.	9-14		xxi.	12-19
				x.	17-22			
112	xiii.	14-23	113	xxiv.	15-28		xxi.	20-24
							xvii.	23, 31
114	xiii.	24-31	115	xxiv.	29-35		xxi.	25-33
116	xiii.	32-37	117	xxiv.	36		xxi.	34-36
				xxv.	13-15		xii.	35-41
				xxiv.	42-46			
118	xiv.	1-9	119	xxvi.	1-13		xxii.	1-2
							vii.	36-40
120	xiv.	3-11	121	xxvi.	6-16		[John xii. 1-8]	
							xxii.	3-6
122	xiv.	12-21	123	xxvi.	17-25		xxii.	7-15...
							xxii.	21-23
124	xiv.	22-26	125	xxvi.	26-30		xxii.	15-20
	[1 Cor. xi. 23-25]						xxii.	39
126	xiv.	27-38	127	xxvi.	31-41		xxii.	31-34
	[John xii. 38]						xxii.	40-46
128	xiv.	39-47	129	xxvi.	42-54		xxii.	47-51
	[Jhn xviii. 10-11]						[John xviii. 23]	
130	xiv.	48-59	131	xxvi.	55-61		xxii.	52-56
							xxii.	66

The sign ... when placed before a verse, indicates that the beginning of the verse is omitted; when placed after a verse, that the end of the verse is omitted.

Table I.—SHOWING THE CONTENTS OF EACH PAGE.

	Mark.			Matthew.		Luke.	
Page.	Chap.	Ver.	Page	Chap.	Ver.	Chap.	Ver.
132	xiv.	60–68	133	xxvi.	62–70	xxii.	56 57
						xxii.	63–65
						xxii.	67–71
134	xiv.	...68–72	135	xxvi.	71–75	xxii.	58–62
	xv.	1–5		xxvii.	1–2	xxiii.	1–5...
				xxvii.	11–14	xxiii.	9–10
136	xv.	6–14...	137	xxvii.	15–23 ..	xxiii.	13–22
138	xv.	...14–21	139	xxvii.	...23–32	xxiii.	23–26
						xxiii.	11–12
140	xv.	22–32	141	xxvii.	33–44	xxiii.	32–43
142	xv.	33–41	143	xxvii.	45–56	xxiii.	44–49
144	xv.	42–47	145	xxvii.	57–61	xxiii.	50–56...
146	xvi.	1–8	147	xxviii.	1–10	xxiii.	...56
						xxiv.	1–11
148	xvi.	9–20					

The sign ... when placed before a verse, indicates that the beginning of the verse is omitted; when placed after a verse, that the end of the verse is omitted.

St. Matthew.

INDEX TO THE PORTIONS PRINTED IN THIS WORK.

Chap.	Ver.	Page	Chap.	Ver.	Page.	Chap.	Ver.	Page.
iii.	1–6	3	viii.	1–3...	9	xiii.	1–12...	25
	11–12	3		...3–4	11		12	23
	13	5		14	7		13	25
	16–17	5		15–17	9		..15...	25
				18	33		18–23	27
				23–28	33		24–32	31
				29–34...	35		34–35	31
				...34	37		[43	28]
							53–58	41
iv.	1–2	5	ix.	1–3	11	xiv.	1–5	45
	11–12	5		4–11	13		6-12	47
	12-13	7		12–17	15		13–19...	49
	17–20	5		18–20	37		...19–29	51
	21–22	7		21–23	39		30–36	53
	23	9		24–26	41			
	24-25	19		27–30	88			
				[32–34	20]			
				35	41			
				36	49			
v.	13	79	x.	1–5...	21	xv.	1	53
	14–16	27		1, 5–15	43		2–9	55 ?
	31–32	81		7..., ...8...	21		10–21	57
				17–22	110		...22–30	59
				26	29		31–39	61
				[33	67]			
				[38–39	67]			
				40, 42	77			
vi.	14–15	95	xi.	10	1	xvi.	1	61
	33	28		15	29		2–9	63
							10–14	65
							15–16	67
							20–27	67
							28	69
vii.	2	29	xii.	1...	15			
	7	95		...1–10	17			
	28-29	7		11–17...	19			
				22–26	21			
				27–32	23			
				38–40	63			
				46–50	23			

The sign ... when placed before a verse, indicates that the beginning of the verse is omitted ; when placed after a verse, that the end of the verse is omitted.

St. Matthew.

INDEX TO THE PORTIONS PRINTED IN THIS WORK.

Chap.	Ver.	Page.	Chap.	Ver.	Page.	Chap.	Ver.	Page.
xvii.	1–8	69	xxi.	1–8	91	xxv.	29	28
	9 16	71		9–14	93		13–15	117
	17–20	73		15–17	95		[31	67]
	…15	73		18–19…	93			
	22–25…	75		20–22	95			
				23–27	97			
				33–35	97			
				36–46	99			
xviii.	1–3	75	xxii.	15–24	101	xxvi.	1–13	119
	3	83		25–36	103		6–16	121
	4-7	77		37–46	105		17–25	123
	8–9	79					26–30	125
	11	75					31–41	127
							42–54	129
							55–61	131
							62–70	133
							71–75	135
xix.	1–4…	79	xxiii.	1–7	107	xxvii.	1–2	135
	4–6	81		11	75		11–14	135
	7	79					15–23…	137
	8–12…	81					…23–32	139
	13–20	83					33–44	141
	21–29	85					45–56	143
	30	87					57–61	145
xx.	17–23…	87	xxiv.	1–8	109	xxviii.	1–10	147
	…23 32	89		9–14	111			
	33–34	91		15–28	113			
				29–35	115			
				36	117			
				42–46	117			

The sign [ ] round any verses denotes that those verses are not printed in full upon the page referred to, but that they may be advantageously considered in connexion with that page.

St. Luke.

INDEX TO THE PORTIONS PRINTED IN THIS WORK.

Chap.	Ver.	Page.	Chap.	Ver.	Page	Chap.	Ver	Page
i.	17	71	vi.	1...	15	x.	1–12	42
	[...37	84]		...1–8	17		4	43
				9–11	19		25	103
				12–16	21		26–28	105
				17–19	19			
				38	29			
iii.	1–4	3	vii.	27	1	xi.	4..., 9	95
	7	3		36–40	119		14–18	21
	15–17	3					16	61
	18–20	45					19-23	23
	21–22	5					29–30	63
							33	27
							43	107
iv.	1–2	5	viii.	4–10	25	xii.	1	63
	13–15	5		11–16	27		2	29
	16–17...	41		17–18	29		[9	67]
	21–24	41		19–21	23		10	23
	28	41		22–27	33		11–12	110
	31–38	7		28–36	35		31	29
	39–44	9		37–44	37		35–41	117
				45–52...	39		50	87
				...52–56	41			
v.	1–2	5	ix.	1–5	43	xiii.	18–19	31
	9	5		6–9	45		22	43
	10–11	7		10–15	49		30	87
	12–13...	9		16–17	51			
	...13–21	11		18–19	65			
	22–30	13		20–26	67			
	31–39	15		27–36...	69			
				...36–40	71			
				41–43...	73			
				...43–47	75			
				...48	75			
				47-50	77			

The sign ... when placed before a verse, indicates that the beginning of the verse is omitted; when placed after a verse, that the end of the verse is omitted.

St. Luke.

INDEX TO THE PORTIONS PRINTED IN THIS WORK.

Chap.	Ver.	Page	Chap.	Ver.	Page.	Chap.	Ver.	Page.
xiv.	[1–6	18]	xix.	26	29	xxiii.	1–5...	135
	[27	67]		28	87		9–10	135
	34–35	79		29–36	91		11–12	139
	35	29		37–38	93		13–22	137
				45–47...	93		23–26	139
				...47–48	95		33–43	141
							44–49	143
							50–56...	145
							...56	147
xvi.	18	81	xx.	1–10	97	xxiv.	1–11	147
				11–19	99			
				20–28	101			
				29–39	103			
				40–45...	105			
				45–47	107			
xvii.	1–2	77	xxi.	1–4	107			
	6	73		5–11	109			
	5–6	95		12–19	111			
	11	79		20–24	113			
	23, 31	113		25–33	115			
	[33	67]		34–36	117			
				37–38	95			
xviii.	15–21	83	xxii.	1–2	119			
	22–30	85		3–6	121			
	31–33	87		7–15...	123			
	35–40	89		15–20	125			
	41–43	91		21–23	123			
				24–27	89			
				26	75			
				31–34	127			
				39	125			
				40–46	127			
				47–51	129			
				52–56	131			
				56–57	133			
				58–62	135			
				63–65	133			
				66	131			
				67–71	133			

The sign [ ] round any verse denotes that those verses are not printed in full upon the page referred to, but that they may be advantageously considered in connexion with that page.

www.ingramcontent.com/pod-product-compliance
Lightning Source LLC
Chambersburg PA
CBHW062042220426
43662CB00010B/1617